# Each Day with Jesus

LARGE PRINT EDITION

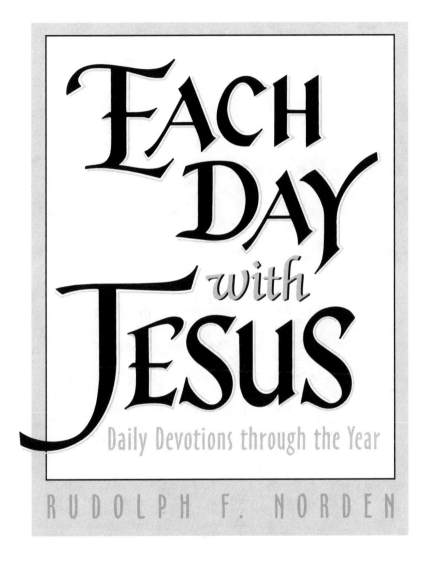

# EACH DAY with JESUS

Daily Devotions through the Year

RUDOLPH F. NORDEN

**CPH.**
SAINT LOUIS

Cover photo: © Orion Press/Natural Selection

All Scripture quotations, unless otherwise indicated, are taken from the HOLY BIBLE, NEW INTERNATIONAL VERSION®. NIV®. Copyright © 1973, 1978, 1984 by International Bible Society. Used by permission of Zondervan Publishing House. All rights reserved.

Scripture quotations marked RSV are from the Revised Standard Version of the Bible, copyrighted 1946, 1952, © 1971, 1973. Used by permission.

Scripture quotations marked NKJV are taken from the New King James Version. Copyright © 1979, 1980, 1982 by Thomas Nelson, Inc. Used by permission. All rights reserved.

Scripture quotations marked KJV are from the King James or Authorized Version of the Bible.

Devotions have been condensed from the original 1994 version.
Copyright © 1994, 1999 Concordia Publishing House
3558 S. Jefferson Avenue,
St. Louis, MO 63118-3968

Manufactured in the United States of America

1  2  3  4  5  6  7  8  9  10      08  07  06  05  04  03  02  01  00  99

*To*
*Olga Norden,*
*my sister*

# Preface

The title *Each Day with Jesus* reminds me as well as you that Jesus is central in each devotion. His person, His preaching and teaching, and especially His work of redemption are the foundation of the Christian faith. Just as we want Jesus to be with us and speak to us, so He wants to share His Word with us.

You are encouraged, therefore, to first read the Bible passage indicated for the day. The meditation is not a substitute for God's own Word, but an aid to applying it to your day's activities. The Prayer Suggestion at the end of the day's meditation hints how you might close your devotion with worship, as you offer to the Lord your petition or thanksgiving.

This book contains enough devotions for an entire year. Most conform to the fixed dates in the church year and the secular calendar; a Christmas reading, for example, is provided for December 25. Readings for occasions such as Mother's Day, Memorial Day, or Veterans Day occur at the approximate time of these dates. A special section at the end contains devotions for the important movable days of the church year: Ash Wednesday, Easter, and Pentecost.

The devotions in this book were presented first in the former "Day by Day with Jesus" radio program, sponsored by the International Lutheran Laymen's League. As I noted in a previous volume of these devotions (*Day by Day with Jesus,* Concordia, 1985), "Through the years ... there has been no change in the Gospel message undergirding every daily devotion. Jesus Christ, who is the same yesterday, today, and forever, has always been 'center stage.' "

*Rudolph F. Norden*

# Janus or Jesus?

January is named after the Roman god Janus, the guardian of doors and gates. The month of January, which opens the door to the new year and closes it to the past, was sacred to him. As a door has two sides, so Janus was represented by having two faces. The doors of his temple in the Forum were shut in time of peace and open in time of war. In Rome's history these gates were rarely closed.

Born when Rome ruled the world, Jesus, the Prince of Peace, also associated Himself with a door. "I am the door; if anyone enters by Me, he will be saved" (John 10:9 RSV).

We do well to commit ourselves to Jesus as January 1 opens the door to the New Year. Time passes, centuries come and go, empires fall, rulers die, idols like Janus are forgotten, but Jesus lives. He is "the same yesterday and today and forever" (Heb. 13:8).

As this year begins, we ask ourselves: Are we for Janus or for Jesus? If we live for the things of this world—its idolatries, its materialism, its sensualism—we are for Janus. If we enjoy a good fight—if not bloodshed in the streets or war at large, then personal and passionate aggression—we are again for Janus.

But if we put the true God on top, seek first His kingdom, work for peace because we know we are forgiven and reconciled with God through the death of His Son, we are for Jesus. We have chosen well, for Jesus is "the author and perfecter of our faith" (Heb. 12:2). He is the only way to the Father, the only door to eternal life. May He guard us this year and always.

***Prayer Suggestion:*** *Declare your trust in the unchanging Christ, asking Him to be with you and your loved ones throughout the year.*

# The Wondrous Name

Many names were given to the Son of God. He was called the Anointed, the Messiah, the Christ. From Isaiah (7:14), Matthew takes the name Immanuel, "God with us," and applies it to Christ. In the virgin's offspring "the Word became flesh and made His dwelling among us" (John 1:14). In Him, "God was manifest in the flesh" (1 Tim. 3:16 KJV).

The hymn writer exclaims:

> Jesus! Name of wondrous love,
> Name all other names above.

Why is the name *Jesus* so wondrous? Because it means Savior. The angel told Mary "You will … give birth to a son, and you are to give Him the name Jesus" (Luke 1:31). The angel told Joseph in a dream: "He will save His people from their sins" (Matt. 1:21).

"His people"—these are primarily the Israelites. In her Magnificat, Mary praises God because in the Messiah "He has helped His servant Israel" (Luke 1:54). But salvation was not to be for the Jews only. The Good Shepherd has "other sheep that are not of this sheep pen" (John 10:16). Through Jesus' obedience and His atoning death, He saved everyone from their sins. St. Peter tells those who were once "not a people" that they are now God's chosen people who have received mercy (1 Peter 2:10).

Jesus' name is wondrous because whoever believes in Him and is baptized into His name will be saved.

***Prayer Suggestion:*** *Ask the Holy Spirit for courage and strength to confess Jesus' wondrous name before the world.*

# God's Steadfast Love

The Muir Woods of giant redwood trees in California are said to be a natural wonder of the world. These trees are believed to be among the oldest living things on earth.

Besides the giant redwood trees, mountains also symbolize permanence. But God by far antedates even them, as Moses declares in Psalm 90: "Before the mountains were born or You brought forth the earth and the world, from everlasting to everlasting You are God" (v. 2).

That would be little comfort if God were forever present to call us to account for our sins. How different to be assured of His unending love! God states through Isaiah: "Though the mountains be shaken and the hills be removed, yet My unfailing love for you will not be shaken, nor My covenant of peace be removed" (54:10).

The steadfastness of God's love—and the steadfastness of God's Word, proclaiming and conveying it to us—is meaningful because we frail creatures are so in need of it. As Moses describes in Psalm 90, people are like grass that is dry and withered in the evening.

God's steadfast love to us rests on the sin-atoning, death-destroying work of reconciliation performed by His Son, Jesus. As the Father is, so is the Son—eternal in the heavens; given to enduring love; and the same yesterday, today, and forever. The giant redwood trees and the mountain peaks, pointing heavenward, remind us that our help comes from the Lord, who sent His Son, our loving and beloved Savior.

*Prayer Suggestion: Speak words of thanks and praise to God for His abiding love extended to you in Jesus Christ, His Son.*

# Grounds for Gratitude

Some years ago in New Jersey, a couple took in a homeless grandson and brought him up. The grandfather eventually turned the deed of his home over to him, with the understanding that he and his wife could stay in it as long as they lived. But in their old age, they were evicted. The grandson sold the house and pocketed the money. What ingratitude!

We find ingratitude stories in the Bible too. Jesus healed 10 lepers, but only one returned to give thanks. The psalmist wrote, "Even my close friend, whom I trusted, he who shared my bread, has lifted up his heel against me" (Ps. 41:9). Jesus quoted these words and applied them to Judas Iscariot, the betrayer.

Our Lord experienced ingratitude on a much larger scale. John writes (John 1:11): "He came to that which was His own, but His own did not receive Him." This applied to a group much larger than His fellow citizens in Nazareth who ran Him out of town. While it is thankless to bite the hand that feeds you, the ultimate ingratitude is to reject the greatest benefactor we have: Jesus Christ, who shed His precious blood for our salvation.

How wonderful is gratitude, a thankfulness for all of God's gifts: life and health; rain and sunshine; food and drink; home and family; parents and children; the love God conveys through other people; and a country that offers an atmosphere favoring the practice of religious faith. Above all, are we thankful for the love of God revealed in Jesus Christ, our Savior? Have you said your thank-You lately for all this?

*Prayer Suggestion: Ask God to give you a truly thankful heart for all His benefits to you, especially for salvation in Christ, His Son.*

# Seeking and Finding Christ

Wise Men searched for the Christ Child. Guided by a unique star, they came to Jerusalem, announcing the nature of their quest: "Where is the one who has been born King of the Jews? We saw His star in the east, and have come to worship Him" (Matt. 2:2). Directed to Bethlehem, they saw the star again, and great was their joy.

"Seek, and you will find." This applies also to the search for Jesus. We seek Him where He is to be found—in His Word. To find Him, we need not scale the highest mountain or descend into the depth of the sea. He is much closer at hand, as St. Paul states, "The Word is near you; … the Word of faith we are proclaiming" (Rom. 10:8).

The Gospel that brings Christ to us is drawn from the Holy Scriptures, which bear witness to Him. The visit of the Wise Men exemplifies this fact. Because the Old Testament prophet Micah had announced that the Messiah was to be born in Bethlehem, the leaders in Jerusalem were able to help the Wise Men find Christ. Throughout the Bible we find testimonies to Jesus Christ, our Savior from sin, the Lord of our life.

The truths of Christ are in that Book where God shows you the road to Christ, your Savior. Because He is cradled in the Holy Scriptures, we can exclaim,

> How precious is the book divine,
> By inspiration giv'n!
> Bright as a lamp its teachings shine
> To guide our souls to heav'n.

*Prayer Suggestion: Ask the Holy Spirit to lead you into the Holy Scriptures, which bear witness to Christ.*

# With Joy They Hailed Its Light

The Wise Men "were overjoyed," Matthew states. They were exceedingly happy when the familiar star they had first seen in the East reappeared in the heavens to guide them to the Christ Child in Bethlehem. They had come to think of this star as a reliable and faithful friend along the way. Now they were sure they would find the newborn King and Savior of Jews and Gentiles.

The Gospel, the Word of God, is a familiar friend, leading us to the most reliable and faithful friend we will ever know: Jesus. Scripture is our guiding light, a bright star directing our footsteps to Him who is the Star of Jacob, the "bright Morning Star," the "Dayspring from on high," the "Light of the world." This we declare of the written Word:

> Bright as a lamp its teachings shine
> To guide our souls to heav'n.

Christians experience a special joy and happiness when the Word of God leads them to the Savior, to Him who is the Word personified. It is a delight to be welcomed into the presence of Jesus Christ, true God and true man. Salvation is found in Him alone. Joy and thankfulness cause us to open our treasures to Him and to serve Him as our King; our joy and gratitude increase each time we do so. The best offering we can bring is the gift of self, as St. Paul wrote of the Macedonians, "They gave themselves first to the Lord" (2 Cor. 8:5).

*Prayer Suggestion: Ask God for the gift of joy that results from putting your trust in Christ, the Light of the world.*

# Christ's Gift to Us: Himself

Biblical novels attempt to fill gaps in the account of Holy Scripture. The reader knows this and therefore does not regard edifying fiction as God's inspired truth. In *The Gifts*, Dorothy Clarke Wilson suggests that Mary and Joseph laid aside the gifts of the Wise Men so some day Jesus might study under Hillel in Jerusalem. But as He got older, so the fiction story goes, He gave the gifts away. The people receiving them did not use them wisely. Disappointed, Jesus realized that He must give a gift greater than gold, Himself, for the salvation of the world.

The main point in the account of Christianity is not that we, like the Wise Men of old, give gifts to Christ—though we will do that out of love to Him—but that Christ is God's gift to us. He is the greatest gift God could bestow. Christ gave Himself for us when He shed His precious blood for the forgiveness of sins. "For you know that it was not with perishable things such as silver or gold that you were redeemed ... but with the precious blood of Christ" (1 Peter 1: 18–19).

Christ, is God's gift to all nations. Simeon in the temple made that clear when he called the Christ "a Light for revelation to the Gentiles." Having received God's Epiphany gift to us—Jesus Christ, His Son and our Savior—we are constrained by the love of God to share this gift with our fellow human beings throughout the world. Our Lord Himself ordained missions when He told us to make disciples of all nations by baptizing them and by teaching them. We may not be able to give gold and silver. We can do better. We offer them God's gift, Jesus Christ.

**Prayer Suggestion:** *Give thanks to God for His unspeakable gift: His Son. Ask God's help to make Christ known in the world.*

# The Two Flights to Egypt

Twentieth-century air travel to distant lands never ceases to amaze passengers. At international airports, flights to Cairo, Egypt, are announced as casually as bus trips to Cairo, Illinois.

Time was when trips to Egypt were slow, difficult, and dangerous. They were made on foot, on mule back, or in carts. In at least two instances in Scripture, such trips were made because Egypt represented a place of refuge.

The first trip was made to save 70 lives from starvation. These famine-driven pilgrims were Jacob and his extended family. The second flight to Egypt was equally urgent. At stake was the life of the infant Jesus. As an angel of the Lord announced to Joseph in a dream, King Herod was "going to search for the child to kill Him" (Matt. 2:13).

Matthew links together the two flights to Egypt. He says that in Jesus' recall from Egypt after Herod's death, there was fulfilled the Scripture from Hosea 11:1: "Out of Egypt I called My Son." The statement applies in the first instance to the Israelite nation, for the Lord directed Moses (in Ex. 4:22–23) to say to Pharaoh, "Israel is My firstborn son, and I told you, 'Let My son go, so he may worship Me.'" Matthew properly applied the statement also to Jesus, for He was the substitute Son who in all things was obedient, where the Israelites, the first son, had been disobedient. Flight Two to Egypt was also a lifesaver—this time for us as well as Jesus. Because Jesus' life was spared, He was able to lay down His life on the cross for our salvation.

***Prayer Suggestion:*** *Thank God for sparing His Son's life in Egypt so later He could save yours.*

# Publishing the Good News

Our Lord had a message to deliver as He visited the cities and villages of the Holy Land. The message, according to the Greek text, was the *euangelion:* the Evangel, the Gospel, the Good News. It announced God's new beginning in dealing with people. Living under condemnation for sin was out. In was God's kingdom or rule of undeserved love—the Good News of the forgiveness of sins based on the perfect obedience and the sacrifice rendered by Jesus Christ, the Lamb of God.

Because of that Good News, all who repent and receive God's forgiveness by faith are at peace with God. They can assuredly put a messed-up life behind them. They can joyfully start life afresh to the glory of God. They are healed persons.

This Good News that Jesus preached also became the message of the 12 disciples, whom He appointed as His spokesmen. Our Lord sent them out on a preliminary mission to preach and to heal only among the Israelites. After Jesus ascended and the apostles received the Holy Spirit, they enlarged their mission to include the Gentiles, as Jesus had instructed: "Make disciples of all nations"; "Preach the Good News to all creation"; "You will be My witnesses" (Matt. 28:19; Mark 16:15; Acts 1:8).

The Christian church follows these instructions today. To preach the total Gospel for the salvation of total persons—that is what our mission is all about. That is the mission we are engaged in when we pray for God's kingdom to come and when by word and deed we support it.

***Prayer Suggestion:*** *Reflect on the phrase of the Lord's Prayer, "Thy kingdom come," and thank God for every opportunity you have to proclaim it.*

# God's Care, Everywhere

It was a series of giant steps that took Harlow Shapley from tiny Nashville, Missouri, where he was born in 1885, to the directorship of the Harvard Observatory in Cambridge, Massachusetts. A world-famous astronomer, his thoughts took him far out into space—to stars, galaxies, nebulae. He spoke of the mind and power of God behind this vast universe.

God is everywhere in our world. The psalmist declares, "Where can I go from Your Spirit? Where can I flee from Your presence? If I go up to the heavens, You are there; if I make my bed in the depths, You are there. If I rise on the wings of the dawn, if I settle on the far side of the sea, even there Your hand will guide me, Your right hand will hold me fast" (Ps. 139:7–10).

No one can escape the all-seeing eye and all-knowing mind of God. However, His presence is also a comfort. God is with us wherever we are, guiding and upholding us—in busy cities or in little communities like Nashville, Missouri, which doesn't even show up on a map.

Jesus promises: "I am with you always" (Matt. 28:20). He can make such a promise because He is the Son of God, our all-present Savior. Once He descended to earth that He might walk the dusty roads of the Holy Land, to preach the Gospel, to heal the sick, to suffer and die for the sins of all people. Then He rose from the dead. As St. Paul summarizes: "He who descended is the very one who ascended higher than all the heavens, in order to fill the whole universe" (Eph. 4:10).

God is there where you are; have no doubt about it!

***Prayer Suggestion:*** *Pray that God may make His presence known to you at all times, especially in time of trouble.*

# Make Room for One More

Recruits in the army have been told, "Always dig your foxholes big enough for two." It takes more effort to do this, but it could save one more life. Making room for one more person in your life is a good principle. The Bible states it like this: "Love your neighbor as yourself."

One plus one: This sets a goal within reach. If you were told to help all humanity, you would say, "How can I possibly make room in my life for billions of people?" But to make your proverbial foxhole big enough for two—big enough for one more—that you can do.

In bearing Christian witness we can "each one, reach one." That is how it worked among the first disciples. Andrew brought his brother Peter to Jesus, and Philip brought Nathanael. This kind of discipling starts right in our own families or friendship circles. Save the world? For one person that is mission impossible, but to reach out to one near and dear is mission possible.

During their training period, the disciples went out two by two. The apostle Paul often made room in his ministry for a fellow missionary. Moreover the one-plus-one formula involves more than companionship; it involves prayer. As Jesus said, "If two of you on earth agree about anything you ask for, it will be done for you by My Father" (Matt. 18:19).

Jesus always made room for one more: for the Samaritan woman at Jacob's well, for Zacchaeus, for the penitent thief on the cross, for you and me—because He died for us all.

*Prayer Suggestion: Ask the Lord Jesus for an increase of love that results in caring for one more needy person.*

# Steps to Success

Actor Jimmy Stewart, a church-going Christian, explained in an interview how advancement used to be made in Hollywood: "You started out with little parts in little pictures, and then you went on to little parts in big pictures, then to big parts in little pictures, and finally to big parts in big pictures."

This kind of professional progress differs from what most people seem to prefer: overnight success. But instant stardom misses the most important ingredient: faithfulness. Jesus' parable of the talents highlights such dedication: "Well done, good and faithful servant! You have been faithful with a few things; I will put you in charge of many things" (Matt. 25:21).

Trustworthiness, giving the assignment your best shot, persisting in good effort—these steps lead to success. Success, however, doesn't necessarily mean gaining wealth or promotions. In God's eyes—and often also in the eyes of people—"success" comes from faithfully using and improving one's talents so better service can be rendered. This brings satisfaction to the individual and gives glory to God.

The letter to the Hebrews declares that Moses "was faithful in all God's house" (3:2–3), but "Jesus has been found worthy of greater honor than Moses" because He was our "merciful and faithful high priest in service to God" (2:17), and "He endured the cross, scorning its shame, and sat down at the right hand of the throne of God" (12:2). Jesus did more than set us an example; by His Spirit, He enables us to find true success in serving God.

*Prayer Suggestion: Pray for the Holy Spirit's gift of faithfulness in the performance of your role in life.*

# God's Eye Is on the Sparrow

When gray-haired Ethel Waters, a former nightclub singer, appeared on a television program, she was asked why she didn't sing "Stormy Weather" anymore. She replied, "There is no more stormy weather in my life, only heavenly sunshine." Having become a Christian, she loved to sing "His Eye Is on the Sparrow," thereby confessing her faith in Jesus Christ.

The song Ethel Waters loved to sing is based on these words of Jesus: "Are not two sparrows sold for a penny? Yet not one of them will fall to the ground apart from the will of your Father. ... So don't be afraid; you are worth more than many sparrows" (Matt. 10:29, 31).

Jesus wants us to use the logic of faith. If the Father's eye is on the sparrow—and our Lord assures us that it is—we are to draw the conclusion that God will all the more watch over us, His dear children. "He who did not spare His own Son, but gave Him up for us all—how will He not also, along with Him, graciously give us all things?" (Rom. 8:32).

The winds of change always blow; into everyone's life some rain must fall. Christians, too, encounter stormy weather, Ethel Waters' certainty of cloudless days notwithstanding. Sorely afflicted, believers sometimes feel worthless and alone, as did the psalmist when he said, "I lie awake; I have become like a bird alone on a roof." But his faith in God's promises rallied, and he said, "[God] will respond to the prayer of the destitute; He will not despise their plea" (Ps. 102:7, 17).

If God's eye is on the sparrow, He will surely take care of us. We have Jesus' word on that.

*Prayer Suggestion: Ask your heavenly Father to strengthen you in your faith so you will confidently rely on His care.*

# Bearing One's Cross after Christ

In truth, no one is by nature or name, by talent or treasure, by acts or accomplishments, worthy of Christ. No one deserved to be created, redeemed, and sanctified. Only God's undeserved love, His grace, prompted these acts of the triune God in our behalf. St. Paul has written, "God demonstrates His own love for us in this: While we were still sinners, Christ died for us" (Rom. 5:8).

When it comes to Christian living, we may speak of a discipleship that conforms to the will of Christ and is, in that sense, "worthy" of Him. When our love for Christ exceeds our love for anyone or anything else, we are at heart worthy of Christ because He loved us above all else. When we take up our cross and follow Him, we are worthy of Him.

The call to Christian cross-bearing is a part of the call to discipleship. Our Lord has in mind such cross-bearing as results from our commitment to Him: renunciation of personal gain for His sake, exposure to the stepped-up temptations of Satan, endurance of the world's ridicule and persecution, even the loss of life itself. All the hatred Christ experienced while on earth, the Christian, too, may expect.

We cheerfully bear our crosses because Jesus bore the cross for us. St. John (John 19:17 RSV) writes of Him as He began the painful journey to Calvary: "He went out, bearing His own cross"—really our cross. Therefore, "Worthy is the Lamb, who was slain, to receive power and wealth and wisdom and strength and honor and glory and praise" (Rev. 5:12).

*Prayer Suggestion: Ask your Lord to help you bear every cross that you must bear, giving you the strength to follow in His footsteps.*

# Christ Removes the Crushing Weight

The newspaper told of Mrs. Maxwell Rogers, who lifted a 3,600-pound car off her son when the jack had slipped. In extreme emergencies people have been known to reach back into a hidden source of physical strength and mental resourcefulness they didn't know they had. Can they do this all by themselves? Or is this help from God that is nothing short of miraculous?

The writer of the epistle to the Hebrews devotes his 11th chapter to Old Testament men and women "who through faith conquered kingdoms, administered justice, and gained what was promised; who shut the mouths of lions, quenched the fury of the flames, and escaped the edge of the sword; whose weakness was turned to strength" (vv. 33–34). It was from God that they drew their strength.

In one dimension of life, however, human strength cannot avail. It does not enable us to save ourselves or others from the power and punishment of sin. By the labors of our hands we cannot fulfill God's demands, we cannot earn salvation. What is more, so the psalmist declares, "No one can redeem the life of another or give to God a ransom for him" (Ps. 49:7). The ransom demanded would be entirely too great.

But what we can't do, our Lord Jesus did for us. He gave His life as a ransom for all, and all who believe in Him as the Savior are freed from the fear of death, from the crushing weight of sin—just as that mother lifted an automobile off her son. Indeed Jesus was lifted up on a cross so He might remove our load and draw us up to Him.

***Prayer Suggestion:*** *Ask your Savior to stand by you with His strength, which is made perfect in your weakness.*

# Practicing and Replenishing Freedom

John Foster Dulles, Secretary of State under President Eisenhower, once stated, "Our institutions of freedom will not survive unless they are replenished by the faith that gave them birth." Likewise our spiritual freedom will corrode unless we nurture and defend it. Wrote St. Paul (Gal. 5:1), "It is for freedom that Christ has set us free. Stand firm then, and do not let yourselves be burdened again by a yoke of slavery."

Christ has freed us from the curse of the Law. The Law said, "The soul who sins is the one who will die" (Ezek. 18:4). Jesus took our place, obeying the Law perfectly. When He suffered death, He took on Himself the punishment for our disobedience of the Law, thus freeing us from the fear of death. We can never give up this freedom, can never exchange it for a yoke of slavery to the Law.

Christ also freed us *for* something. Our salvation in Him sets us free to serve Him. It motivates and enables us to do His will, not from a feeling of compulsion but because of love. Christ has set us free to be His voluntary servants, even as He Himself is the Servant and Savior of us all. Set free from cares and worries, we are enabled to worship our God with joy and to find happiness as sons and daughters in His family.

Consider all the institutions founded on the exercise of Christian freedom: our homes, churches, schools, and more. What Mr. Dulles said applies to Christian freedom as well: We daily need to replenish our Christian institutions with the faith that gave them birth.

***Prayer Suggestion:*** *Thank God for the freedom you have in Christ and ask His help for its right use.*

# Faithful Stewards of God's Gifts

James Cash Penney, the founder of the J. C. Penney Company, was a minister's son who grew up in Hamilton, Missouri. Despite his name, money did not play a prominent part in his boyhood days, when he worked for 10 cents a day in a local dry-goods store. But he was thankful, later refusing to open his own chain store in town until his former boss had gone out of business. Penney, active in the Christian laymen's movement, was a generous giver to projects, including a special provision for retired church workers.

God blesses His people in many ways, wanting them to be a blessing to others. Consider Abraham, whom God blessed with material wealth. He does not promise riches to everyone, but He does expect each of us to whom He has given some ability or gift or treasure to share it. God expects His people to be faithful stewards, or managers, over everything He has entrusted to them: treasure, talents, time.

"God loves a cheerful giver," writes St. Paul (2 Cor. 9:7)—a cheerful giver not only of money but of other things as well. God loved Moses, who was a faithful servant in His house. God loved the widow, who gave her mites. He loved Dorcas, who used her time and talent to sew garments for the poor. He loved the early Christians in Macedonia, who, poor but generous, "gave themselves first to the Lord" (2 Cor. 8:5).

As Christians we make our contributions in response to the love of Jesus Christ, who gave all for us when He died on the cross and rose again. The love of Christ constrains us to be faithful stewards of all that God has entrusted to us.

**Prayer Suggestion:** *Ask for God's help to be a better steward of all His gifts to you.*

# Caring about People

Pastor Harold Bell Wright, suffering from tuberculosis, moved to Branson, Missouri, where, at a place called Inspiration Point, he lived in a tent to get plenty of fresh air. While there, he wrote *The Shepherd of the Hills*, the story of a pastor serving people of the hill country.

A good shepherd cares about the sheep. A hired hand, though, leaves the sheep and flees when the wolf comes because he cares nothing for the sheep, said Jesus (John 10:13). He says: "I am the Good Shepherd … I lay down My life for the sheep" (vv. 14–15). All human beings are as lost in sin as sheep in the wilderness. But Jesus, the Good Shepherd, delivered us, leads us, and supplies all our needs.

Just as Jesus cared for the lost, so we also care for people who are lost in sin and for those who are in great need. This caring, this Christian love, can be practiced in our own family, where we have wonderful opportunities to care about one another: parents for children, children for parents, and brothers and sisters for each other.

There is also God's larger family, the community of believers, the Christian church, whose members are at times in need. Jesus identifies them as His brothers and sisters (Matt. 12:50).

In a still larger circle, people who suffer bodily and spiritual needs are our concern. We are Christ's representatives in caring for them. Because Christ, our Good Shepherd, laid down His life to redeem us from sin and death, we are enabled to lay down our lives for all who are in need.

*Prayer Suggestion: Pray for God's help as you care for people and fulfill their needs.*

# The Stork: A Bird on Schedule

When the people of Jeremiah's time failed to repent, ignoring the time of return to the Lord, the prophet exclaimed, "Even the stork in the sky knows her appointed seasons. ... But my people do not know the requirements of the Lord" (Jer. 8:7). The stork, wintering in Africa and returning to Palestine in spring, migrated as regularly as the seasons changed.

The word for stork in the Hebrew Bible is derived from *chased*, the term for God's love and compassion. The stork was thought to be affectionately attentive to its young. Perhaps that's why the stork is associated with babies, who certainly need much loving care.

The stork, like all migratory fowl, knows the times, the prophet said. Do we know our times? Jesus once shed tears over the Holy City because its unholy people did not know the time of their visitation. St. Paul writes, "The hour has come for you to wake up from your slumber, because our salvation is nearer now than when we first believed. The night is nearly over; the day is almost here. So let us put aside the deeds of darkness and put on the armor of light" (Rom. 13:11–12).

"Clothe yourselves with the Lord Jesus Christ," the apostle goes on to say. Christ is the armor of light, the proper attire for the day in which we live and work. Of ourselves we have no righteousness. So God clothes us in the robe of righteousness that Jesus Christ gained for us when as our substitute He kept God's law and by His death atoned for the guilt of our disobedience.

*Prayer Suggestion: Take a moment to ask God in Jesus' name to forgive all your failings and to clothe you with Christ's holiness.*

# Jesus, Our Physician

Visitors to historic Calvary Cemetery in St. Louis have reason to pause at the grave of Dr. Thomas Dooley III, who established village hospitals in Laos and founded MEDICO, now part of Care, Inc. He died of cancer before he reached his mid-30s.

"Physician, heal thyself," goes the old saying. A Christian man, Dr. Dooley would be the first to admit that this is not always possible. Doctors, too, are mortal, subject to the same diseases they seek to cure in their patients.

Only one is exempt from sin and sickness, and that is Jesus Christ. When He was on the cross, the crowd taunted Him by saying, "He saved others, … but He can't save Himself" (Mark 15:31). This insult contained truth and error. Jesus did save others—from bodily sicknesses and, above all, from sin and death. But it was untrue to say, "He can't save Himself." As the almighty Son of God, He could easily have done so, but He chose not to. The time had come for Him to heal us by His wounds and then to rise again.

By His resurrection, Jesus showed that He was true God and our Savior indeed. Death was defeated because sin was defeated by His self-sacrifice on the cross. Jesus, our Good Physician, is Himself beyond the power of sin and death.

Dr. Tom Dooley, even with his great devotion to the sick and suffering, was limited in what he could do. God in His wisdom and love called him home while still a young man, leaving so much, humanly speaking, undone. But Jesus Christ lives forever, now making intercession for us before His heavenly Father.

*Prayer Suggestion: Ask God, for Jesus' sake, to forgive all your iniquities and to heal all your diseases.*

# Completing the Father's Work

In 1821, Moses Austin, a Missouri resident, received a Texas land grant to colonize 300 families. But he died, so his son, Stephen F. Austin, planted the first settlement in Texas. After him, the father of Texas, the city of Austin is named.

It is not uncommon for a son to take over and complete his father's work. In the Bible we read that King David made plans to build a temple, but the actual construction fell to his son Solomon.

The foremost father-and-son relationship takes us to heaven. It involves God the Father and God the Son. So close were they that Jesus, even while on earth, could say, "I and the Father are one" (John 10:30). They were also of one mind and will with regard to the redemption of the sin-fallen human race. At Jacob's well, where Jesus had drawn the Samaritan woman into a deep conversation, He forgot all about eating His noon lunch. He said: "My food … is to do the will of Him who sent Me and to finish His work" (John 4:34). And finish it He did, not stopping until He could exclaim on the cross, "It is finished" (John 19:30). The price for the redemption of the whole world had been paid.

There remains much work for us to do, not the work of earning our salvation—Jesus has done that—but the work of proclaiming the saving Gospel and of showing people their spiritual home. All of us can join Jesus in saying that we must do the Father's work while it is day, for the night comes when no one can work.

*Prayer Suggestion: Ask for God's help in continuing to proclaim the Gospel.*

# New Use for Your Abilities

Some concepts developed for war have been redirected into delightful peace-time pursuits. For example, ski troops with guns turned up as a sport in the 1984 winter Olympics in Yugoslavia.

Centuries ago, in Spain, the Lipizzan horse was developed for war; now, in Austria, these beautiful, graceful white horses are trained to put on highly skilled performances. So also the Jeep, originally developed for war, has many peace-time uses.

We can take this lesson into our personal lives. Words, for example, can be used for oral warfare—to hurt, to cut, to strike inner wounds. But a Christian uses words to express love.

Energy, a gift of God, has been used by some to destroy, to build up a dishonest business, to advance sinful causes. In the Bible we read about Saul the Pharisee, who was full of misdirected energy and zeal and made war on Christians. After he was converted near Damascus, he labored to reconstruct what he had destroyed. He proclaimed Jesus Christ, who by His death and resurrection made peace between God and sinners.

Consider what you can do to find new uses for your abilities, how you can convert them from war use to peace. To use the language of the prophets, you too can beat your swords into plowshares and your spears into pruning hooks. Figuratively speaking, instead of a fighter you are now a farmer who sows, cultivates, and feeds the world.

*Prayer Suggestion: Ask for the Holy Spirit's guidance and strength to redirect your energy to the glory of Christ and the good of His people.*

# Cure for Sin-Sick Hearts

*Crimes of the Heart,* Beth Henley's Pulitzer Prize-winning play, tells about three scheming sisters in a small Mississippi town who grow up in the shadow of their mother's death.

Long before any modern play or story was written on the subject, the Bible said that not only open crimes but also hidden, sneaky sins have their source in the heart. Jesus said, "Out of the heart come evil thoughts, murder, adultery, sexual immorality, theft, false testimony, slander" (Matt. 15:19). Our Lord puts His finger on the same human heart for the failure of love toward God: idolatry, profanity, neglect of worship.

"What has happened to sin?" Dr. Menninger asks in his book on human behavior. He answers: Nothing has happened to sin; it is still very much with us, as it has been from the beginning—only our recognition of sin has blurred. "Every inclination of [man's] heart is evil from childhood," the Lord said to Noah (Gen. 8:21).

This young person's confession, has a familiar ring: "There was a pear tree near our vineyard. In the dead of night we crept up to it—a gang of youthful good-for-nothings—to shake it down and despoil it … to throw the pears to the pigs. We did so only to be doing something which would be pleasant because it was forbidden." The youth was St. Augustine.

There is a cure for the sins of the heart, and St. Augustine personifies it. Through the Gospel, the Holy Spirit leads us to faith in Jesus, the Redeemer from sin, and grants us a new heart, out of which flow thoughts, words, and deeds of love.

***Prayer Suggestion:*** *Pray that the Holy Spirit may create in you a new heart and renew a right spirit within you.*

# Different, Yet the Same

People who feel frustrated or inferior because they aren't good in everything should remember Albert Einstein. While he was a promising violinist and at age 11 did college-level work in physics, he flunked French in his college entrance exam. A mathematical genius, he sometimes miscounted his change when making purchases.

No one is best in everything; there's always something that someone else does better. For purposes of God's glory and for our usefulness to others, God does not distribute personal gifts to all in the same kind and to the same degree.

We see from the world He has created that God loves variety. If He planned a new subdivision, He would, very likely, not build identical houses, as though they were stamped out by the same machine. When God made man and planned for succeeding generations, He did not have in mind to clone all of Adam's descendants. He provided for great variety, not only as to size, skin color, and physical appearance, but also as to gifts of the mind.

Created different, we complement and serve one another with our unique gifts, as do the members of a human body. The church is Christ's body. He is the Head and we are His members, serving Him and one another.

In an important respect, however, we are all the same. We are all sinners and need a Savior. Jesus Christ, the Cross-bearer and Cross-Sufferer in our stead, is that Savior. Because we are thankful for our common salvation, we serve Him with our varying talents.

*Prayer Suggestion: Thank your Maker and Redeemer for His gifts to you, and ask His guidance for their proper use.*

# St. Paul's Conversion, a World Event

Tourists who these days visit the Three Fountains in Rome may be standing on the very ground where St. Paul was martyred on the traditional date of January 29, sometime in the mid-60s. Another event in the life of the apostle, which caused his martyrdom in the first place and which the church observes on January 25, was his conversion. It took place on the outskirts of another city—Damascus. In Rome, St. Paul dies; in Damascus, he was spiritually born.

In St. Paul's life, Rome and Damascus stand for opposites. To Rome the apostle was led as a prisoner for Jesus Christ. To Damascus he had gone to take Christ's disciples prisoners. The voyage to Rome, perilous as it was, was made in consuming love for Christ; the expedition to Damascus in misguided zeal.

What makes so great a change in a person? It is conversion, a 180-degree turn-around. It is nothing less than that. It is becoming a "new creation" in Christ. It takes place when the Holy Spirit, through the Gospel and the washing of Holy Baptism, turns sinful human beings from despair or self-reliance to full dependence on the redeeming love of Jesus Christ for salvation. In no sense does a person participate or cooperate in his or her conversion. Think of Saul the Pharisee on the Damascus Road. Had not Jesus confronted him personally and turned him around, Saul would have stayed Saul.

The conversion of St. Paul, while of utmost significance to him, was a world event. Because he became a Christian, multitudes have heard the saving Gospel and found peace with God in Christ.

***Prayer Suggestion:*** *Give thanks to Christ for converting St. Paul and for making Himself known to you as the Savior.*

# The Day of Salvation Is Now

On a phone-in radio program dealing with alcoholism, a caller said, "I pray the good Lord to keep me from driving while drinking." To this the show host replied, "Why don't you ask the Lord to keep you from drinking?"

Many people seemingly enjoy sin so much that they refuse to go to the root of their problem. They say, "Someday, Lord, I'm going to get out of this dishonest business I'm in, but not for the present; I'm enjoying the money I'm making." Similar reasoning is brought to other vices: using drugs, living in sinful sexual relationships, cheating on one's income taxes, stealing, and the like.

People who think and speak this way are a variety of "tomorrow Christians"—tomorrow they will repent and make their peace with God; tomorrow they will give their heart to God. Right now, however, sinning is too much fun to quit.

The Lord takes a dim view of such reasoning. He reminds us that for many there is no tomorrow, no opportunity to set one's house in order. Therefore His urgent invitation to listen to His voice today! He declares through the holy writer, "Now is the time of God's favor, now is the day of salvation" (2 Cor. 6:2).

True enjoyment and happiness are not found in sinning but in serving Jesus Christ, who in love died on a cross to save us. Angels might well envy us the opportunity to choose the ways we serve the Savior. There is perhaps only one regret on the part of those who have turned to Christ, and that is this: "Alas, that I so late have known Thee, Who are the Fairest and the Best."

**Prayer Suggestion:** *Pray for God's help so you can serve Jesus more.*

# "Where Is the Rest of Me?"

In the 1941 movie *King's Row,* a man's legs were amputated by a vengeful surgeon. When the patient woke up and became aware of his loss, he asked, "Where is the rest of me?" The actor was Ronald Reagan, who in 1965 chose that question as the title of his autobiography.

"Where is the rest of me?" is a good question to ask in my relationship to God. When I am in church, my body is present, but where is my mind? As a disciple I have given only a part of myself to the Lord—perhaps my words but not my deeds, some of my possessions but not my heart. In my daily work I go through the motions of doing my job; I work with my hands but not with my full mental talents.

Jesus rules out the possibility of dividing one's loyalty, giving half of it to Him and half to the god of worldly wealth. During His earthly ministry, He encountered people who wanted to go with Him only a part of the way.

Our Lord was wholeheartedly committed to His mission and ministry as the world's Savior. He declared, "The Son of Man did not come to be served, but to serve, and to give His life as a ransom for many" (Matt. 20:28). When we reverse the reference numbers, we get Matt. 28:20, where Jesus commits us to the Great Commission of making disciples for Him.

The familiar hymn "Take My Life," goes into detail: Take my moments, days, hands, feet, voice, intellect, will, heart, love, and then also my silver and my gold.

Where is the rest of me? Lord, it's all here—here with You and for You.

**Prayer Suggestion:** *Pray for greater love for your Lord so you may be moved to serve Him with all your heart, soul, and mind.*

# God, the World's Owner and Keeper

Some years ago, the supreme court of Switzerland settled the question of who owns Matterhorn mountain and the surrounding resort area. It ruled that it belonged to the community as a whole, not just to the descendants of families who in 1618 purchased feudal rights to the land.

Such a dispute taken to court leads Christians to the ultimate question: Who is the real owner of the world? Who owns all the mountains? Who owns the world's valuable minerals, its fruitful valleys, its rivers and fountains of water, its forests, its flora and fauna, and the air so easily polluted?

The psalmist replies, "The earth is the LORD's, and everything in it, the world and all who live in it" (24:1). God owns the universe and everything in space by reason of the fact that He is its Maker and Preserver. We put up fences, stake out our claims, build cities, and the like, but God is the ultimate Proprietor; He is the one in charge.

What then is our role as the world's inhabitants? We are stewards, caretakers, just as Adam, the first human being, was appointed supervisor of the Garden of Eden. As citizens of the earth, we have the duty to preserve God's earth—its land, water, air, natural assets, its beautiful sights. As Christians, we, however, also have every motivation to do so, for He who is the Maker of heaven and earth is also our Redeemer—the Sender of His only Son, Jesus Christ, to reclaim from sin and conserve for service God's greatest possession: people. We belong to God because He made us, redeemed us, and sanctifies us.

*Prayer Suggestion: Pray for the wisdom and the incentive of faith in Christ to use your gifts and belongings to God's glory.*

# Strength through Faith

Since Sunday school days we've known about the giant Goliath. With the two armies—the Israelites and the Philistines—occupying opposite mountaintops, Goliath would enter the valley below and challenge an Israelite to a duel. Called a "champion," he stood nine feet tall and would have been any coach's dream as a basketball player.

But Goliath was not as big and strong as he thought. David, the shepherd boy, easily felled him, and from that time on it was David who stood tall. The sculptor Michelangelo seemingly indicated this in his famous "David" statue in the Gallery of Fine Arts, Florence. But the real David was great because of his faith in God. He said to Goliath, "I come against you in the name of the LORD Almighty, the God of the armies of Israel, whom you have defied" (1 Sam. 17:45).

How does God save? The prophet Zechariah replies: " 'Not by might nor by power [of man], but by My Spirit,' says the LORD Almighty" (4:6).

The New Testament epistle to the Hebrews devotes its entire 11th chapter to a recital of what men and women of faith accomplished. Faith has great strength—it makes giants of people, not because it relies on human resources but because it takes God at His word; it trusts in His promises. St. Paul declares that the Word of promise, the Gospel, is the power of God for the salvation of everyone who believes in Jesus Christ as the Savior.

This strength is available to you. Believe in the Lord Jesus Christ and you will know this strength.

***Prayer Suggestion:*** *Pray that God may increase your faith so you may be able to meet every challenge in your life.*

# One Person Is Important

During a 25-year period, a church near Glasgow, Scotland, received only one new member: David Livingstone, through whom many Africans were won for Christ. All churches want to gain many new members, but when that is not possible, we should not lose hope. God's arithmetic doesn't always agree with ours. Sometimes He sets aside for Himself one person that through that one, He might gain many more.

From every viewpoint, one person is important in God's sight. On many occasions Jesus addressed large crowds, but that did not keep Him from attending to individuals. He gave much of His time to 12 men, who would after His resurrection and ascension gain many converts. What is more, our Lord often gave His full attention to one person, like the shepherd seeking his one lost sheep. He did this, for example, at Jacob's well, where He conversed at length with a Samaritan woman (John 4:4–42). In fact, one of the finest sermons that Jesus preached had this audience of one person. Through her He gained many followers in that village.

Every person we meet is important. God created each one, Jesus Christ shed His precious blood for each one, and the Holy Spirit wants to make each one a holy temple.

This applies also to each one of us. We can feel good ourselves because we know that we have worth in God's sight and are the instruments of His love toward others. St. Paul said, "The Son of God … loved me and gave Himself for me" (Gal. 2:20). This fact prompted the apostle to reach out to others with Christ's love.

*Prayer Suggestion: Say, "Lord, teach me the worth of myself and of every person entering my life."*

# Problems: Their Source and Solution

A survey conducted at a church-related college found that those 1,500 students had 3,165 problems—something like 2.09 problems per student. Of course, people of all ages and walks of life have problems—many of them more than two or three.

Sometimes problems are interrelated, and when they come, they descend on us in clusters. The Japanese say that a man will weep three times in his lifespan. Many people weep more often than that, and sometimes for extended periods of time, as the psalmist declares: "My tears have been my food day and night" (42:3).

What is the source of human problems? Some people create their own problems. Jesus said in a parable that some who hear the Word of God soon lose it because they permit their faith to be choked by "life's worries, riches and pleasures" (Luke 8:14). Sin lies at the root of human problems—not necessarily one particular sin but sin in general. In the beginning Adam and Eve sinned. The result of their disobedience was a whole cycle of problems that still affect us today.

But there is a solution to sin, and that eases our problems. In Jesus Christ we have redemption through His shed blood; we have the forgiveness of sins. In Christ, God has become our heavenly Father, who loves us and cares about us. Because we are God's sons and daughters, we can confidently come to Him in prayer and cast all our cares and burdens on Him. Our problems are much easier to deal with when we stand in a loving relationship to God.

**Prayer Suggestion:** *Ask God to give you the wisdom and strength to deal with your problems, trusting in His power to help you.*

# No Hometown Welcome

Homer, the Greek epic poet who flourished in the ninth century B.C., had to beg to stay alive. Only after he was long dead—and famous—did various cities each claim him as their "famous son." Hence the rhyme: "Seven cities claimed old Homer dead, In which the living Homer begged his bread."

Perhaps it is different when a hero has established himself in his lifetime. Towns and cities like to bestow honor on former or present residents who have found success in the world. On occasion they may plan special celebrations to say nice things to them. The folks at home like to bask in reflected glory. Supposedly the hometown is to be credited for producing an outstanding individual.

If this is so, why was Nazareth so inhospitable to its "native son" Jesus? And why did Jesus say, "No prophet is accepted in his hometown" (Luke 4:24)?

Gaining a reputation in the world at large is not the same as gaining it in one's hometown. The local people are inclined to say, "This person is just as we are. We know his ability, his circumstances, his family. Surely he can't be someone special."

Further, the Nazarenes seemed to feel slighted because Jesus had brought fame to Capernaum and other cities by doing His mighty works there instead of in Nazareth. They overlooked that it was their unbelief that kept Jesus from proclaiming His Word and doing His deeds in their midst.

Unbelief always shuts the door to Christ, who in love died for us. His is a standing offer of grace: "Here I am! I stand at the door and knock" (Rev. 3:20).

***Prayer Suggestion:*** *Bid Jesus welcome in your heart and home that He may share His blessings with you.*

## Spiritual Fitness

Ours is an age of physical fitness. People exercise, jog, watch their diet, and want air, earth, and water to stay clean for the sake of good health. Bodily fitness, so closely related to mental and emotional fitness, is very important.

All-around good health includes spiritual fitness. It deserves top rating because it pertains to one's relationship to God for time and eternity. St. Paul advises young Timothy to guard his health but adds, "Train yourself to be godly. For physical training is of some value, but godliness has value for all things, holding promise for both the present life and the life to come" (1 Tim. 4:7–8).

Jesus in His youth grew not only physically and intellectually but also in favor with God—that is, spiritually. Throughout His life, He cultivated close communion with His heavenly Father.

What Jesus did suggests what we, too, can do to stay spiritually fit. He prayed fervently, He immersed Himself in the teachings of Holy Scripture, He regularly attended worship in God's house, He exercised Himself in love toward others.

What is more, Jesus made it possible for us to become spiritually fit—fit to be accepted by God—when He died to atone for our sins. Then, having risen from the dead and ascended into heaven, He sent His Holy Spirit on Pentecost and still sends Him into our hearts so we can grow in holiness from day to day.

Christ invites us all to follow His spiritual fitness program as outlined in His Gospel.

**Prayer Suggestion:** *Pray that God may bless your efforts to attain spiritual fitness.*

# When Hardship Strikes

Rupert Hughes (1872–1956) was a prolific writer of fiction and drama. Among his works are *We Can't Have Everything* and *The Uphill Road.* These titles indicate that life is often a struggle, that some things are beyond our reach.

Christianity does not promise us a primrose path through life. St. Paul says: "We must go through many hardships to enter the kingdom of God" (Acts 14:22). Here is bad news and good news. The bad news is that life is a passage through tribulations. The good news is that we enter the kingdom of God—the kingdom of grace now and the kingdom of glory later.

Jesus likewise says, "In this world you will have trouble. But take heart! I have overcome the world" (John 16:33). The Greek word for "hardship, trouble, or tribulation" means pressure, a pressing or rubbing together, oppression, distress—not unlike a mother's birth pains that are forgotten once the baby is born. Jesus urges us to be cheerful at the good news that He has overcome the world. Our Lord Himself passed through great hardships; He was in all points tempted and tested as we are. But He, having passed through His suffering and dying in our behalf, rose from the dead, giving us hope and newness of life amid all our hardships.

Perhaps you have experienced life as an uphill road. Remember: Christ gives you the strength to keep climbing. You know also that you can't have everything—you may lack riches, great honor, close family ties, health. Don't worry! Be thankful, happy, and content with what you have. Be glad that Christ is in your life and that your life is found in His.

***Prayer Suggestion:*** *Pray that Christ's strength may be made perfect amid your weakness.*

# With Rights Go Responsibilities

While serving as U.S. Senator from Maine, Margaret Chase Smith told a group of teenagers, "Don't demand special privileges under the guise of equal rights." Rights and privileges do go together—but so do rights and responsibilities.

The Bible speaks of the rights and privileges of Christians. St. John records (1:12), "To all who received [Christ], to those who believed in His name, He gave the right to become children of God." St. Paul states (Rom. 8:17), "If we are children, then we are heirs—heirs of God and co-heirs with Christ." St. Peter writes (1 Peter 2:9), "You are a chosen people, a royal priesthood, a holy nation, a people belonging to God."

Jesus Himself focused on the rights of those who follow Him—the right to live in the freedom of truth, the right to pray to the heavenly Father, the right of living in fellowship with Him. All these rights are the fruits of Christ's redemption, along with the forgiveness of sins, the deliverance from the fear of death, and the gift of peace with God.

The reverse side of the coin shows the responsibilities of being a Christian—not thereby to earn salvation but as evidence that we have it. The responsibilities of being Christ's disciple are to serve Him with a life of piety and of good works. Among these are, in the words of St. Peter, that we "declare the praises of Him who called you out of darkness into His wonderful light" (1 Peter 2:9).

The apostle adds that we have received mercy. This is a great privilege. It prompts us to express our thankfulness by carrying out our responsibilities with joy.

***Prayer Suggestion:*** *Pray for a greater awareness of your rights and of the responsibilities accompanying them.*

# Waiting for God

Samuel Beckett, in the play *Waiting for Godot*, wrote of two tramps patiently waiting for Mr. Godot to show up. But he doesn't come. At long last a boy comes on stage and tells the tramps, "Mr. Godot can't come today, but surely tomorrow." One gets the impression that on the next day the same non-events will be repeated.

Is God like His near namesake, Godot? Does He promise things but fail to fulfill them? Do we wait in vain for an answer to our prayer? Is worship—and the Christian faith as a whole—an exercise in futility?

One fact we must always bear in mind: God bids us wait and be patient. God is God, and He will act at His own good time. He said to the prophet Habakkuk, who expected an answer from God: "Though [the vision] linger, wait for it; it will certainly come and will not delay" (2:3).

Throughout Scripture, but especially in the psalms, we find exhortations to patience. God tells us through the psalmist, "Wait for the LORD; be strong and take heart and wait for the LORD" (v. 14). When we tend to grow impatient, we hear the voice of Jesus: "My time has not yet come" (John 2:4).

God rewards our patience with an outpouring of His blessings. Surely He who in love gave us the greatest Gift of all—His own Son, Jesus Christ, as our Savior—will not deny us the lesser gifts we need. While we wait, we can occupy ourselves with doing our Lord's work. Said St. Paul, "Let us not become weary in doing good, for at the proper time we will reap a harvest if we do not give up" (Gal. 6:9).

***Prayer Suggestion:*** *Pray for patience as you await God's answer to your prayer.*

# Intelligent Believing and Obeying

Hiroo Onado, a lieutenant in the Japanese army during World War II, hid out in the jungles of the Philippines for 29 years, waiting for orders to return to Japan. What obedience! By way of contrast, in 18th-century Austria, a special order of merit was given to soldiers who used their minds, even when it sometimes meant disobeying orders.

What kind of disciples are we to be? obedient? intelligent?

Human reason is not the source and criterion of faith. It cannot fathom "the deep things of God." At the same time, the human mind—knowledge, intelligence, reason—plays a part in Christianity. Jesus said, "Love the Lord your God with all your heart and with all your soul and with all your mind" (Matt. 22:37). The saving faith in Jesus Christ is not possible when a person's mind rejects the facts of salvation. But when faith is added to knowledge, conviction ensues. St. Peter bids us, "Grow in the grace and knowledge of our Lord and Savior Jesus Christ" (2 Peter 3:18).

The right use of the mind is called for also in Christian life as it flows from the saving Christian faith. It is not blind conformity nor is it a mindless performance that God desires. Rather it is intelligent, joyful, and willing obedience. When Christians, out of love to God and in appreciation of His mercies, yield themselves body and soul to obedience, they are performing a service that St. Paul describes in the Greek as "logical," that is, proper to the spiritual commitment they have made to Christ.

*Prayer Suggestion: Pray that God may open your understanding more to the love He has shown in Christ and to the love you can render in response.*

# God Looks on the Heart

In Peter De Varies' story *The Glory of the Hummingbird* one of the characters declares, "There has been enough of personality; it is time for character." The cult of personality, the preoccupation with good outward appearance and skin-deep beauty, the greater emphasis on style than on substance—we've had enough of these. It is time for upright character, truth, reality. As Jesus said of the Pharisees, "You clean the outside of the cup and dish, but inside they are full of greed and self-indulgence. ... You are like whitewashed tombs, which look beautiful on the outside but on the inside are full of dead men's bones and everything" (Matt. 23:25, 27).

People are sometimes impressed by what they see. So it was with the prophet Samuel, whom God sent to Bethlehem to anoint as king one of the sons of Jesse. Samuel was impressed by the oldest son. But God said, "Do not consider his appearance or his height, for I have rejected him. The LORD does not look at the things man looks at. Man looks at the outward appearance, but the LORD looks at the heart" (1 Sam. 16:7).

The psalmist declares, "O LORD, You have searched me and You know me" (139:1). God is aware of what goes on in our lives. He sees the saving faith in those who believe in Jesus Christ, their Savior and Lord. He knows the feedback of love they have toward Him and to His brothers and sisters in need. He looks upon our hearts and knows our own needs.

Yes, it is time to put away appearances—time to cultivate Christian character and honesty of heart.

*Prayer Suggestion: Ask the Lord to cleanse your heart of all pride and deceit and to grant you the uprightness of faith in Jesus Christ.*

# More Power to You!

Plato, the Greek philosopher, once said, "Only those who do not desire power are fit to hold it."

What a contrast to Pontius Pilate, who represented the power of the Roman government. An administrator with the army at his command, Pilate was cruel. At various times he ordered people slaughtered. He ordered Jesus scourged and then sentenced Him to the cross, though he himself had pronounced Jesus innocent. Pilate desired power, the power of the sword, and he proved himself unfit to hold it.

Jesus told Pilate, "You would have no power over Me if it were not given to you from above" (John 19:11). This saying of Jesus reflects His conviction that the superior will of the heavenly Father had to be done so, in fulfillment of the Scriptures, He might yield His life for the salvation of all humankind. Pilate was under divine authority, and while he was an instrument in the hands of God, he was fully responsible for the misuse of his power in sentencing Jesus to death.

Our Lord submitted to the power of Pilate so the greater power of the love of God might rule our lives. The power of the Roman government is long gone, but our Lord's kingdom of grace and love flourishes still. It is not the power of the sword that Jesus wields or that He wants His church to wield. It is the power of the Gospel, which alone changes human hearts and frees people from sin and enables them to serve the living God.

When you believe in Jesus, a great power comes into your life: the power of the love of God in Christ.

***Prayer Suggestion:*** *Pray that the Holy Spirit may strengthen your faith in Jesus and, as a fruit of that faith, give you the power of love.*

# God, the Giver of Life

Marlin Perkins, through his TV program "Wild Kingdom" as well as his *Animal Faces* and other writings, encouraged us, as coinhabitants of this world, to treat God's creatures with care.

The proper care of wildlife is part of the stewardship life God wants us to lead. We are caretakers both of inanimate things—gold, silver, soil, water, forests—as well as living things—the fish of the sea, the birds of the air, the fauna. God Himself provides for them, and He wants us to help in this by preserving the environment that supports wildlife.

In the Old Testament, God made provision for soil conservation for a purpose, saying through Moses, "For six years you are to sow your fields and harvest the crops, but during the seventh year let the land lie unplowed and unused. Then the poor among your people may get food from it, and the wild animals may eat what they leave" (Ex. 23:10–11).

In His talks, many of them held outdoors, Jesus referred often to life around Him, to fig trees and the lilies of the field as well as to sparrows, foxes, camels, sheep, oxen, and the like. While He indeed valued them as creatures God made, His greater love went to human beings made in the likeness of God. Not the animals but Adam sinned in the beginning, and it was for all of Adam's descendants that He gave His life.

Having received life from Christ—eternal life beginning now—we are enabled to see all of life in a new perspective, wildlife included.

*Prayer Suggestion: Ask for God's guidance as you evaluate life around you in this world.*

# In the Eyes of the Public

Does it matter what people think of us? After all, the standards by which people judge vary greatly. Further, the information on the basis of which opinions are formed is usually very limited. Consequently, we sometimes must take special measures to make clear our intent or state of mind.

Sometimes we have to do something special to correct possible misconceptions. For example, the morning was cold when King Charles I of England was to be executed for treason. Since he didn't want his enemies to think that he was shaking from fear, he wore two shirts to keep warm.

Does it make a difference what the general public thinks of Christians? The apostles thought that it did. They urged first-century Christians to cultivate peaceful relations with their heathen neighbors so the light of the Gospel would shine through them and bring warmth into a cold world. Their love, not only to one another but also to their enemies, made a deep impression on their contemporaries.

Of early Christians it was said, "See how they love one another!" This was said in high praise and admiration. Showing love brings the saving faith in Jesus to light. In love Jesus walked the Calvary road all the way to the cross so He might redeem us not only from something—from sin and the fear of death—but also for something—for living uprightly in this world as His disciples.

**Prayer Suggestion:** *Pray that your life in Christ may show through clearly and strongly in all you say and do.*

# Christ Is the Connection

During World War II more than 16,000 prisoners of war died while building the so-called "death railroad" and bridge over the River Kwai. The purpose of the project was to connect Thailand and Burma.

Connections are sometimes made at a tremendous price. If that is so with regard to the bridges we build, the canals we dig, and the dams we construct, think of the cost required to build a bridge between fallen humankind and the holy God! A far greater effort would be demanded than what any one human being—or the whole human race, for that matter—could put forth. Sinners cannot reunite themselves with God by what they do or leave undone. They cannot redeem themselves nor offer to God a ransom for others.

It all has to begin with God, and from Him must come the completion of the reunion. And come they did. He built the bridge from earth to heaven, and the name of that bridge is Love. As Jesus declared, "For God so loved the world that He gave His one and only Son, that whoever believes in Him shall not perish but have eternal life" (John 3:16).

St. Paul adds his testimony in writing to Timothy: "There is one God and one mediator between God and men, the man Christ Jesus, who gave Himself as a ransom for all men" (1 Tim. 2:6). The apostle introduced this passage by saying that God wants all people to be saved and to know the truth.

A yawning gulf was created by sin that human beings could not bridge. But God bridged it when He sent His Son, Jesus Christ, into the world as Savior. Now we are again connected.

*Prayer Suggestion:* Thank God for sending His Son to be the Way, the Truth, and the Life. Ask His help as you seek to direct others to this way.

# We Know Whom We Have Believed

It should not surprise us when people speak negatively about Jesus Christ and His Gospel. Our Lord's enemies accused Him before Pontius Pilate of perverting the nation, of telling people not to pay taxes, and of proclaiming Himself a temporal king. They said many evil things also against the apostle Paul, as though he were a common criminal and should be punished as such. They considered the Gospel to be foolishness.

Abraham Lincoln was criticized severely. A Chicago newspaperman wrote this about the Gettysburg Address: "The cheek of every American must tingle with shame when he reads the silly, flat, and dish-watery utterances of the man who has been pointed out to intelligent foreigners as the president of the United States."

Harsh criticism about Christ, Christians, and Christianity need not upset us. We can say with St. Paul: "I know whom I have believed" (2 Tim. 1:12). He knew Jesus, who had appeared to him on the road to Damascus and who turned his life around. The apostle declared after his conversion, "The life I live in the body, I live by faith in the Son of God, who loved me and gave Himself for me" (Gal. 2:20).

We, too, have come to know Jesus Christ as our dearest friend. We have experienced His love and the love of those who serve Him. We have found God's Word to be true—the Word of the Law that convicts us of sin and the Word of the Gospel that brings the good news of our salvation. We know Jesus; that is all that matters.

***Prayer Suggestion:*** *Pray that you may grow in the grace and knowledge of your Lord and Savior, Jesus Christ.*

# Above and Beyond the Call of Duty

The following help-wanted ad for a garage foreman once appeared in a St. Louis, Missouri, newspaper: "Qualifications: Patience of Job, leader of men, a lover of people, nerves of steel, six hands, twelve ears, ability to be in four places at once. Experience. See John H … "

It is evident that the garage owner resorted to an over-statement, even to a touch of humor, in listing the qualifications. But he also made it plain that an employee will at times render services above and beyond the call of duty.

The Lord is that kind of an employer. When Jesus called 12 men to be His disciples and later His apostles, He didn't promise that "the livin' is easy" and the work always pleasant. Instead He said this: "I am sending you out like sheep among wolves. Therefore be as shrewd as snakes and as innocent as doves" (Matt. 10:16).

Christ's full-time workers today know that their work doesn't always fall into a neat daily schedule. They are prepared to agree to the aforementioned qualifications of the garage foreman: "Patience of Job, leader of men, lover of people …"

So what else is new? This: Every Christian, as a servant of Jesus Christ, is expected to go above and beyond the call of duty, to be hassled and harassed in Christ's behalf and for the good of His brothers and sisters. Why are Christians willing to go the second, even the third and the fourth, mile? Because they believe that this is what Jesus did in their behalf. He endured suffering, even death on the cross, for their eternal good, for your eternal good.

***Prayer Suggestion:*** *Pray for strength to render that extra Christian service in critical situations.*

# The Book We Need

While it's interesting to know that *Gone with the Wind* is the only book Margaret Mitchell ever wrote, it's imperative to know that the Bible is the only Book God ever wrote. Of course, God did not write it with His own hand. God employed a great many writers, from Moses, who wrote the first five books of the Old Testament, to St. John the Divine, author of Revelation, the last New Testament book. He did not use the dictation method; if He had, all the writers would have written in the same style. God inspired the writers. As St. Peter declares (2 Peter 1:21), "Men spoke from God as they were carried along by the Holy Spirit"—and wrote from God. St. Paul adds, "All Scripture is God-breathed" (2 Tim. 3:16).

We cannot know or explain the process of the Bible's divine inspiration, but we do know what the Bible is—the Word of God—and we know why it was written—to instruct us for salvation through faith in Christ Jesus. Jesus said, "The Scriptures ... testify about Me" (John 5:39). They testify that Jesus is God's Son, who died for our sins and rose again.

Because the keynote of salvation is so clear in the Bible, it was not necessary for God to write other books on this theme. Whatever is clearly and concisely stated in creeds, confessions, and catechisms is drawn from the Bible; they are not bibles to be added to the Bible.

The Bible is the one book God wrote. No other book from the pens or typewriters of human authors can ever replace the Bible.

***Prayer Suggestion:*** *Pray that the Holy Spirit may enlighten you as you read God's Word and that He may draw you closer to Jesus.*

# The Bible Leads Us to Christ

Some years ago Dr. Nelson Glueck, then president of Hebrew Union College—Jewish Institute of Religion, Cincinnati, stated that the copper mines of King Solomon had been found in the southern part of Judea. He said the presence of metals had been indicated in Moses' words that the Promised Land was "a land where the rocks are iron" (Deut. 8:9). Glueck added, "I have always gone on the assumption that the historical statements of the Bible are true."

Long before Glueck, when the Wise Men came to King Herod to ask where the newborn Messiah could be found, the biblical scholars in Jerusalem acted on the conviction that the prophetic statements of the Bible were true. Since the prophet Micah had said that Christ was to be born in Bethlehem, Herod sent the Wise Men to Bethlehem—and there they did, in fact, find Him.

The Bible can be depended on—above all, to lead us to the greatest treasure of all: Christ the Savior. No one ever goes astray when he or she accepts as true that all people are sinful and in need of the Savior. You will never be disappointed when you follow the scriptural road signs that direct you to Jesus Christ. When He calls Himself the Way, the Truth, and the Life, believe it! When He bids you, burdened with many a care, to come to Him for rest, believe it and go! When the unanimous voice of the apostles proclaim Him the Lamb of God offered for the sins of all, including your sins, believe it!

Remember: The statements of the Bible concerning Jesus are true!

***Prayer Suggestion:*** *Pray that the Holy Spirit may open to you the Scriptures to lead you to Christ.*

## Glimpses of Heaven

Before Moses died, God led him to the top of Mount Nebo to show him the beauty and bounty of the land that the children of Israel were to possess. In his play *The Green Pastures*, Marc Connelly has God say to Moses concerning heaven, which he was soon to enter, "Moses, it's a million times nicer than the land of Canaan."

Of all the beautiful sights and places we may have seen in our travels—impressive waterfalls, flora and fauna in their natural setting, a colorful sunset, the majestic mountains—we can say heaven is a million times nicer.

Who on this side of heaven can really say what it is like? Our minds are too limited to comprehend and describe heaven. Heaven is like the perfect paradise in which Adam and Eve lived before they fell into sin. It is a place of reunion with loved ones. Jesus speaks of heaven as the Father's house of many mansions. The book of Revelation affords a glimpse into heaven by means of pictures and symbols: a well laid-out city with jeweled walls, streets of gold, gates of pearl. The holy seer tells us of sad experiences that will not be repeated in heaven: no more tears, no mourning, no more pain, no death.

The most consoling fact is that in heaven we will be in the presence of Jesus Christ, our dearest friend. Our Lord prayed for this, "Father, I want those You have given Me to be with Me where I am, and to see My glory, the glory You have given Me because You loved Me before the creation of the world" (John 17:24). Fellowship with Jesus is something we have known on earth. It is a foretaste of eternal life; it is a glimpse of heaven.

*Prayer Suggestion: Pray for steadfastness in faith so you may be with Jesus forever.*

# Gaining Life through Serving

Jim Elliott, a missionary, wrote this as a theme of his life of self-surrender: "He is no fool who gives what he cannot keep to gain what he cannot lose." He gave and received to the fullest when he, along with several associates, was killed by Auca Indians in Ecuador.

Not everyone is divinely called to be a missionary. Most of us work as parents, wage earners, caregivers, and the like. It is in the context of that life that Christians fulfill their calling, in the words of St. Paul, "to live lives worthy of God, who calls you into His kingdom and glory" (1 Thess. 2:12).

Whatever their vocation, Christians are set free by Jesus Christ to live a life of service where they are. Once enslaved by sin and the fear of death, they are redeemed by the blood of Christ not only from something, but also for something

This makes Christian living an adventure, regardless of outward circumstances. The challenge is to live according to the will of the heavenly Father, who in Christ made them His sons and daughters. This is spiritual enrichment through voluntary self-denial. It is finding through losing—as Jesus said, "Whoever loses his life for My sake will find it" (Matt. 10:39). And with this goes the promise of a reward of grace: eternal life.

What shall I do with my life? This is St. Paul's answer: "I have been crucified with Christ and I no longer live, but Christ lives in me. The life I live in the body, I live by faith in the Son of God, who loved me and gave Himself for me" (Gal. 2:20).

*Prayer Suggestion: Tell the Lord Jesus Christ that you, too, want to do something with your life.*

# Distinguishing Trivia from Treasure

One February day in 1975, the despondent head of a large company deliberately broke a window in his skyscraper office. Careful to pick out the glass so as not to cut himself, he crawled through the window and leaped to his death.

There is such a thing as being careful in little things but utterly without regard to the big things or acts that can destroy one's life. Jesus referred to such an inconsistency when He said to the punctilious Pharisees, "You blind guides! You strain out a gnat but swallow a camel" (Matt. 23:24). Again, He asked what it profits a person if he or she gained earthly trinkets but lost the treasure of greatest value: one's very self, the soul, the wealth and health of the life in Christ (Mark 8:36).

People consult their doctors about minor aches and pains, but are sometimes neglectful about the major disease that can deprive them of life hereafter: sin. Judas Iscariot was greatly concerned about a little thing in life: money. For that reason he stole from the disciples' treasury and, in the end, betrayed his Lord for 30 pieces of silver. In so doing, he forfeited God's greatest gifts: physical and eternal life.

Jesus put things in the right perspective for us by bidding us to be enriched in Him, the Pearl of great price. He became our Savior of priceless worth when He laid down His life for our salvation and then assumed it again in His resurrection. He teaches us the difference between life's trifles and life's treasure.

*Prayer Suggestion: Pray that you may be enriched through a greater knowledge and appreciation of Christ's love for you.*

# Jesus, Our Healer

In the 1860s the Hawaiian Islands established a leper colony on an isolated peninsula of Molokai Island. One man, Father Damien, a missionary from Belgium, ministered to those in the colony until he himself died of leprosy.

Leprosy infects the skin and the surface nerves, causing disfigurement. This dreaded disease is often mentioned in the Bible. When Jesus was asked whether He were the promised Messiah, He said, "The blind receive sight, the lame walk, those who have leprosy are cured, the deaf hear, the dead are raised, and the good news is preached to the poor" (Matt. 11:5). These were to be the Messiah's works, according to Isaiah's prophecy.

Great was Jesus' compassion for the sick, including the leprosy sufferers. On one occasion He healed a walking colony of 10 lepers and was pleased when one of them, a Samaritan, returned to give thanks.

Jesus effected an even greater healing when He healed us from the leprosy of sin. This He could do because He was the sinless Son of God and had power over sin, death, and Satan. Had He been subject to sin, He Himself would have succumbed to the disease. But Jesus was set apart from all sinners by His holiness and was able to conquer sin.

Molokai, once known as the "Lonely Island," is today called the "Friendly Island." Our world, too, has changed because Jesus was here in the flesh and is still with us in His unseen presence. Truly we can sing, "What a Friend we have in Jesus, All our sins and griefs to bear!"

*Prayer Suggestion: Pray that Jesus, the Healer and Helper of the helpless, may come into your heart and home with His love.*

# Different, yet Much the Same

Many movies have been made that portray brothers living on different sides of the law or track. The story line is true to life. The great theologian John Calvin, for example, had a brother who was a bum. The same parents and the same home environment do not guarantee the same personality.

The Bible, a mirror of human nature and behavior, reflects this fact. Of the first two sons ever born, Cain was a killer. Jesus in several parables draws sharp distinctions between brothers, as in the parable of the prodigal son. At another time He spoke of a son who readily agreed to do what the father said but didn't do it, while the other son was the reverse; he at first said no, then changed his mind and obeyed his father.

Despite great differences, even among brothers, all people have something in common. The bond that unites us all is sin—sin of one kind or another. The prodigal son sinned when he blew his inheritance, but his unforgiving, self-righteous brother was also a sinner. In today's world we still have killers like Jack the Ripper. But we also have those who, with their tongues, rip up the good name and reputation of others. Some rob by pressing a gun against their victims' ribs, others by committing white-collar crimes.

Since we are all brothers and sisters under the skin, none of us can be proud or self-righteous. All of us need the salvation and forgiveness of Jesus Christ. He forgave the coarse thief on the cross; He also forgave the crooked tax collector Zacchaeus. Because Jesus forgives all who come to Him, there is hope for you and me.

*Prayer Suggestion: Pray that Christ may make you more fully His own, forgiving you and prompting you to serve Him.*

# What Is Past Is Past

Lola, the woman in William Inge's play *Come Back, Little Sheba*, tries to recapture the past. Sheba, her runaway dog, will not come back. Even if it did, it could not (though Lola wishes it could) substitute for her long-dead baby.

To paraphrase a poem: The moving finger writes, and having writ, moves on. Not all our piety or wit can lure it back to cancel half a line, nor all our tears wash out a word of it.

There is no purpose in worrying about the present or future. The psalmist declares, "In vain you rise early and stay up late, toiling for food to eat" (127:2). Jesus tells us: "Do not worry about your life, what you will eat or drink; or about your body, what you will wear" (Matt. 6:25). And it is just as futile to worry about what might have been. Clock and calendar cannot be turned back. Contentment with what we are and have is the key word in every stage of life.

If our past sins give us concern—which is good if it keeps us from recommitting them—we can turn to God in repentance and rest assured of His forgiveness. St. Paul writes, "We are justified freely by [God's] grace through the redemption that came by Christ Jesus. God presented Him as a sacrifice of atonement, through faith in His blood. He did this to demonstrate His justice, because in His forbearance He had left the sins committed beforehand unpunished" (Rom. 3:24–25).

Jesus Christ died for our sins. In Him we have forgiveness for sins that are past. We can be of good cheer!

*Prayer Suggestion: In your prayer confess your sins to God, asking Him to forgive you for Jesus' sake. God will grant your request.*

# God Is There

The remains of Charles A. Lindbergh (once known as the Lone Eagle) rest on Maui of the Hawaiian Islands. The epitaph on his headstone reads, "If I rise on the wings of the dawn, if I settle on the far side of the sea, even there Your hand will guide me, Your right hand will hold me fast" (Ps. 139:9–10). These are fitting words for the man who, in 1927, took the wings of a small plane and flew across the Atlantic ocean.

God is everywhere. That means, on the one hand, that none can escape Him. David declares, "Where can I go from Your Spirit? Where can I flee from Your presence? If I go up to the heavens, You are there. If I make my bed in the depths, You are there" (Ps. 139:7–8).

God is present, even if we can't see Him. People can run away from members of their family, but they cannot run away from God. Jonah found this out when, instead of going to Nineveh, he boarded a freighter bound for Tarshish. God found him, even when the crew had cast him into the sea.

God is everywhere. This fact is also a consolation, as David writes in another psalm, "I will fear no evil, for You are with me" (23:4). Wherever we are—on a journey, at home, at work, in a hospital—God is there too. God is always present.

God's presence comforts us because He is our Immanuel, our God-with-us Savior. In Him, who gave His life for us, we are reconciled, forgiven, accepted. He has promised, "I am with you always, to the very end of the age" (Matt. 28:20).

*Prayer Suggestion: If you feel lonely, ask God to assure you of His presence as you seek Him in His Word and in the company of His people.*

# Son and Servant

Among the Old Testament titles given to the coming Messiah are Son and Servant. Both titles apply to Jesus, the promised Messiah. At His Baptism the voice from heaven said, "This is My Son, whom I love; with Him I am well pleased" (Matt. 3:17). Further, Jesus was the Servant who said, "The Son of Man did not come to be served, but to serve, and to give His life as a ransom for many" (Mark 10:45). Jesus said this when the mother of James and John had asked that her two sons be seated to His right and left in His kingdom. It was their pride that spoke here—the desire to rule, to be served, rather than to serve.

Perhaps we, too, have at times preferred the crown of a ruler to the towel of a servant. If so, we need to see our position in a clear light. We are God's sons and daughters. The heavenly Father adopted us into His family for Jesus' sake. As His children we will inherit eternal life. Is that not sufficient reason to serve God? We are not God's slaves, compelled to serve; we are His willing servants, doing God's will because we want to.

In Japan, women used to regard it the highest honor to serve in the emperor's palace. How similar to Christians! We are to serve Christ who redeemed us. So we sing:

> Then all that you would have me do
> Shall such glad service be for you
> That angels wish to do it too.
> Christ Crucified, I come.

*Prayer Suggestion:* Thank God for adopting you as His child, then ask Him to show you how and where you can serve Him.

## Jesus: Innocent, yet guilty

After World War I, when feelings against foreigners ran high, two Italian-born men, Nicolo Sacco and Bartolomeo Vanzetti, were tried for the murder of a paymaster and his guard at a Massachusetts shoe factory. They were executed August 23, 1927. Many people believed that the verdict was directed more by prejudice than evidence.

In the case of Jesus Christ (Luke 22–23), there is no doubt but that hateful emotion carried the day. The charge against Him in the Sanhedrin was that of blasphemy: By calling Himself the Son of the Highest, Jesus was speaking blasphemy. In the hearing before Pontius Pilate, the charge was that of political subversion: fomenting against taxes and proclaiming Himself king. Those who accused Him cared little about the specific charges; they simply wanted Him pronounced guilty and executed. Pilate declared, however, "I find no basis for a charge against this man" (Luke 23:4); He is innocent.

In a sense, Jesus was guilty—because He took the place of every sinner. St. Paul teaches clearly, "God made Him who had no sin to be sin for us" (2 Cor. 5:21). In His role as the substitute Sinbearer, Jesus assumed the guilt of the whole human race. He was the greatest sinner who ever lived. Why did He change places with us all? "So that in Him we might become the righteousness of God."

Here are two truths side by side: (1) Jesus is innocent of any wrongdoing; and (2) Jesus has assumed the guilt of us all. The effect on our life: We give thanks by Christian living in word and deed.

*Prayer Suggestion: Thank your Lord Jesus for assuming your guilt and setting you free to serve Him.*

# There Was a Man on the Cross

During the late evening hours some years ago, a crowd gathered before a tall building in downtown Chicago. People were looking up to the cross atop the 556-foot steeple of the Chicago Temple. Someone had been heard to say that a man was ascending the cross. As it turned out, it was all an illusion caused by the interplay of light and shadows.

Another time there actually was a man on the cross, and this was no illusion. That one—the Son of God become man—was Jesus Christ, crucified for you and me. In full sight of a curious crowd outside Jerusalem's walls, He atoned for the sins of the whole world and opened the doors to eternal life.

Sometimes, when the night shadows of doubt descend, people may wonder whether Jesus ever went to the cross for the purpose stated. They may ask, "Are we just imagining that He died on Calvary for our salvation?" Some have even claimed that no man on a cross could atone for others' sins. Bear in mind, though, that the Bible states the facts simply: "God was reconciling the world to Himself in Christ" (2 Cor. 4:19). Christ is the Lamb of God bearing everyone's sins. Be assured that God took all your sins and nailed them to Christ's cross.

Because there was a man on the cross, there is now less of a cross on man—whether suffering, sickness, losses, insults, mental anguish, loneliness, or reproach for the sake of Christ. Because Christ bore the big cross, we can carry our crosses after Him. This is our calling. As our Lord said, "If anyone would come after Me, he must deny himself and take up his cross and follow Me" (Matt. 16:24).

*Prayer Suggestion: Tell your Lord that you are filled with a thousand thanks for ascending the cross in your behalf.*

# When the Smallest and Greatest Are Equal

What a great difference in size between these two men: Mihaly Meszaros, who is less than 33 inches tall, and the 8-foot, 2-inch Don Koehler!

In their relation to God, however, people have much in common. By the standards of God's evaluation, two important facts stand out, both of which equalize the smallest and the greatest of people. The first is the fact of sin. Sin blankets all people. All are sinners, and they fall short of God's expectations.

The fact of sin would bring all people into divine judgment if it were not for the second fact that puts the least and the greatest on the same footing: God's grace. Human merit does not count with God; good works do not avail because "by grace you have been saved, through faith—and this not from yourselves, it is the gift of God" (Eph. 2:8).

In the light of divine grace, there can be no boasting. St. Paul, that great missionary, called himself "the least of the apostles" (1 Cor. 15:9). John the Baptist, the forerunner of Christ, was a most humble man despite his important role. Jesus said of him—and this paradox is typical of the effect of God's grace—"Among those born of women there has not risen anyone greater than John the Baptist; yet he who is least in the kingdom of heaven is greater than he" (Matt. 11:11).

So if you feel you don't cut much of a figure in the world, don't feel sorry for "poor little me." God looks on your heart, and if in your heart you believe that Jesus lived, died, and rose again for you, you are great in God's sight.

*Prayer Suggestion: Begin your prayer by thanking God for every grace He has bestowed on you.*

# Feeling Good about Doing God's Will

In a daytime soap opera, a married woman involved in an illicit romance declares, "I wouldn't feel this good if it weren't right." We have heard the claim that might makes right. Others say, "If the deed is to your advantage, or to that of your in-group, it is right." And still others base everything on their feelings: If you feel good about what you did, it is right.

If these claims were carried out to their fullest in every arena of life, we would live in a world of utter chaos. If human insights and feelings decided moral issues, we would have each one going his or her own way in seeking self-fulfillment, but we could not have a family, a community, or a nation. Such things exist only when a common standard is upheld.

The actress in the soap opera should have reversed her terms: Do what is right—right according to the Ten Commandments—and then you will feel good about it. "The precepts of the LORD are right, giving joy to the heart," declares Psalm 19:8. In Psalm 1 the psalmist tells about the truly happy person, one who has delight in the will and Word of God and meditates on it day and night.

Jesus felt the same way about life under the Father. St. John records Him saying (6:38), "I have come down from heaven not to do My will but to do the will of Him who sent Me." Jesus the Messiah was joyfully obedient to the heavenly Father's will, going all the way to the cross for our redemption. In faith we look up to Him, the author and finisher of our faith, so we too can do God's will and feel good about it.

***Prayer Suggestion:*** *Pray for the help of the Holy Spirit to give you joy and peace in following the guidance of God.*

# A Life of Service

General John J. Pershing, the commander-in-chief of the U.S. expeditionary forces in World War I, knew that living a life of service requires sacrifice. But he did not expect to lose his wife and two small children in a fire at the Presidio in San Francisco.

Contrast that to the sacrifice willingly chosen by our Savior Jesus Christ. He Himself declares, "The Son of Man did not come to be served, but to serve, and to give His life as a ransom for many" (Mark 10:45). Not only did He deny Himself during His three-year ministry as He served people by day and night, but the redemption He came to achieve demanded self-sacrifice on the cross as atonement for the sin of the world. John the Baptist called Him the Lamb of God, and St. Paul comes back to this theme when he tells the Corinthians, "Christ, our Passover Lamb, has been sacrificed" (1 Cor. 5:7). It would not do for the Son of God to send someone else—an angel, a superman—to serve and to sacrifice; this was something He Himself had to do and wanted to do. His resurrection shows that He succeeded.

Christ has called us to be His disciples. It means that we deny ourselves, take up our cross, and follow Him. This isn't easy. No bed of roses, no rose garden is promised. But consider the blessings: peace with God, a purpose in life, the joy of living, and eternal life in the world to come. Yes, following Jesus is a joyful, self-fulfilling experience.

**Prayer Suggestion:** *Pray that you may find joy in serving Jesus and His people in need.*

# Brought Us into His Kingdom

Back in 1912, Champ Clark (1850–1921) narrowly missed the nomination for U.S. president. In fact, it took 46 ballots before the other man, Woodrow Wilson, was nominated.

Close may count in horseshoes and hand grenades, but usually a miss is as good as a mile. In any endeavor of life, one can be so near and yet so far away.

This is true also of Christianity. After St. Paul had pleaded the case for the Gospel (Acts 26:27–28), he made this appeal, "King Agrippa, do you believe the prophets? I know you do." Then Agrippa said to Paul, "Do you think that in such a short time you can persuade me to be a Christian?" Almost, but not quite—in fact, not at all! If the king died in his unbelief, he was just as surely lost as if he had never been near.

One time, when a scribe remarked that love to God and the neighbor was "more important than all burnt offerings and sacrifices," Jesus told him, "You are not far from the kingdom of God" (Mark 12:33–34). Not far—that again implied that the man was near God's kingdom but not in it. And not to be in the kingdom means to miss out on salvation.

Left to ourselves, we would all be, at best, almost-Christians—people not far from but still without the saving faith in Jesus Christ. But here is what God did: "Now in Christ Jesus you who once were far away have been brought near through the blood of Christ" (Eph. 2:13).

What happened to Champ Clark in politics did not happen to us. God not only nominated but also elected us in Christ to be His children now and forever.

*Prayer Suggestion: Ask the Holy Spirit to give you faith in Christ that you may not only live close to Him, but in Him.*

# When It's Moving Time

From boyhood days in rural Nebraska, this writer recalls that March 1 was always an important and interesting day. March 1 was moving day in that community. Anyone who had bought or rented a farm took possession on this date. What fun to watch the wagons loaded with household goods and farming equipment pass by.

Moving is not so bad—it can even be fun—when a person has a place to go, perhaps better than the one he had before. It is a different story when an eviction notice finds a family with no prospect of a home.

Our moving days on earth are a prelude to the final day when we all receive our eviction notice. The day will come when death will tap each one of us on the shoulder and say, "Friend, it is time for you to vacate these premises."

The Son of God left His home above to come to this earth. As St. John writes (1:14), "The Word became flesh and made His dwelling among us." His mission was to seek and save the lost, to give His life as a ransom for all. He who was born in another's stable died on the cross for our salvation and was buried in another's grave. Although He was the Lord of all, nothing was really His.

Jesus came to this vale of tears that we might be with Him "in heaven's fair homes," as the hymn declares. We can be sure of this: When the time comes for us to leave this world, there is a place to which we can move. The new home, heaven, is ready and waiting for those who are Christ's own.

***Prayer Suggestion:*** *Thank your Lord Jesus for having made a reservation for you in the Father's house of many mansions.*

# Our Guide for Moral Living

When Harry S. Truman died, a newspaper writer stated that he may have been the last U.S. president to make decisions in clear-cut terms of right and wrong. Perhaps his simple life as a youth helped him. Born in 1884 in the little Missouri town of Lamar, he spent 11 years helping his father manage a farm at Grandview. He was not afraid to make decisions and assume personal responsibility for them. "The buck stops here," read his Oval Office motto.

Ours has become a very complex age, one in which it is hard to feel even 51 percent right in some choices. Despite our feelings, God has given us a clear-cut standard in His Word: the Ten Commandments. They, of course, demand 100 percent compliance in thought, word, and deed—which we cannot render, and therefore, we deserve God's punishment. But Jesus Christ, the Son of God and perfect Man, obeyed the Law for us, and by His endurance of death on the cross, He paid the penalty for our sins. While we were thus freed from the demands of the Law for salvation, we don't discard it; we still need it as a guide to God-pleasing living. The Ten Commandments tell us what God's will is for those whom Christ has redeemed.

It is in the light of God's revealed will—and under the promptings of the love God has revealed to us in the Gospel of Jesus Christ—that Christians make their decisions. When choices are made in this way, they are responsible choices.

***Prayer Suggestion:*** *Pray that God may give you the wisdom and willingness to make decisions in keeping with His will as revealed in His Word.*

# Jesus—the Friend Who Sets Us Free

In 1857 a slave named Dred Scott sued for his freedom on grounds that his owner, an army surgeon in St. Louis, had taken him into free territory. The U.S. Supreme Court threw out the case, saying that a black slave is not a citizen and therefore can't sue. Scott, however, eventually went free because he was bought and set free by his friend Taylor Blow.

In a spiritual sense, all human beings were the slaves of sin. That slavery began when our first parents in the Garden of Eden obeyed the voice of Satan and sinned against God. By that disobedience they lost their holiness and righteousness. In place of it came corruption, came death in a full sense, came bondage to Satan. There was nothing human beings, individually or collectively, could do to set themselves free.

But just as Dred Scott had Taylor Blow as a friend to set him free, so we have Jesus Christ as our friend and liberator. The Bible tells us that Jesus took on Himself our human nature "that by His death He might destroy him who holds the power of death—that is, the devil—and free those who all their lives were held in slavery by their fear of death" (Heb. 2:14).

Now we are free from the slavery of sin, from the fear of death, from the power of Satan. We are free to serve our heavenly Father. Such freedom is not a license to sin. It is not a free ticket to live as we please, but, in love, to follow Jesus. Our Lord tells us, "If you hold to My teaching, you are really My disciples. Then you will know the truth, and the truth will set you free" (John 8:31–32).

*Prayer Suggestion: Ask the Holy Spirit to confirm you in your Christian freedom lest you backslide into sin's slavery.*

## Ecce Agnus Dei

"Behold, the Lamb of God, who takes away the sin of the world!" (John 1:29 RSV). This was the Gospel witness John the Baptist bore of Jesus.

John also proclaimed and applied the Law of God in all its sharpness. His words of judgment were like a surgeon's scalpel cutting away a person's hopes of self-salvation: religion without repentance, leaving undone the works God desires, leaning on one's family connections. But in all this, John intended to show people their need for Christ and assure the penitent ones that in the Lamb of God all their sins were forgiven. His interjection, "Behold," turned attention away from John and focused it on Christ, the world's only Savior.

Why the designation "Lamb"? The implied reference is to the lamb that Israelites were to offer at the Passover in the Old Testament. "Each man is to take a lamb for his family. … [a lamb] without defect" (Ex. 12:3, 5). Jesus is our true Passover Lamb whose precious blood, like that of a "lamb without blemish or defect" (1 Peter 1:19), ransoms us.

Jesus, who is "holy, blameless, pure, set apart from sinners, exalted above the heavens" (Heb. 7:26), is the Son whom God the Father designated as the Reconciler. He is indeed the "Lamb of God," the Agnus Dei. This is the Anointed and Appointed One, the Lord of Easter, the Christ of Christmas, whose coming the prophets announced. "Worthy is the Lamb, who was slain, to receive power and wealth and wisdom and strength and honor and glory and praise!" (Rev. 5:12).

*Prayer Suggestion: Say in your prayer to Jesus that you are laying your sins on Him, who bore them all.*

# Destination and Directions

In His farewell talks with His disciples (recorded in chapters 14, 15, and 16 of John's gospel), Jesus was preparing them for His imminent departure. He spoke words of comfort to them.

For the orphaned disciples, life would be a difficult journey traversing "field and fountain, moor and mountain" and finally leading through "the valley of the shadow of death" (Ps. 23:4)—a violent death for all of them except John. But the journey would be worthwhile because of its glorious destination.

The goal toward which Christ's followers still strive is not anything in this world. It is not what man's hands can build, the kind of houses people want today and already wanted in the time of Amos—"winter house," "summer house," "houses adorned with ivory," "mansions" (3:15). To come face to face with our Father in heaven—that is also our goal.

But it would be purposeless for Jesus to point to the destination if He didn't also give us the directions for getting there. Jesus says, "I am the way and the truth, and the life" (John 14:6). Jesus is the Way, the only road leading to the Father, and all who believe in Him as their Savior have found the way. He is the Truth, the Revealer of the true God and of His good and gracious will for our salvation. He is the Life, the Giver of eternal life beginning here and now and reaching its fullness in heaven.

Destination and directions for getting there—heaven as the goal and Christ as the road—that is what our Lord still reveals to us in His wonderful Gospel.

*Prayer Suggestion: Ask that God not only heighten your desire for the heavenly home but also show you the right road: faith in Jesus Christ, the Savior.*

# Going in the Right Direction

One day in 1938, Douglas Corrigan presumably intended to fly his plane from New York to California. Instead of going west, he went east and landed in Dublin, Ireland. For that he earned the nickname "Wrong Way Corrigan."

Of course, others have gone in opposite directions. The prophet Jonah, told by God to go east to Nineveh to preach repentance, caught a ship to sail west, across the Mediterranean Sea, to Tarshish (Jonah 1:1–3).

"Going in the opposite direction" accurately describes sin. Already in the beginning, Adam and Eve did the opposite of what God desired. That is what sin still is today. God says, "Come to Me," but people go away from Him, as the prodigal son went away from his father and home. Does it get them anything good? No, only unhappiness, disillusionment, death.

Christian obedience means going in the right direction, going God's way, which He presents to us in His Word. All His commandments are summed up in the word "love": Love God totally, and love your neighbor totally. When we love, we avoid the pitfalls and pratfalls of sin.

But we are imperfect in our love and would lose our way if left to our own sense of direction. Knowing this even better than we do, God sent His Son into the world. He sent Jesus Christ to be the Way, the Truth, and the Life. Not only does Jesus point out the right way, not only does He set us a good example, He Himself is the Way to peace with the Father and to eternal life. Believing in Him as our Savior and Peacemaker, we are on the right road, we are going in the right direction.

*Prayer Suggestion: Ask God to keep you on the right road by strengthening your bond with Jesus Christ, who is the Way to the Father.*

# Treasures More Precious than Gold

In Shakespeare's *The Merchant of Venice*, a wealthy father has prepared three chests—one of gold, one of silver, and one of lead. Into one of them he has placed a picture of his daughter. The suitor who on the basis of clues chooses the right chest gets to marry the daughter, Portia. The prince of Morocco chooses the golden one, and the prince of Aragon the silver one. Both lost. But Bassanio, unaware of how the others have guessed, chooses the lead casket (as hinted at by Portia) and wins her hand. He loved a person, not a precious metal.

Shakespeare then observes, "All that glitters is not gold." The same is true of life itself. A lame man at the temple gate in Jerusalem asked for alms. Peter told him, "Silver or gold I do not have, but what I have I give you. In the name of Jesus Christ of Nazareth, walk" (Acts 3:6). The love of God that sent Jesus Christ into the world to heal all people from the sickness of sin—and in this instance to affect also a physical cure—is of far greater worth than all the silver and gold in the world.

You can make your own list of human values that exceed the value of treasure chests of gems and jewels. Money cannot comfort you, but a friend can. All the gold in Fort Knox is no substitute for the love of a husband, wife, father, mother, or child. Millions and billions of dollars cannot bring peace with God, cannot open heaven. But faith in Christ can. Therefore, Peter tells people that through suffering and trials they have come to appreciate "your faith—of greater worth than gold" (1 Peter 1:7). These riches can be yours!

*Prayer Suggestion: Ask that God may grant you the treasures of faith and love to share with people around you.*

# From Dreams to Deeds

Ralph Waldo Emerson said, "Good thoughts are no better than good dreams, unless they are executed." Excellent ideas can come to people as they sit and think—what kind of house to build, where to go for vacation, how to improve one's worth—but these are idle daydreams unless translated into action.

To think, to meditate, to plan, to learn, to listen—we need to do these things to raise our sights and deeds above the shallow routines of daily living. The words of St. James give emphasis to this: "Do not merely listen to the word. … Do what it says" (James 1:22). Jesus spoke often of doing the will of God: "Not everyone who says to Me, 'Lord, Lord,' will enter the kingdom of heaven, but only he who does the will of My Father who is in heaven" (Matt. 7:21). Again, "Everyone who hears these words of Mine and puts them into practice is like a wise man who built his house on the rock" (Matt. 7:24).

The will of God to be done is embodied in the Ten Commandments. In summary they tell us to love God and love our neighbor. Such love goes far beyond words. St. James declares that a brother or a sister, ill-clad and lacking of daily food, is not helped with the words "Go, I wish you well; keep warm and well fed" (James 2:16). The goal of love is reached, says St. James, by giving people the things needed.

Jesus performed many deeds of love, not only with His healing miracles but also by His teaching. What is more, Jesus fulfilled the Father's will to the utmost by offering up Himself on the cross for the salvation of all. Jesus not only spoke the words of life but also did the works of life.

***Prayer Suggestion:*** *Pray that God may grant you holy desires, good counsels, and just works.*

# God's Abiding Love

Mount McKinley in Alaska, more than 20,000 feet high, is the highest peak in North America. Compared in size, Calvary, though sometimes called a mount, is only a mole-hill. One hymn calls it a "green hill," but very likely it was a desolate knoll. Yet Calvary, or Golgotha, towers above the world's tallest mountains. Because our Lord earned eternal salvation there for us all, it still will have meaning when every mountain range has vanished.

Every physical thing, even a mountain, is temporary. Only the Word of God and the salvation in Christ that it promises are eternal. St. Paul tells us, "So we fix our eyes not on what is seen, but on what is unseen. For what is seen is temporary, but what is unseen is eternal" (2 Cor. 4:18). We cannot see God and the love in His heart, but it is real. Through Isaiah the Lord tells us, "Though the mountains be shaken and the hills be removed, yet My unfailing love for you will not be shaken nor My covenant of peace be removed" (Is. 54:10).

God's covenant of love and peace in Christ abides. 1 Corinthians 13 extols Christian love that outlasts prophecies, knowledge, and certain extraordinary gifts. God's love abides, exceeding everything we have experienced or known.

This is a truth worth contemplating every day. We have troubles, problems, cares; they will disappear. God's love is steadfast. We do well to cling to it. The hymn writer, Paul Gerhardt, summarized it all in the refrain of one of his hymns:

All things else have but their day,
God's great love abides for aye.

***Prayer Suggestion:*** *Thank the heavenly Father for His unfailing love to you, especially appreciated during times of trouble.*

# The Christian's New Self

The woman on whose experience the book and movie *The Three Faces of Eve* were based has stated that over a period of 45 years she had 22 distinct personalities. Not just outward faces but deep psychological problems were involved.

That psychosis, however, is not the same as simultaneously having what Scripture describes as sinful nature and the new self. Through a spiritual rebirth we receive a new nature, which does not replace the old, sinful nature but does prevent it from taking over the converted person. Christian growth means that the old self is increasingly overcome by the new self, which is modeled after Jesus who dwells within us.

St. Paul writes to the Colossians (3:8–10), "You must rid yourselves of all such things as these: anger, rage, malice, slander, and filthy language from your lips. Do not lie to each other, since you have taken off your old self with its practices and have put on the new self, which is being renewed in knowledge in the image of its Creator." And to the Ephesians (4:24), St. Paul writes, "Put on the new self, created to be like God in true righteousness and holiness."

The Holy Spirit, through the Gospel, creates faith in us, so we rely on the redemption from sin by Christ. Given a new heart and mind, we serve Him. Sometimes there is tension between the old self and the new self. But with God's help coming to us through Word and sacrament, the new self restores inward peace.

Being a Christian is more than improving bad outward habits. It goes much deeper: God changes the heart.

***Prayer Suggestion:*** *Ask God's help to conquer the old sinful self and to grow more and more in the new self after the likeness of Christ.*

# Upholding Tired Arms

After nearly a century of holding up its torch in the harbor of New York City, the Statue of Liberty was closed for repairs and renovations. On July 4, 1986, it was reopened with the torch again being held up for all to see.

When the Israelites were fighting the Amalekites, Moses, accompanied by Aaron and Hur, was on a nearby hill praying. As long as his arms were raised in prayer, Israel was winning. But Moses' arms grew tired, so Aaron and Hur held up his arms until Israel won.

St. Paul declares (1 Tim. 2:8) that throughout Christendom people "lift up holy hands in prayer," but they sometimes grow tired. It remains for us to uphold the praying arms of our spiritual leaders. We, who are likewise concerned about the outcome of the battle against evil, can play the role of Aaron and Hur.

Many are the occasions in God's kingdom when Christians help those doing the Lord's work—pastors, teachers, congregational officers, missionaries, institutional chaplains. Support through prayer and personal participation is called for also in our everyday community life. The more people join in the performance of needed services, the greater is the prospect of favorable outcomes.

We are indeed willing to uphold the arms of those who lead us in church and country—in appreciation of what Jesus Christ did when He extended His arms on Calvary's cross for our salvation. That arm still guards us, and we join in the hymn lines, "I fear no harm, For with His arm He shall embrace and shield me; So to my Lord I yield me."

*Prayer Suggestion: Ask God for strength to join others in their labors and prayers.*

# Response to God's Welcome

America's welcome on the Statue of Liberty reads, "Give me your tired, your poor, your huddled masses yearning to breathe free, the wretched refuse of your teeming shore, Send these, the homeless, tempest-tossed to me: I lift my lamp beside the golden door." Since the time this was written, America's welcome to refugees has been muted.

One welcoming invitation that will never change is that of Jesus, "Come to Me, all you who are weary and burdened, and I will give you rest" (Matt. 11:28).

Countries can become so overpopulated and jobs so scarce that newcomers are no longer wanted, but the kingdom of God always has room. It offers to all the same privileges and gifts of grace. Seniority is not a factor. While God does indeed bless persons for their long-term, faithful services in His kingdom, He does not exclude recent converts from the blessings of salvation. A place in paradise awaited even the penitent thief on the cross.

As you read your Bible, you find many "come" invitations—in Isaiah 55:1, "Come, all you who are thirsty, come to the waters"; in Matthew 22:4, "Come to the wedding banquet"; in John 6:35, "He who comes to Me will never go hungry"; in Revelation 22:17, "The Spirit and the bride say, 'Come!' And let him who hears say, 'Come!' Whoever is thirsty, let him come; and whoever wishes, let him take of the free gift of the water of life."

Charlotte Elliott—and all who sing her hymn—respond to that invitation by saying, "O Lamb of God, I come, I come."

*Prayer Suggestion: Complete this prayer: Lord Jesus, I thank You for inviting me to come to You...*

# Prayer for Good Government

A stable government, even if imperfect, is a blessing of God. Government derives its authority from God, who has all power. The fact that we have a government of, for, and by the people takes nothing away from God as the ultimate authority. It is through the people that God's authority is conveyed to the duly elected representatives.

Governments at all levels do not exist for their own sakes but are God's servants "to do you good," as St. Paul writes to the Romans (13:4). The fact that governments have power—the power of the sword, no less—causes no fear to law-abiding citizens. But law-breakers—thieves, murderers, traitors, and the like—have reason to be afraid because the government has the power to punish them.

When Jesus was asked whether it was right to pay taxes to the Roman government, He replied, "Give to Caesar what is Caesar's, and to God what is God's" (Matt. 22:21).

This is a most helpful statement because it makes a proper distinction, and it indicates what our action is to be in both spheres: Caesar's and God's. The kingdom of God is spiritual, not political. We render to God what is properly His when we pray to Him, acknowledge Him as our Creator and Preserver, serve Him, and above all, accept the love that He showed when He sent His Son, Jesus Christ, to make us God's children by His reconciling death. God and government—we need them both.

**Prayer Suggestion:** *In your prayer, enumerate the blessings God has conveyed to you through the government, then give thanks.*

# Carrying the Torch for Christ

In preparation for the 1984 Summer Olympics in Los Angeles, more than 10,000 relay runners took turns carrying the Olympic torch on a 9,000-mile journey across the United States—through 41 major cities in 33 states.

Similarly, our Lord wants His Gospel—a light, a burning torch—to be carried to all nations to dispel the darkness of sin. To that end He appointed 12 apostles, telling them to make disciples of all people by teaching and baptizing them. In addition, He called St. Paul as an apostle to the Gentiles.

But the apostles needed other Gospel runners to assist them and eventually succeed them. They enlisted men and women who, like Olympic torchbearers, carried the light of the Gospel to many communities. St. Paul, too, covered a lot of ground himself. But he couldn't keep on doing this, so he named many helpers: Timothy, Titus, Silas, Mark, and Luke among others. And Paul prepared people everywhere for spreading the Good News about Jesus.

Because generation upon generation has passed on the torch, you and I have come to know the love of Jesus. How happy we are that we are not orphans and victims of blind fate but are the children of our heavenly Father!

It would be tragic, however, if the progress of the Gospel stopped with us. We don't want that to be so; therefore, we pass the torch of God's truth on to others—to our children, neighbors, coworkers, and the like. In doing this, we keep the torch moving as it leads people to the ultimate destination: to their heavenly home.

*Prayer Suggestion: Ask the Holy Spirit to keep the torch of your faith burning and to make you a shining light in the world.*

# Christ Alone Can "Make It Up"

On the fateful night that President Abraham Lincoln was shot, the assassin, John Wilkes Booth, having suffered a broken leg in jumping from the presidential box onto the stage of Ford's Theater, rode off into Maryland. There a country doctor, Dr. Samuel A. Mudd, set the leg, apparently without asking any questions. For aiding and abetting a criminal, Dr. Mudd was sentenced to prison. A few years later, when an epidemic broke out at Fort Jefferson in the Florida Keys, Dr. Mudd rendered heroic services and was in 1869 pardoned by President Andrew Johnson. In a way, the doctor made up for his misdeed, if such it was.

In the Bible, sins are sometimes called errors. The psalmist writes, "Who can discern his errors? Forgive my hidden faults" (19:12). Again, St. James: "Whoever turns a sinner from the error of his way will save him from death" (5:20).

Sins, errors, trespasses, transgressions (or whatever we call them)—can we ever make up or atone for them by doing good? The writer of "Rock of Ages" states, "Not the labors of my hands, Can fulfill Thy law's demands … All for sin could not atone; Thou must save, and Thou alone." Jesus did save us by offering Himself as the ransom for all sinners. Redemption is complete; nothing can be added by good works. That would be like trying to pour water into a full glass.

St. Paul said it briefly but clearly, "Believe in the Lord Jesus, and you will be saved" (Acts 16:31).

*Prayer Suggestion: Pray that God the Holy Spirit may give you a faith that relies completely on Christ's redemption, a faith that in gratitude prompts you to do good works.*

# The Whole Armor of God

The historic USS *Constitution* earned the nickname "Old Ironsides" because in a sea battle the shots of the British *Guerriere* glanced off its heavy planking, causing a British sailor to say: "Her sides are made of iron."

Are our sides made of iron? St. Paul tells Christians to put on the armor of God: the belt of truth, the breastplate of righteousness, the shoes of peace, the shield of faith, the helmet of salvation, and the sword of the Spirit, which is the Word of God (Eph. 6:13–17). "That is cumbersome armor," some will say. "We can get along with our own defenses, our know-how." But St. Paul reminds us that we are not contending with physical forces, but with spiritual enemies (v. 12).

We do need God's armor—all of it. The two most important weapons are the shield of faith and the sword of the Spirit, one defensive and the other offensive. With the shield of faith—faith in the victory of Jesus Christ over sin, death, and devil—we "can extinguish the flaming arrows of the evil one" (v. 16). The devil's darts are unbelief, doubt, temptation, indifference, or outright hostility to God. Equipped with faith, we can turn the shots aside. The other weapon is the sword of the Spirit, that is, the Word of God. God's Word, supported by the Holy Spirit, conveys God's power, and against it Satan cannot prevail.

Because of God's Spirit working in us, we can be called "Old Ironsides," having the protective armor of faith and the sword of God's Word to put Satan to flight.

*Prayer Suggestion: Pray that God may equip you with the spiritual weapons you need to win in the battle for your faith.*

# A New Creation in Christ

In 1779, Ned Ludd of England and his followers, the Luddites, tried to reverse the Industrial Revolution by destroying labor-saving machines and burning factories. Their efforts failed.

Just as futile are other attempts to correct unwanted situations by using destruction. In Revelation 2:1–7 we read about the teachings of a would-be religious sect called the Nicolaitans, especially active in the church at Ephesus. They agreed that human nature is admittedly evil and subject to drives such as sex. However, they said the way to solve this is to exhaust the body by excessive eating and drinking and by the free exercise of sex. That works about as well as when people try to correct economic problems by smashing the machines.

God has a better plan. He knows that human nature is sinful, that it will twist and bend its drives and appetites into all kinds of aberrations. But God does not want the body and mind destroyed for that reason. His solution is much more positive and constructive. He offers conversion, regeneration, the new birth. This comes about by the power of the Holy Spirit working through the Gospel. Born anew is such a sinner who repents and believes in Jesus Christ as the Savior, who gives us new spiritual life within.

Instead of destruction, there is reconstruction; instead of deformation, transformation. Christians are the new creation in Christ. They serve God with renewed minds and bodies.

*Prayer Suggestion: Ask God the Holy Spirit to create a new spirit in you, directing you to use body and mind to God's glory and the good of the human race.*

# Teachings from Two Mounts

On Mount Sinai God gave the Ten Commandments. If God's people then—and those who were to become His people from among the Gentiles—had been able to keep the commandments perfectly, salvation would have been theirs, and there would have been nothing more for God to do.

But we know that human beings cannot fulfill God's holy will perfectly. Consequently they face severe punishment: "The soul who sins is the one who will die" (Ezek. 18:4). But finding no pleasure in the death of the wicked, God made provision for all of them to come to the knowledge of the truth as revealed in His Son. This Son, Jesus, declared that all who believe in Him shall have eternal life.

How shall those who believe in Him live? How shall they be, and what shall they do—not to be saved but because they are saved? For a reply we go to another mount, where, as a counterpart to the Law of Mount Sinai, Jesus delivered His Sermon on the Mount. How gracious, our Lord's words of truth and wisdom! The sermon begins with the Beatitudes—10 statements beginning with "Blessed"—for example, "Blessed are the merciful, for they will be shown mercy" (Matt. 5:7).

Jesus also declares that Christians are the salt of the earth and the light of the world. Read more of the Sermon on the Mount (Matt. 5–7), comparing it with the giving of the Law on Mount Sinai (Exodus 20). Note Jesus' "Blessed" and the Law's "Cursed." The more you compare, the more you will agree with what St. John has written, "The law was given through Moses; grace and truth came through Jesus Christ" (John 1:17).

***Prayer Suggestion:*** *Ask Jesus to shower you with the blessedness of believing in Him and living for Him.*

# A Needle Instead of a Harp

In Eugene Field's poem "Grandma's Prayer," an elderly woman says that in heaven she would prefer a needle to a harp because "Plain sewing's been my line." She would be content "if asked to mend The little angel's britches."

The Bible speaks of a woman in Joppa who sewed garments for the poor. Her name was Tabitha or Dorcas. She was called a disciple, which means that she plied her needle out of love for Christ and to the least of His brothers and sisters. She also might say, "Give me a needle instead of a harp."

Is such a picture of life in heaven realistic? In heaven we will be in the presence of Jesus Christ and see our heavenly Father face to face. Our greatest happiness will be to give thanks and praise to our Lord and Savior for giving His life on earth so we might have eternal life. This thankfulness can be expressed in many ways, certainly in singing hymns of praise—and the singing will undoubtedly be accompanied by harps, as St. John writes in the book of Revelation (5:8).

The ability to play musical instruments is a great talent by which we glorify God. But there are other talents by which we can praise God and serve Him. These may include painting pictures, composing verses, growing flowers, or plying the needle. Is such a picture of life in heaven realistic? Perhaps.

In the meantime, as far as our present life is concerned, we live out St. Paul's words, "So whether you eat or drink or whatever you do, do it all for the glory of God" (1 Cor. 10:31).

*Prayer Suggestion: As you consider what you might enjoy doing in heaven, pray for the Spirit's guidance in using that talent in this life for God's glory.*

# What Our Daily Bread Teaches

At times, God may grant something for which we asked, but for a reason completely opposite of our own. For example, in Deuteronomy 8:2–3 we read, "Remember how the LORD your God led you all the way in the desert these forty years, to humble you and to test you in order to know what was in your heart, whether or not you would keep His commands. He humbled you, causing you to hunger and then feeding you with manna … to teach you that man does not live on bread alone but on every word that comes from the mouth of the LORD."

No matter the what or why of God's possible answers, we keep on praying, realizing that we are dependent on God for everything. By His creative Word He gave us a world of rain, sunshine, and good soil so it might yield seed to the sower and bread to the eater. By His power He gave us Adam and Eve, and after them—through many generations—our own parents to provide for us.

We know that things for the body but especially those of the soul come from God. Our spiritual lives depend "on every word that comes from the mouth of God" (Matt. 4:4). God's Word calls us to faith in Jesus Christ, the Bread of life. To this Word Jesus Himself was obedient when Satan tempted Him. To this Word Jesus was obedient to the point of death so we might live, both now and eternally.

When you reach for another piece of bread, remember that God gives you bread to teach you that life is more than bread—more than money, cars, television sets, computers—and that your life depends on His creating, saving Word.

*Prayer Suggestion: Thank God for your daily bread, and pray that Jesus may more and more become the Bread of Life for you.*

# Keeping God's Temple Clean

Tourists in Athens, Greece, are sure to visit the Parthenon, an ancient temple on an elevation called the Acropolis. The temple was all but destroyed when, in a military siege in 1687, gun powder stored there exploded.

Now shift your attention to another temple. According to St. Paul, Christians are to regard their bodies as dwelling places of the Holy Spirit. He writes, "Do you not know that your body is a temple of the Holy Spirit, who is in you, whom you have received from God? You are not your own; you were bought with a price. Therefore honor God with your body" (1 Cor. 6:19–20).

But as happened in Athens, people sometimes bring the gun powder of sin into this temple, and unspeakably great damage results when it explodes. The temple is ruined by acts of immorality, drunkenness, overindulgence, covetousness, and all kinds of spiritual warfare against God.

We have every reason to think highly of our body and to honor God with it. God is our Creator and owner. Further, Jesus Christ redeemed us from sin; He bought us with a price of His own blood. Then through the Gospel, the Holy Spirit cleaned out the rubbish of sin and sanctified us—made us God's instruments. By creation and re-creation, our body is His.

In urging Christians to serve only God, St. Paul asks, "What agreement is there between the temple of God and idols? For we are the temple of the living God" (2 Cor. 6:16). Clean-living Christians are God's works of art. In body, soul, and spirit, they reflect well on their Maker, Redeemer, and Sanctifier.

*Prayer Suggestion: Pray that the Holy Spirit may dwell in your heart and keep you clean within.*

# Jesus, the Perfect Savior

In these verses that compare persistent Christianity with running a race, St. Paul declares that he himself must be concerned about staying in condition. Having preached to others, he does not want to become a castaway himself. These words came to mind when reading that Jim Fixx, who popularized jogging with his best-selling book *The Complete Book of Running,* died while jogging.

Life is full of similar occurrences, all pointing to the fact that it is hard to practice what we preach. Physicians often die from causes they seek to correct in others. Some teachers fault pupils for poor performances but themselves fall short of good scholarship. Parents tell children not to do this or that, then they become guilty of the same errors.

We are reminded that people who are themselves sinful human beings succumb to the same fate from which they want to save others. The psalmist declares, "No man can redeem the life of another or give to God a ransom for him" (49:7). The payment that would be required would be too great. In fact, even if one were to die for another, he could not redeem him from sin, as noble as that attempt would be.

Only Jesus Christ, the Son of God and sinless human being, could sufficiently suffer and die to redeem us from the guilt of sin and the power of death. And Jesus, risen from the dead, did redeem, giving His life as a ransom for all. Only as the perfect Savior was He able to do this. So we fix our eyes on Jesus, the author and perfecter of our faith.

*Prayer Suggestion: Give thanks to Jesus Christ for His perfect redemption, asking Him for strength to follow in His steps.*

# In Business with God

Quite often father and son are together in a business. When the father steps down, the son continues the firm. This is so in other walks of life. For example, Walter Damrosch succeeded his father, Leopold, as conductor of the New York Orchestra.

Such father-and-son connections remind us of the perfect union of God the Father and God the Son. Jesus often referred to this unique relationship. He said, "My Father is always at His work to this very day, and I, too, am working" (John 5:17). As a 12-year-old lad, He said He had to be about His heavenly Father's business. At the end of His three-year ministry, He said in His High Priestly Prayer that He had finished the work the Father had given Him to do. With His resurrection our Lord announced the fulfillment of this work.

Through the Gospel, the Holy Spirit, the third person of the Holy Trinity, comes into our hearts to grant us faith and to make us the children of God, partners in the work of the Father and the Son. The work of salvation, of course, is finished, and we cannot add anything to it. But we can make known the Good News of salvation. We can say to our fellow human beings: God sent His Son to lay down His life for all sinners so they might become the sons and daughters of God. St. Paul considered himself and those with him as coworkers with God in this sense.

The church is a divine institution where Father, Son, and Holy Spirit are at work, and much of what they want done—the proclaiming, the teaching, the comforting, the serving—is done through us. Yes, we are in business with God.

***Prayer Suggestion:*** *Pray that your life continue and promote the "business" begun by your heavenly Father.*

# Your Lease on Life

The lease that the British Crown Colony of Hong Kong had with China expired in 1997. This caused uneasiness in what is the third largest financial center of the world. On a smaller scale, you may have seen a sign in a local store, "Lost Our Lease, All Goods on Sale."

People are beset by uncertainties, and one of these pertains to the length of life. As it were, God has given us a lease on life. We are not the owners of what we have; we are lessees, stewards. Not only our goods but life itself is given us on loan. Only God knows when we must come before Him to give an account of our stewardship.

We can be joyful and thankful that God has given us life and, with it, opportunities to serve Him. Not only when we work but also when we vacation and see God's wonderful works in nature, we can be glad that God continues to give us a lease on life as a gift to be used to His glory and the good of others.

Further, the thought that our lease on life will one day expire should not fill us with fear. We know that all our days and years are in God's hands. When in His infinite wisdom and love He wants us and our dear ones to come home, we can say, "We are ready, Lord!"

We can say this when by faith in Jesus Christ we have become God's children. By His life, death, and resurrection Jesus has reconciled us. He has made us the heirs of heaven. So when the one lease expires, a much better one awaits us. We have a clear title to our place in the Father's house.

*Prayer Suggestion: Thank God for entrusting life to you and for the many opportunities it affords to serve Him.*

# Jesus, Lamb and Shepherd

In tribute to the exalted Jesus, one of the elders in the book of Revelation declares with respect to the heavenly multitude, "The Lamb at the center of the throne will be their shepherd" (7:17). Here two roles are ascribed to Jesus.

As the Lamb of God, Jesus was sacrificed on the altar of the cross for the sin of the world. All of sin, original and actual, is rolled up into a big bale and loaded on the shoulders of Jesus. All sin is atoned for; the total debt is paid. What remains is that you and I believe in Jesus, whose blood was shed for our sins.

But in the Bible, Jesus is also called Shepherd. In the passage cited from the book of Revelation, this Shepherd "will lead [the believers] to springs of living water." This echoes Psalm 23, "[The Lord] leads me beside quiet waters, He restores my soul" (vv. 2–3). Jesus declared in John 10 that He is that Good Shepherd. He knows us, His sheep; He provides for us, protects us. Having risen from the dead and ascended into heaven, He prays for us, sends the Holy Spirit to lead us into all truth, fills the hearts of the faithful so as His representatives they look after the needs of His brothers and sisters. He supplies His church with pastors and teachers to lead us to the green pastures of God's Word.

Jesus, Lamb and Shepherd. Of Him as the Good Shepherd we sing:

> The Lord my Shepherd is,
> I shall be well supplied;
> Since He is mine and I am His,
> What can I want beside?

*Prayer Suggestion: Pray that you may ever remain a member of Christ's flock to be blessed by Him.*

# Jesus, the Rose of Sharon

Some farmers complain about a certain thorny plant, almost a weed, that seems to destroy pastureland: the multiflora rose. It was deliberately introduced in the United States in the 1880s to deter erosion and serve as a wildlife cover. Apparently, it got out of hand.

Sin is like this plant. When sin was introduced into the world, the devil made it seem very attractive. From our first parents, sin spread to their children and then to all generations born after them. The first son ever to be born, Cain, became a killer.

One dreads to think what this world would be like if God had not taken measures to counteract sin. In love and compassion He sent a Second Adam to atone for the sin of the first Adam. This Adam II is Jesus Christ, God's own Son, conceived by the Holy Spirit and born without sin from the virgin Mary. Through His preaching and teaching He bore witness to the reality of sin. Through His death on the cross He made salvation from sin a reality. Through faith in this Savior, we live in Him and for Him, bringing forth much fruit.

If sin is like the thorny, spreading multiflora rose, then the Savior from sin can be compared to a true rose. Of Him we sing:

> Fair are the meadows,
> Fair are the woodlands,
> Robed in flow'rs of blooming spring;
> Jesus is fairer, Jesus is purer,
> He makes our sorr'wing spirit sing.

*Prayer Suggestion: Ask God to let your heart become a beautiful rose garden to His glory and for the delight of people around you.*

# While It Is Day

It is true what the hymnist wrote, "Swift to its close ebbs out life's little day." But for all of us, including those approaching eventide, it still is day, and we have the opportunity to do worthwhile things. Whatever we do is made more pleasant when we look at it as an opportunity rather than an obligation.

"Work," of course, can apply to whatever we do, not only in the fields and in factories but also other worthwhile activities: reading a good book, writing a letter to a lonesome person, helping the neighbor with a project, making life a little more pleasant for someone. Now is the time for doing this, for we know one thing for sure: Night is coming, when we can no longer do it.

It is still day for another important thing: Becoming reconciled with someone with whom we are on the outs. St. Paul writes, "Do not let the sun go down while you are still angry" (Eph. 4:26). Make peace while you have the opportunity!

For all this we have the example of Jesus, who said (John 9:4–5), "As long as it is day, we must do the work of Him who sent Me. Night is coming, when no one can work." In going on to say, "While I am in the world, I am the light of the world," our Lord is not only our exemplar but also our enabler to work while it is still day. As the Light comes from God, Jesus enlightens us, enabling us to follow in His steps. He became the Light of the world when, by His reconciling work on the cross, He overcame the darkness of sin and the fear of death. With the light of the Gospel He shines into our lives while it is still day.

*Prayer Suggestion: Pray for wisdom and strength to do God's will and work while the sun of your life is still shining.*

# The Lord Looks for Lost People

You have heard of "the ten lost tribes of Israel" who were carried away into Assyria and there disappeared. On a smaller scale, something similar took place on Roanoke Island. In 1587, Sir Walter Raleigh settled a colony there. Three years later, a ship bringing supplies could find no trace of the settlers.

In a spiritual sense, all people are lost—lost in sin. In one parable, Jesus refers to His contemporaries as lost sheep from the house of Israel. As the Good Shepherd, Jesus sought to save all the lost. He gave up His life so He might give life to the spiritually dead.

One of England's famous old churches includes this inscription, "John Newton, a clerk, once an infidel and libertine, a servant of slavers in Africa, was by the rich mercy of our Lord and Savior Jesus Christ preserved, restored, pardoned, and appointed to preach the faith he had long labored to destroy." This was the man who wrote the hymn: "Amazing Grace! How Sweet the Sound."

Jesus Christ seeks every one of us today, regardless of who we are or what we have done or left undone. We all hear:

Oh, the height of Jesus' love,
Higher than the heav'ns above,
Deeper than the depths of sea,
Lasting as eternity!
Love that found me—wondrous thought—
Found me when I sought Him not.

*Prayer Suggestion: Give thanks to Christ for finding you, and pray that many other lost ones may be found.*

# What an Exchange of Roles!

As a student in Magdeburg, Germany, Martin Luther was shocked at seeing a member of a religious order carrying a sack and begging in the streets. Because of the discipline to which the man had subjected himself, he was a thin, wasted figure—nothing more than "animated bones." What was remarkable about this man was that he had been Prince William of Anhalt, a German state. He voluntarily exchanged his luxurious life as a nobleman for a miserable existence.

Far from approving of what this man did, we can refer to his self-denial as descriptive of someone else's far greater exchange of roles in our behalf. In Philippians 2:5–8, St. Paul declares that Jesus Christ, who was God's true Son and thus "in very nature God," took the form of a servant, not only to serve but to become obedient unto death, even death on a cross.

When you read about Jesus in the gospels—how He was despised, spat upon, crowned with thorns, and nailed to a cross—you get an inkling of what it meant for the Son of God to leave the glory of heaven to become our Savior here on earth. Christ's self-chosen humiliation was far greater than that of Prince William of Anhalt, who probably did it to earn his salvation. Jesus did it to earn someone else's salvation—ours!—for we could not save ourselves. What love!

How do we benefit? St. Paul tells us in 2 Corinthians 8:9, "You know the grace of our Lord Jesus Christ, that though He was rich, yet for your sakes He became poor, so that you through His poverty might become rich"—rich in forgiveness and peace with God!

*Prayer Suggestion: Say a prayer of thanksgiving to Christ for what He did in your behalf.*

# Spiritual Giants

We hear legends of giants today. In the Hubei Province of China some claim to have seen Le Ren, a seven-foot wild man. In the Himalayas one hears reports about Yeti, the Abominable Snowman. Sasquatch, or Bigfoot, supposedly lives somewhere in the Pacific Northwest.

While the Bible speaks of giants such as Goliath, it also speaks of other kinds of giants—people who stand tall because of their faith in God. The woman of Canaan—to whom Jesus said, "You have great faith" (Matt. 15:28)—was such a spiritual giant. She believed that Jesus could and would free her daughter from a demon. The 12 apostles were giants because they turned the world upside down for Christ. Chapter 11 in the book of Hebrews enumerates many heroes of the faith: Abel, Noah, Abraham and Sarah, and many more.

There are such giants today, and we can be among them. But how does one reach such a stature? First, we go to Calvary's cross and see God's great love shown in the sacrifice of His Son, Jesus Christ, for our sins. In the acceptance of so great a salvation lies the beginning of spiritual growth.

Physically we may be weak, but God's strength is made perfect in our weakness. Our reliance on Christ increases our capacity for bearing heavy burdens, for overcoming personal problems, for conquering sinful passions, for befriending people undeserving of love. Such a giant accepts what life brings, not only bearing the load courageously but also turning it into a spiritual plus. As St. Paul said (2 Cor. 12:10), "When I am weak, then I am strong." His strength came from Christ.

*Prayer Suggestion: Pray for a greater measure of faith in Christ so you may receive His strength working in and through you.*

# The Three *P*s of Divine Grace

The grace God reveals to us in Jesus Christ can be seen as taking the form of special gifts, each one beginning with a "p."

The first of God's gifts is *pardon* for the past. For the sake of Jesus, God forgives us the sins of yesterday. St. Paul wrote (Col. 2:13–14), "[God] forgave us all our sins, having canceled the written code, with its regulations, that was against us and that stood opposed to us; He took it away, nailing it to the cross"—the cross of Jesus.

A further gift of God is *power* for the present. God's power is made perfect in our weakness. God gives us the strength to lead a Christian life. He not only clears our past record, He gives us power for the present so we don't stumble into the same old sins. He enables us to cope with present problems, to fulfill our daily duties as husband and wife, parents and children. When it seems that we cannot go one step further, God taps resources in us we didn't know we had.

A third evidence of God's grace is His *promise* for the future. God declares that He will not leave us nor forsake us. Our Savior has affirmed that He will be with us always. God's promise rests on His great act of not sparing His own Son, but delivering Him up for us all. The promise of Christ, the greatest Gift, was fulfilled. If God has done this, should He not grant us also the lesser gifts we need? As St. Paul wrote, "No matter how many promises God has made, they are 'Yes' in Christ" (2 Cor. 1:20).

Rejoice, then, over the three *p*s: pardon for the past, power for the present, and promise for the future.

***Prayer Suggestion:*** *Pray for greater assurance that in Christ pardon, power, and the promise of peace are yours.*

# A Foolish Farmer

Despite April Fool's Day, no one enjoys being called a fool. Yet in His wisdom and love, God does use that term for some people. He declared through David, "The fool says in his heart, 'There is no God.' "

To act the fool often occurs when people do not act on the basis of the knowledge they possess. Certainly the five foolish virgins in Christ's parable (Matt. 25:1–13) knew that lamps won't burn unless they have oil. Yet because of carelessness or preoccupation with other things, they expected to participate in the marriage festivities by bringing lamps without oil.

In another parable (Luke 12:13–21), Jesus spoke of a man who likewise has to be called a fool because he did not act on the knowledge he had. He undoubtedly knew that "a man's life does not consist in the abundance of his possessions" and that barns full of grain cannot satisfy the soul's hunger. This rich landowner knew also that death was inevitable. Yet he failed to prepare to meet his Maker. So God said to him, "You fool! This very night your life will be demanded from you."

To know what God's will is and to act rightly on it—this is wisdom. As Solomon's proverb says (3:7), "Do not be wise in your own eyes; fear the LORD and shun evil." The highest wisdom, however, is to be "wise for salvation through faith in Christ Jesus" (2 Tim. 3:15). Do you have this wisdom? When we are right with God through our faith in Jesus Christ, we have wisdom for all of life because we have the guidance of God's Word in all situations.

*Prayer Suggestion:* *Ask the Holy Spirit to give you light from above to guide you in all your ways.*

# Evaluating a Human Being

Fame can be very elusive and unpredictable. To some it comes early in life, to some later, and to others only after death. Take, for example, Mozart, the highly honored musician and composer. When he died, only a handful of people followed the hearse to the cemetery, where the body, wrapped in a sack, was unceremoniously put into an unmarked, mass grave in Vienna. Today no one knows the place where he is buried.

"Give everyone what you owe him … if respect, then respect; if honor, then honor," writes Paul (Rom. 13:7).

The giving of honor should begin at home, where all the members of the family love and respect one another. Sometimes the expression of affection and esteem comes a little late—after the damage of neglect has been done or after death has taken its toll.

We do well to recognize the worth of each person within our circle—family, church, community—and to recognize the value of that person's service, great or small. For this, we do not rely on the fame, or the lack of fame, that the general public attributes to that individual. Fame, as indicated, can be fickle.

What is our guide for the proper appreciation of those around us? God's Word gives us the true basis of a person's worth. It tells us that God made me and all others, that Jesus Christ died for me and all others. Can anyone for whom Christ shed His precious blood be contemptible?

Fame can pass away, wealth and health can be lost, and human affection can grow cold, but God's love in Christ abides. It is our guide for estimating human worth.

***Prayer Suggestion:*** *Pray that you may grow in faith toward Jesus Christ and in love toward those whom He loves.*

# Forgiving Oneself

In the practice of forgiveness, we need to forgive ourselves too. In a conversation in James Baldwin's *Another Country,* Cass tells Rufus, "When you're older, you'll see, I think, that we all commit our crimes. The thing is not to lie about them—to try to understand what you've done, why you've done it ... That way, you can begin to forgive yourself. That's very important. If you don't forgive yourself, you'll never be able to forgive anybody else, and you'll go on committing the same crimes forever."

The power for forgiving—ourselves as well as others—comes from God's forgiveness of us as proclaimed in the Gospel: "In [Christ] we have redemption through His blood, the forgiveness of sins" (Eph. 1:7). This forgiveness is available to all who repent and, by faith, look to Jesus for grace.

Because God has forgiven us all our trespasses, we are compelled by God's love to forgive those who trespass against us.

But what about forgiving ourselves? Many drag themselves through life bearing a burden of guilt. Others make excuses of all kinds for their wrongdoing. But that is not the right way to forgive ourselves. Rather, we can say with the hymn writer in repentance and faith, "I lay my sins on Jesus, the spotless Lamb of God; He bears them all and frees us from the accursed load."

Having laid our sins on Jesus, we are rid of them. Our consciences are cleared of guilt, our hearts relieved of their burdens—all this because for Jesus' sake we have forgiveness and have forgiven ourselves.

*Prayer Suggestion: Pray that God may give you the assurance that, for Jesus' sake, all your sins are taken away.*

# Speak the Truth in Love

Sociologist John Hutchinson has written, "By the time word reaches the fourth person, a message is likely to contain no more than five percent of the whole story."

Truth was terribly distorted at the trial of Jesus. His accusers claimed He wanted to destroy the holy temple in Jerusalem because He said, "Destroy this temple, and I will raise it again in three days" (John 2:19). Jesus, of course, was speaking of the resurrection of His body.

Many false rumors start when a statement is misunderstood or wrongly interpreted. Sometimes no malicious intent is involved. We have to reckon with human imperfection in speaking and hearing. That's why the English courts distinguish between truth as it is spoken and truth as it is heard.

Because we are all fallible human beings, we need to speak plainly and to listen carefully when the good name and reputation of the neighbor is at stake, lest we do someone an injustice. God's commandment tells us not to bear false witness against the neighbor, and St. Paul writes this: "Each of you must put off falsehood and speak truthfully to his neighbor, for we are all members of one body" (Eph. 4:25).

As we, in love, refrain from uttering untruth, so we in the same love also speak the truth of correction when required.

Jesus is the Truth personified. He not only spoke the truth but also did the truth, fulfilling the work the heavenly Father had given Him to do. He is our Exemplar and our Enabler of truth-speaking, giving us the willingness and power to speak the truth in love.

*Prayer Suggestion: Ask God to keep you from speaking falsehood and to help you always to speak the truth.*

# The Right Treatment

Shakespeare's *The Tempest* includes the line, "You rub the sore when you should bring the plaster."

In medicine, every doctor tries to avoid treatments that have an effect opposite of the one intended. So, too, the good Samaritan in Jesus' parable poured oil and wine—not salt—into the victim's wounds.

It is wrong treatment when, in a figurative sense, we rub our own or other people's sores when we should apply a healing, soothing agent. Since most people feel bad enough when they have failed, to berate them with negative criticism adds insult to injury. Unless positive instruction is given, criticizing an employee for poor performance will hardly do any good. One wonders how many marriages are eventually wrecked because, in some instances of failure, the explosive bomb of anger is used instead of a healing balm.

Criticism has its place—even sharp criticism when the culprit's skin is as thick as an elephant's. But criticism, if it is not to have a traumatic effect, should be accompanied by commendations spoken in love. Martin Luther used an apt expression when he said that a disciplining father should hold the rod in one hand and the apple in the other.

Jesus Christ is the Good Physician, the perfect pharmacist. He applied the Law to hardened sinners but the sweetest Gospel to wounded hearts. That Gospel, in capsule form, is this: "God so loved the world that He gave His one and only Son, that whoever believes in Him shall not perish but have eternal life" (John 3:16).

*Prayer Suggestion: As one whose soul Jesus has healed, pray that He may use you to heal others through the Gospel.*

# Controlling One's Love

Love is sometimes misdirected. People sometimes lack proper judgment—as in the case of an oil heiress who left her $12 million estate for the care of stray dogs. The last dog to survive was Musketeer, who lived in a $26,000 dog house. Or consider the millionaire who opened a hotel window and threw fistfuls of dollar bills to the crowd below.

The Bible speaks of misdirected love that values things more than people, like the rich man who let Lazarus starve or the rich farmer who was concerned about crops and barns to house them. They loved all right, but they loved things.

Jesus also says that with wrong love often goes wrong zeal, with the result that good intentions are claimed for doing wrong deeds, "A time is coming when anyone who kills you will think he is offering a service to God" (John 16:2).

How are you handling your love? Keeping it locked up inside? Extending it only to friends and to those who can return the favor? Withholding it from the needy at your door?

What about in your family? Love is misapplied when parents lavish material gifts on their children but fail to give themselves. The meaning of love is misunderstood when parents practice a permissive love of anything goes. True love considers the well-being of the person to whom it is directed.

True love comes from God, St. John tells us. God is not only the source of love, God is love. This He proved when He gave His Son into death for our salvation while we were still sinners. Such divine love awakens the love in our hearts and with it the wisdom to use it rightly.

*Prayer Suggestion: Pray that love may be a force in your life but always in keeping with the love and will of God.*

# A Way to Top One's Weaknesses

Because of sickness or advancing age, some people are weak, and to match them up with the strong would be unfair competition—like sending a Little League team against major leaguers.

The apostle Paul, a man of great energy and zeal, knew about weakness. Given a thorn in the flesh (perhaps a sickness), he was kept from doing what he wanted to do. Three times he prayed for the removal of the affliction, but this was the answer he received from God (2 Cor. 12:9): "My grace is sufficient for you, for My power is made perfect in weakness." The result was that a power much greater than Paul's—the power of Christ—took over in his life.

Then St. Paul states a truth far superior to Murphy's law or the Peter principle: "When I am weak, then I am strong." This was so because, in his weakness, Paul relied on Christ.

God knows our strengths and weaknesses. He knows that we are sometimes like young children and that we would not survive if pitted against adults. So He prevents it. He knows what our capacity is and keeps us from being overloaded.

The Christ in our lives is both mighty and merciful, bidding all who labor and are heavy laden to come to Him. In Him we have a friend, all our sins and griefs to bear. When He traveled the Calvary road that led to a cross, He carried our load. Having done that, He also will help us take up and carry our smaller crosses.

**Prayer Suggestion:** *Pray that with every challenge God may make His grace powerful amid your weakness.*

# Healed from the Sickness of Sin

Thanks to medical research, polio, tuberculosis, and other diseases are under control. Years ago, populations were ravaged by yellow fever and cholera. In 1866, for example, 175 men of the 56th U.S. Infantry were exposed to cholera and died in St. Louis. The same city was the scene of 57 yellow fever deaths in 1878. Now such large-scale plagues can be prevented.

How wonderful if spiritual and moral evils—the sickness of sin—could be stamped out! Sin is to the soul what leprosy is to the body—it destroys. In his time the prophet Isaiah declared about his contemporaries, "Ah, sinful nation, a people loaded with guilt ... Your whole head is injured, your whole heart afflicted. From the sole of your foot to the top of your head, there is no soundness—only wounds and welts and open sores" (1:4–6). Worst of all, if left alone, the sickness of sin has fatal results: "The wages of sin is death" (Rom. 6:23).

The holy Christian church is God's hospital where the spiritually sick are made well. There Jesus Christ, the Good Physician, heals them. How? Isaiah, speaking of the Messiah, "Surely He took up our infirmities and carried our sorrows ... He was pierced for our transgressions, He was crushed for our iniquities; the punishment that brought us peace was upon Him, and by His wounds we are healed" (Is. 53:4–5).

Thank God for Christ's clinic where sinners are made healthy and happy through faith in Him! He invites all who labor and are heavy laden to come to Him for rest.

*Prayer Suggestion: Pray that, through Word and Spirit, Christ may reveal to you more of Himself as the Good Physician.*

# Still Fruitful

Laura Ingalls Wilder wrote her first book, *Little House in the Big Woods,* when she was 65 years old—and continued writing until age 83. Grandma Moses began painting after age 75.

Not all can do creative work in old age, but all can be encouraged to use the talents and powers God continues to give them. In Psalm 92 (vv. 12–14), God has this promise for His people: "The righteous will flourish like a palm tree, they will grow like a cedar of Lebanon; planted in the house of the LORD, they will flourish in the courts of our God. They will still bear fruit in old age." Note the words that apply to young and old: "grow," "flourish," "bear fruit."

Someone has said that the elderly should not lapse into a mood called "transcendental vegetation." They still have minds to think, hearts to love, hands to do something purposeful, feet to go on missions of mercy. With more time, they can give greater expression to their interests and talents.

Along with the opportunities to serve, God gives special promises to those advancing to life's eventide. He declares through Isaiah, "Even to your old age and gray hairs I am He, I am He who will sustain you" (Is. 46:4).

Whether we are young or old, God's promise of total salvation in Christ carries us safely. As Paul wrote, "In Him we have redemption through His blood, the forgiveness of our sins, in accordance with the riches of God's grace" (Eph. 1:7).

*Prayer Suggestion: Ask God to help you lead a fruitful life, whether young or old.*

# Who Is a Success?

A West Point graduate once tried to make a living on his farm near St. Louis, Missouri, but he failed. Then he tried to sell real estate, again to no avail. So he moved to Galena, Illinois, to go into business with his brothers. Soon after, the Civil War broke out. This West Point graduate became the top Union general, then the president of the United States—Ulysses S. Grant.

Most people have to put up with some failure. The question is, however, how do we deal with it? Christians try to put their life and life's work into perspective. First, they do their best, bearing in mind what the Bible says, "Whatever your hand finds to do, do it with all your might" (Eccl. 9:10).

Second, Christians realize that they need God's blessing on their work, and they pray for it. The psalmist declares, "Unless the LORD builds the house, its builders labor in vain" (127:1). We recall the words of Peter the fisherman in Luke 5:5, "Master, we've worked hard all night and haven't caught anything." But Peter went on, "But because You say so, I will let down the nets." How different was the outcome then because the Lord abundantly blessed the efforts of the fishing disciples.

Christians keep this truth in perspective: Success in this world isn't everything. So they seek first Christ's kingdom and His righteousness. True discipleship is of the greatest importance because they want to live for Him who redeemed them with His blood. By Christ's standards, all who are strong in faith and rich in good works are a success.

*Prayer Suggestion: Pray that God may uphold you when failure threatens you in your work or in life as a whole.*

# Christians: Twice Buried, Twice Raised

When the *Mary Rose,* an English warship, sank near Portsmouth on July 19, 1545, several hundred men were buried with it in a watery grave. Then, after the ship had been raised, they were raised, too, and were given a church burial on land in 1984—439 years later.

These men, buried twice, will be raised twice—the second time when Christ returns on the last day (assuming they were Christians). Jesus said, "My Father's will is that everyone who looks to the Son and believes in Him shall have eternal life, and I will raise him up at the last day" (John 6:40). Our Lord was Himself raised from the dead. St. Paul, linking the Christian's resurrection to Christ's, says, "God raised the Lord from the dead, and He will raise us also" (1 Cor. 6:14). Almighty God gave us life once, and He can and will do it again.

In the meantime, we already have been raised from spiritual death. By nature all are dead in trespasses and sins, but God raised us up by the power of the Holy Spirit, who caused us to be born anew through the Gospel. St. Paul reminds us, "We were therefore buried with [Christ] through baptism into death in order that, just as [He] was raised from the dead through the glory of the Father, we too may live a new life" (Rom 6:4).

Buried twice, raised twice? Yes. From the grave of sin and spiritual death we have been raised, and we will someday rise from our cemetery graves. This is the second resurrection, which will take place when Christ returns to take us home with Him to heaven, our heavenly Father's house.

*Prayer Suggestion: Pray that Christ may strengthen the life of faith in you and in the end give you eternal life.*

# Ministering Spirits

The beautiful baroque church in Bavaria (Germany) known as the Wies makes an artistic statement about Christ's atonement. Its artwork also shows the role of angels. One wall painting over the altar depicts angels showing God the Father the symbols of Christ's suffering: the crown of thorns, the hammer and nails, the sponge on a reed, the spear.

Angels were involved in God's plan for our salvation. They announced the birth of Jesus to the shepherds at Bethlehem. At the empty tomb they proclaimed His resurrection. Angels did not come to redeem sinners—that is Christ's work—but they rejoice in heaven when one sinner repents. The Good News that is preached throughout the world, writes Peter in his first epistle, contains things into which the angels long to look.

The angels themselves, firmly established in their blissful position, have nothing to gain from the blessings God intends for human beings. Nevertheless they are joyful and willing messengers of God, as the rhetorical question in the epistle to the Hebrews states, "Are not all angels ministering spirits sent to serve those who will inherit salvation?" (1:14). The final service they render is to carry the believers' souls to heaven.

Angels surround the throne of God, praising Him for His mercy. On the ceiling of the Wies church, a heavenly scene shows Christ's judgment seat to be empty, as if to say there still is time for those who have not yet believed.

We have angels waiting on us, serving us, protecting us, rejoicing with us—just one more reason to be thankful to God, the Father of mercies.

**Prayer Suggestion:** *Thank God in your own words for the protection He has given you through His guardian angels.*

# The Road That Gets You There

Early in the 1800s, when many people were migrating westward, the so-called National Road was well traveled. Beginning in the Baltimore area, it crossed the Alleghenies, then ran to Wheeling, Columbus, Indianapolis, and beyond. Along the way were supply stores, inns, taverns, and toll stations. At the time the National Road was very important, taking people where they wanted to go to settle down.

The all-important spiritual road that takes us through life to our heavenly home above is the road of faith in Jesus Christ. Along the way are places where life's travelers can rest and be refreshed: Christian churches, schools, homes. But there are no toll stations. Offerings are taken, yes, but these are gifts gladly given for the spread of the Gospel. The road to eternal life is free. It was built by Jesus Christ, the pioneer and perfecter of our faith. It came into existence when He Himself walked the Calvary Road to be sacrificed on the cross for our sins.

The National Road had difficult passages as it ran through mountains, across swollen streams, and over steep grades. Similarly, the road that Christ walked and that He bids us take is beset by obstacles. Our Savior has told us, "Enter through the narrow gate. For wide is the gate and broad is the road that leads to destruction. … But small is the gate and narrow the road that leads to life" (Matt. 7:13–14).

The question is not whether Christ's way is an easy one, but is it the right one? Our Lord settled this question for us when He called Himself the Way, the Truth, and the Life—the only way to the Father. Christ is the road that gets you there.

***Prayer Suggestion:*** *Ask God to lift the fog and darkness in your life and show you the road that leads to Him.*

# Jesus Christ: Villain or Victor?

The June 28, 1914, assassination of Archduke Franz Ferdinand of Austria-Hungary ignited World War I. Many considered the assassin, Gavrilo Princip, as a villain, but in his native land he was considered a national hero. He even has a statue erected in his honor.

In His time, Jesus Christ was looked upon in the same way. When they brought Him to Pontius Pilate, His enemies said, "If He were not a criminal … we would not have handed Him over to you" (John 18:30). His accusers charged, "We have found this man subverting our nation. He opposes payment of taxes to Caesar and claims to be Christ, a king" (Luke 23:2). On the basis of these charges the accusers demanded His death.

In the end it comes down to the question of whose side you are on. Those who are Christ's followers see Him as the victor—the liberator from sin and the fear of death. They regard Him as their benefactor and join Peter in saying, "He went around doing good and healing all who were under the power of the devil, because God was with Him" (Acts 10:38).

As with Jesus, so it is with His Gospel. Paul writes, "The message of the cross is foolishness to those who are perishing, but to us who are being saved it is the power of God" (1 Cor. 1:18). Christ, who rose victoriously from the dead, gave us the Gospel that raises us from death and gives us life forever.

Jesus Christ: villain or victor? That's the real question behind the one Jesus asked (Matt. 22:42), "What do you think about the Christ? Whose Son is He?" Since He is the Son of God and our Savior, we cannot but hail Him as the victor.

***Prayer Suggestion:*** *Ask the Lord Jesus to draw you closer into friendship with Him and to bless you with His grace.*

# Faith and Form 1040

The federal income tax is one of many taxes citizens must pay. The Internal Revenue Service does what it can to lighten the task of figuring one's tax. Even so, a great deal of agony attends the ritual of filling out Form 1040.

Paying taxes to a despotic Roman emperor was a painful experience to oppressed people. Yet Jesus told them, "Render … to Caesar the things that are Caesar's" (Matt. 22:21 RSV). In the book of Romans, St. Paul says much the same, "Give everyone what you owe him: If you owe taxes, pay taxes; if revenue, then revenue" (13:7).

Paying taxes to our country is not as hated as it was in Jesus' land. But hated or not, we Christians know that God is involved in the office of government. As St. Paul said (Rom. 13:4), the government "is God's servant to do you good." Thus for a moral reason—for the sake of conscience—citizens want to obey the "powers that be," and the payment of taxes is part of that obedience. Yes, faith in God determines our attitude toward Form 1040 and all it stands for.

Christians find motivation for good citizenship in their faith. The love of Christ that controls them also compels them to render their appropriate dues to both government and God. Jesus is our enabler in this respect. Having redeemed us from sin at the cost of His own life, He elicits from us the response of obedience to God and to all who represent Him.

*Prayer Suggestion: Pray that God may always bless our country with a stable, morally responsible government that administers wisely and well the taxes we pay.*

# Mountain Climbing

Climbing mountains is a challenge that is not without perils. The "outback" Ayres Rock in Central Australia, for example, has claimed the lives of 15 people who tried to climb it.

Spiritual mountain climbing can be hazardous too, that is, when people try to climb Mount Sinai (the Law) to earn forgiveness of sins, peace with God, and a place in heaven. This is the attempt to be right with God by following a be-good-do-good religion. The Bible stresses that salvation cannot be gained by good works, regardless of the hard effort put forth. Sinai, where the Law was given to Moses, is not a mountain to climb. St. Paul, speaking of it as a spiritual mother, states that it "bears children who are to be slaves" (Gal. 4:24).

The same apostle teaches, "It is by grace you have been saved, through faith—and this is not from yourselves, it is the gift of God—not by works, so that no one can boast" (Eph. 2:8–9).

Marvelous, amazing grace! Salvation is God's free gift. But grace is not cheap. It cost the Son of God, our Savior Jesus Christ, His life. He did the mountain climbing on our behalf—carrying a heavy cross, climbing Mount Calvary, atoning for our sins. Faith in Christ saves, not doing the works of the Law.

Therefore, it is not a chore, not a hazardous journey, for us to undertake good deeds for Christ. Having said that we are saved by grace, St. Paul goes on, "We are God's workmanship, created in Christ Jesus to do good works, which God prepared in advance for us to do" (Eph. 2:10). For Christians, doing good works is a pleasure trip.

*Prayer Suggestion: Thank Christ Jesus for fulfilling the Law for you so you are now free to serve Him with good works.*

# Christian Witness in a Jail

The Bible tells us of one potential prison riot that never came off. In the city of Philippi, Paul and Silas had been imprisoned after driving an evil spirit out of a slave girl. Her owners had made money from using her for prophesying and fortune-telling.

At midnight a sudden earthquake shook the prison to its very foundations, opening the doors and unfastening the prisoners' stocks. All elements were present for a riot, including prisoners who could turn on their jailer.

But the outbreak—and breakout—never took place because of the two Christians there, Paul and Silas, who earlier had prayed and sung hymns within the prisoners' hearing. The two missionaries had enough influence to keep the others from rioting and fleeing. When the jailer, thinking all the prisoners had fled, was about to commit suicide, St. Paul could say (Acts 16:28) in behalf of all prisoners, "Don't harm yourself! We are all here!"

In the darkness of that prison, Paul and Silas let their light shine as they witnessed to the other prisoners and to the jailer, telling the latter as he asked about the way of salvation, "Believe in the Lord Jesus, and you will be saved" (v. 31).

Everywhere in our world, people are sitting in sin's darkness and in the prison of their own making: selfishness, fear, anxiety, doubt, unbelief. We say to them, "Jesus Christ died to set you free. Believe in Him and be saved!"

*Prayer Suggestion: Pray the Holy Spirit to enlighten you so you, too, can let your light shine to the glory of Jesus Christ, your Savior.*

# The Worth of Works that Abide

George Caleb Bingham, a struggling artist, painted the life of fur traders and riverboat people in Missouri. A hundred years after his death, when people finally appreciated his work, his "Flatboatmen" canvas sold for $980,000 in Los Angeles. For some people, recognition comes only after they have passed from the scene.

God has not promised us fame and fortune. He has promised that work faithfully performed—especially work done in building the lives of others—will outlast structures built of stone and steel. Parents who bring up their children to believe in God and to walk in His ways are building for eternity. They leave a heritage that endures from generation to generation.

All of us today, whether we realize it or not, are standing on the shoulders of those who have gone before us. The founding fathers and mothers of our cities, communities, churches, and other organizations may not have been able to foresee everything in the future. But they laid well the foundations, enabling us to continue their work and ours. As our Lord has said, "Others have done the hard work, and you have reaped the benefits of their labors" (John 4:38).

Jesus, in the words of the epistle to the Hebrews (12:2), is "the author and perfecter of our faith, who for the joy set before Him endured the cross, scorning its shame, and sat down at the right hand of the throne of God." He left us a treasure, a finished redemption, the charter of salvation, the title to our place in the heavenly Father's spacious condominium.

*Prayer Suggestion: Ask God to help you to continue in the work He wants you to do, even if you cannot as yet see the outcome.*

# God Blesses the Offerings of Faith

One often reads of children banding together to raise money for a worthy cause. In some of those instances, the inspiration undoubtedly comes out of Christian gratitude, giving "as unto the Lord."

Consider the motivation for Abel's gift offering. God was greatly pleased with it, "bearing witness [of this] by accepting his gifts" (Heb. 11:4 RSV). God did not consider the size or amount of the gift, but the spirit—the faith—in which it was given. This fact is stressed when St. Paul points to the Macedonian churches as examples of generosity because they had first given themselves to the Lord (2 Cor. 8). Because that is so important, the apostle does not prescribe the exact amount, such as a tenth of one's income. Nor does he say that the gifts should be cash, though money is probably the most convenient form. Gifts of food and drink, clothing and shelter, also are spoken of in Scripture.

God has promised to bless also our small love offerings, multiplying them so many are benefitted. We can be sure that God blessed both the widow and the mites contributed in God's house. God blesses all our faith offerings, including the cup of cold water, the loaf of bread, the garment, the deed and word of kindness.

God blesses our efforts not because we deserve it, but because of His grace, the same amazing grace or love that sent Christ Jesus into the world to bring us forgiveness and peace. It is in response to that grace that we share what we have with the needy.

*Prayer Suggestion: Pray that God may richly bless your offerings of love, however small and in whatever form they are.*

# On Being Well-Dressed

In Revelation 16:15 the Lord declares through St. John the Divine, "Behold, I come like a thief! Blessed is he who stays awake and keeps his clothes with him, so that he may not go naked and be shamefully exposed." Thus Christ describes His sudden coming, calling on us to be prepared to meet Him.

The garment in which we appear before God as well-dressed people is the robe of the righteousness of Jesus Christ. Our Savior, by His obedience of the Law for us and by His endurance of the death penalty we as sinners had deserved, has gained a righteousness that is ours by faith. Our concern as Christians is to be clothed in this garment. St. Paul speaks for us all when he expressed the earnest desire to "be found in [Christ], not having a righteousness of my own that comes from the law, but that which is through faith in Christ—the righteousness that comes from God and is by faith" (Phil. 3:9).

Do we really need this garment? The Russian writer Leo Tolstoy says this about someone who had renounced his Christian faith: "He felt suddenly like a man who has changed his warm fur cloak for a muslin garment and, going for the first time into the frost, is immediately convinced, not by reason but by his whole nature, that he is as good as naked."

One cannot endure a Russian winter dressed in a flimsy muslin material, nor can one endure the rigors and hardships of life unless he or she is properly dressed in the robe of Christ's righteousness. Wrapped up in the love of Christ, we are warm and safe from life's cold climate.

*Prayer Suggestion: Thank your Lord for numbering you among those who wash their garments and make them white in Jesus' cleansing blood.*

# Putting Oneself in Another's Place

Students of American literature study the life and poetry of Walt Whitman, whose best-known work is perhaps *Leaves of Grass.* What may not be known is that Whitman was a great humanitarian. During the Civil War he did volunteer work among some 80,000 wounded soldiers. Out of that experience grew his empathy, "I do not ask the wounded person how he feels; I myself become that wounded person."

In Jesus' parable, the Good Samaritan played such a role (Luke 10:30–37). He put himself in the place of the wounded man by the wayside and rendered all possible assistance.

It can be said that all of us are spiritually wounded. We are the victims of combat with sin and Satan. Left to our own devices, we would perish. We would likewise perish if someone merely asked us, "How do you feel?" and then did nothing about our situation.

But there is one who comes to our rescue: Jesus Christ. He sees how badly we are wounded, and instead of passing by on the other side, He Himself becomes what we are—wounded. Isaiah says it plainly, "He was wounded for our transgressions … and with His stripes we are healed" (53:5 RSV). St. Peter takes up the same theme in his first epistle as he writes, "[Christ] Himself bore our sins in His body on the tree, so that we might die to sins and live for righteousness; by His wounds you have been healed" (2:24).

To live for righteousness is to love by doing what is right. It is not asking a wounded person how he or she feels, but becoming that wounded person.

***Prayer Suggestion:*** *Pray that out of love for Jesus you, like Him, may become more sensitive to the hurts of others.*

# Christ, the Key to the Bible

Like an anvil, the Bible has worn out many a hammer. Despite all attacks made against it, every day thousands upon thousands of copies of the Bible are sold.

More important than the selling of the Bible is the reading of it. It does no good to buy the book, then let dust gather on it. But when we read, mark, learn, and "inwardly digest it" (as one of the prayers of the church puts it), great blessings are given to us. It is a storehouse containing food for the spiritually hungry. It is a fountain where thirsty souls can drink the fresh water of life. It is a treasure chest from which God's precious truths can be learned and applied.

The Bible is precious because it bears witness to Jesus Christ. It testifies that all people are lost in sin but that God has organized a rescue mission—and the leader of the search-and-save party is Jesus Christ. As it is written, "God so loved the world that He gave His one and only Son, that whoever believes in Him shall not perish but have eternal life" (John 3:16). As long as we live, we can sing with our children, "Jesus loves me, this I know, for the Bible tells me so."

Christ the Savior is the key to the Holy Scriptures. With that key the Holy Spirit opens our hearts and minds to understanding and believing the greatest story ever told. Wanting others to know about Jesus, we translate the Bible into many languages. Now people in almost every nation can read God's Word. It makes them wise unto salvation through faith in Christ Jesus, who went to the cross to atone for sin and rose again on our behalf.

**Prayer Suggestion:** *Pray that the Holy Spirit may lead you closer to your dearest friend, to Jesus, through the Holy Scriptures.*

# Christian Fruitfulness

Child and spousal abuse seem to abound in our society. It should not be so. While the writer of Proverbs 13:24 does say that "he who spares the rod hates his son," he goes on to say, "but he who loves him is careful to discipline him." Discipline can help a youngster overcome bad tendencies. But to bring out the good in him, something else is needed: love that comes in response to God's love.

That is illustrated by many biblical examples. Hannah, the mother of the prophet Samuel, raised a godly son (1 Sam. 1:20–28), not by trying to beat the good out of him but by praying with and for him, by teaching him the Word of God, by bringing him to the temple. In the New Testament, Eunice and Lois, mother and grandmother of Timothy, prepared him for a life of service, not by beating him but by sharing their faith with him. Thus, as St. Paul reminds Timothy, he knew from childhood the Holy Scriptures, which made him wise unto salvation through faith in Jesus Christ (2 Tim. 1:5 and 3:15).

And as for a man's relationship to his wife, Scripture says, "Husbands, love your wives, just as Christ loved the church and gave Himself up for her" (Eph. 5:25). Such love comes in response to the love of God in Jesus Christ that reaches into our lives and makes them productive. It makes us like trees planted by streams of water that yield their fruit in their season.

*Prayer Suggestion: Pray that in love to Jesus Christ, your Savior, you may become more fruitful in good thoughts, desires, words, and works.*

# The Cross, God's Judgment Tree

At the Daniel Boone home near Defiance, Missouri, stands a dead elm tree under which Boone, as the representative of the Spanish government, held judgment sessions between Indians and white people. It is called the Judgment Tree.

Many things have been transacted under trees. Under the Washington Elm in Cambridge, Massachusetts, George Washington took command of the Continental troops. Under the Treaty Tree in Texas, Stephen F. Austin signed boundary agreements with the Indians. The Peace Tree on San Juan Hill in Cuba marked the spot where Col. Theodore Roosevelt and the Rough Riders dislodged the enemy from its stronghold.

No tree saw a greater event than the accursed tree—Calvary's cross. There Jesus was crucified, having been made a curse for us that we might be redeemed from the curse of the Law. Then He rose again. St. Peter told the council members who voted for Jesus' death, "The God of our fathers raised Jesus from the dead—whom you had killed by hanging Him on a tree" (Acts 5:30).

On the cross Jesus endured the judgment of death, which the righteous God demanded of all sinners. Jesus, the sinners' substitute, suffered death on the cross. But by that act sinners escape the judgment of death through faith in Jesus as their Savior. The Judgment Tree becomes the Peace Tree, the tree that brought peace with God.

The cross loses its horror and the threat of divine judgment when we keep in mind what St. Paul has written, "Therefore, since we have been justified through faith, we have peace with God through our Lord Jesus Christ" (Rom. 5:1).

***Prayer Suggestion:*** *Pray that God may give you firm faith in the sin-forgiving power of Christ's cross.*

# Where Is He?

Many people today, influenced by the scientific approach to life, look for evidence of the Christian faith. They say they would be impressed if somehow Jesus Christ could be brought before them and they could question Him directly about His teachings—the way a notable person is quizzed on various television programs.

Obviously that is not possible. Jesus Christ, after His duly-attested resurrection, ascended bodily into heaven and now sits at God's right hand. However, He is still with us in His unseen presence. He said (Matt. 28:20), "I am with you always." "Where two or three are come together in My name, there I am with them" (Matt. 18:20). But in His visible presence, Jesus is no longer on earth.

Where can we find Jesus today? How can we be in touch with Him? Our Lord is present with us in Word and sacraments. When the Gospel of our salvation from sin is proclaimed, then we hear the Word that He also proclaimed. Believing that Word, which in the sacraments is accompanied by outward signs (water in Baptism; bread and wine in Holy Communion), we are in personal fellowship with Him. Then He is in us and we are in Him. When this has taken place, the Holy Spirit gives us the inner testimony that Jesus Christ is the Son of God and that His teaching is the truth. Having this conviction, we no longer need to ask where Christ is or to lay eyes and hands on outward evidence. We simply say with Thomas, "My Lord and my God!" (John 20:28).

*Prayer Suggestion: Speak to Jesus, your Savior and friend, asking Him to keep coming to you in His Word and to abide in your heart.*

# Red Sails in the Sunset

Lake Tiberias, also known as Lake Gennesaret (Lake Kinneret today) and the Sea of Galilee, was an appropriate setting for the reinstatement of Peter as an apostle. At this lake Jesus had recruited him in the first place.

The waters of this lake were familiar to Peter. As a fisherman he had often hoisted his sails here for launching out into the deep to let down his nets. To be in a position for night fishing, he had to make all his preparations before sunset.

As an apostle—as one sent by Christ to be a fisher of men—Peter had to prepare also for his spiritual fishing expeditions. His mission journeys by land and sea would take him to many places, even Rome itself. We can picture him at eventide asking Mark, his traveling companion, whether all was in readiness for setting sail in the morning.

The "red sails in the sunset" theme applies especially to the end of Peter's life. As the risen Savior foretold, "You will stretch out your hands" (John 21:18). Just as his Lord had been made to extend His hands on a bloody cross, so this disciple would glorify God with a martyr's death by crucifixion. Peter accepted the reappointment. He looked forward to the morning—to the morning of an eternal day when he and all believers would be with Christ in heaven.

We all are sailing on the sea of life. Sometimes the voyage is everything but smooth. Evening comes, and we must get ready for another day of hard work. When sails are red in the sunset, we can go on because Jesus goes with us.

*Prayer Suggestion: Tell Jesus, your Lord and Savior, how much you desire His presence as you come and go, work and rest.*

# Forgiveness, the Breath of Life

A headstone inscription in Mount Olives Cemetery at Hannibal, Missouri, records this grim fact:

Leaves have their time in Fall
And flowers to wither at the north wind's breath;
And stars to set, but all—
Thou hast all seasons for thine own, O Death.

Another headstone records this expression of faith:

And when thou art refreshed in death,
Christ will give thee back thy breath.

It was in a tomb in "Joseph's lovely garden" that our dead and buried Lord was given back His breath. On Easter morning the angel announced, "You are looking for Jesus, who was crucified. He is not here; He has risen, just as He said. Come and see the place where He lay. Then go quickly and tell His disciples: 'He has risen from the dead'" (Matt. 28:5–7).

Christ was given back His breath so His presence might serve as a living proof of His victory over sin and death. At His reunion with His disciples, He breathed on them and said, "Receive the Holy Spirit. If you forgive anyone his sins, they are forgiven" (John 20:22–23). Here we have the great news to be proclaimed: the Gospel of the forgiveness of sins in the name of Jesus. To forgiveness is linked the promise of eternal life. Forgiveness gives peace and hope in life and in death. It brings joy because the promise of life comes from Christ, who pronounces Himself the Resurrection and the Life. Because He lives, we, too, shall live, even as we already live in Him now by faith.

*Prayer Suggestion: Ask God the Holy Spirit to strengthen your faith in Christ's promise of forgiveness and of life eternal.*

# Pardon, Peace, and Life

As the Messiah, Jesus declared, "The kingdom of God is near. Repent and believe the good news" (Mark 1:15). Applying the prophet Isaiah's words (61:1–2) to Himself, Jesus stated the purpose of His mission was to minister to those who repented and accepted the good news of God's forgiveness.

As the Healer of hearts, Jesus found many spiritual patients in a group of social and religious outcasts called tax collectors and sinners. The tax collectors were hated for working with the oppressors, as well as for their greed in overcharging oppressed taxpayers. "Sinners" was a catchall category for an assortment of wrongdoers, including irreligious persons, adulterers, the heathen, and those who made themselves ceremonially unclean by consorting with the heathen.

These were the people who responded to the Lord's invitation to bring their spiritual sicknesses and to be healed. In answer to those who objected to His "chaplaincy" to outcasts, Jesus said, "It is not the healthy who need a doctor, but the sick. I have not come to call the righteous, but sinners" (Mark 2:17).

Well for us that Jesus does not discriminate against sinners like us, who have need of His healing ministry.

> We deserve but grief and shame,
> Yet His words, rich grace revealing,
> Pardon, peace, and life proclaim.
> Here our ills have perfect healing;
> We with humble hearts believe
> Jesus sinners will receive.

***Prayer Suggestion:*** *Express your gratitude to Jesus for inviting you to come to Him "just as you are."*

# Reunion in Galilee

The angel at the empty tomb announced to the woman that the crucified Jesus "has risen from the dead and is going ahead of you into Galilee." The risen Lord Himself told the women on their homeward way, "Go and tell My brothers to go to Galilee; there they will see Me" (Matt. 28:7, 10).

Galilee—what memories it held for Jesus and His disciples! There, in Nazareth, He grew up. There, on the shore of the Sea of Galilee, He found His first disciples. There He opened His preaching and healing ministry, and there, in Cana, He performed His first miracle. Galilee entered into the events of the final week. When on Palm Sunday people asked "Who is this?" the reply was, "This is Jesus, the prophet from Nazareth in Galilee" (Matt. 21:10, 11). Pontius Pilate, on learning that Jesus was a Galilean, sent Him to Herod for judgment (Luke 23:7).

It is not surprising that the risen Lord sought a rendezvous with His disciples in Galilee. It was familiar territory. The mountaintop to which Jesus had directed them was undoubtedly a locale where He had previously met with His disciples. The well-known scene would help identify the risen Savior as indeed the Jesus of Galilee.

The Galilee where Jesus Christ meets with us today is His Word, the Holy Scriptures. This Word bears witness that Jesus "was delivered over to death for our sins and was raised to life for our justification" (Rom. 4:25). And His message to us is this, "If you hold to My teaching, you are really My disciples. Then you will know the truth, and the truth will set you free" (John 8:31–32).

***Prayer Suggestion:*** *Thank the risen Savior for seeking a reunion with you in His Word.*

# Communicating the Easter News

Communication is written large in the Easter story. Angels are sent to inform the women at the tomb that Jesus has risen from the dead. The women are to pass the word on to the disciples, and the disciples are in turn instructed by the risen Christ to proclaim the Good News in all the world. The gospel accounts by Matthew, Mark, Luke, and John, in which we read all this, are themselves a vital part of this proclamation.

To be told and then to tell—that is why we call pastors, build churches, and assemble in those buildings for worship. In God's house the message of Christ is communicated anew, "Peace be with you." Present with us, Jesus gives the peace He has won for us. He gives us faith that appropriates and makes our own the gift of salvation—forgiveness of sins, reconciliation with God, newness of life in Him. This is what is preached in our churches.

Having been told the Good News, we now tell others. That is the mission inherent in the Easter event. The risen Savior comes into our midst with the charge, "As the Father has sent Me, I am sending you" (John 20:21). As His latter-day disciples we communicate to today's generation "that Christ died for our sins according to the Scriptures, that He was buried, that He was raised on the third day according to the Scriptures" (1 Cor. 15:3–4).

Sing we to our God above,
Praise eternal as His love;
Praise Him, all you heav'nly host,
Father, Son, and Holy Ghost. Alleluia!

*Prayer Suggestion: Ask the risen Savior for willingness and ability to tell others the Easter news.*

# Singing Instead of Sighing

Just about every human experience today has been endured before and is reported in the Bible. The psalmist prays, "May the groans of the prisoners come before You; by the strength of Your arm preserve those condemned to die" (79:11).

In Venice, a bridge that spans a water street in Venice is called the Bridge of Sighs because it connects prison cells with the court rooms. Through the ages many prisoners have sighed or groaned as they were led back after sentencing.

All of us, prisoners or not, have bridges of sighs to cross. Many are the bridges of grief because of losses and failures, tensions in marriage and family, sickness and death. And St. Paul writes (2 Cor. 5:10) that we must all appear before the judgment seat of Christ; what sorrow is ours because of sins that bring us into judgment!

How comforting to know that Jesus, who has crossed all the bridges of sighs Himself, goes with us through life! He was a prisoner in our stead, being sentenced to death on a cross to redeem us from sin and to enable us to stand blameless before the throne of God. The prophet Isaiah foresaw the redemption of God's people, saying, "The ransomed of the LORD will return. They will enter Zion with singing; everlasting joy will crown their heads. Gladness and joy will overtake them, and sorrow and sighing shall flee away" (35:10).

Christ, who set us free from the captivity of sin, is pleased when we help others, including prisoners, turn their sighing into singing. He declares, "I was in prison and you came to Me" (Matt. 25:36).

***Prayer Suggestion:*** *Ask God to help you bring the joy of Jesus Christ into the lives of people you know.*

# Keeping Christ in Control of Your Life

Some people claim to have dual, even multiple, personalities. St. Paul seemed to be two persons with opposing wills. Two contradictory principles were at work in him, as he writes (Rom. 7:15), "What I want to do I do not do, but what I hate I do." It was the sin in him that opposed the good he wanted to do. He had once been Saul the Pharisee; now he was Paul, the Christian apostle. Once an enemy of Christ, he was now at peace with Christ. He was now dead to the Law—he knew he could not be saved by doing the perfect deeds it required—and alive to Christ: "I have been crucified with Christ and I no longer live, but Christ lives in me. The life I live in the body, I live by faith in the Son of God, who loved me and gave Himself for me" (Gal. 2:20).

The apostle was not a perfect saint. Sin still lived in him and wanted to gain the upper hand. Both flesh and spirit, the old nature and the new nature, still dwelt in him.

In that sense, all Christians are composite people, which is different from being split personalities. The old sinful drives of greed, selfishness, and lovelessness are still in us, creating tensions. But in Christians, in whom the Holy Spirit lives, sin is no longer in control. The new nature, which came into being with conversion, is calling the shots. Faith in Jesus Christ, which God works in Christians through the Gospel, produces love and many other fruits. Sin still plagues us, but Christ is in charge. That's why Christians are not spiritual schizophrenics but integrated persons, growing in their commitment to Christ.

**Prayer Suggestion:** *Pray that, amid the many voices clamoring in you for your attention, the voice of Christ may prevail.*

# Project Jonah

These days, a number of environmental groups are trying to save whales and related sea animals. These efforts bring to mind how, in a reversal of roles, it was once a large fish that saved a man—Jonah.

In today's Bible reading, it was neither the fish nor Jonah whom Jesus was trying to save, but the people around Him. He claimed that His "unorthodox" message came from God. So the people demanded tangible proof that He, in effect, had come from God. Jesus, however, said, "None will be given [this evil and unfaithful generation] except the sign of [the prophet] Jonah" (Matt. 16:4). Our Lord wanted people to draw a lesson from Jonah.

What was the lesson? Earlier in Matthew's gospel, when a similar demand was made of Him, Jesus explained, "As Jonah was three days and three nights in the belly of a huge fish, so the Son of Man will be three days and three nights in the heart of the earth" (Matt. 12:40).

Jonah's survival, of course, proved nothing about Jesus. Instead, His own death, burial, and resurrection are sufficient "proofs" that He is God's Son and our Savior. As St. Paul writes, "Christ died for our sins according to the Scriptures, that He was buried, that He was raised on the third day according to the Scriptures" (1 Cor. 15:3–4).

Christ's Word and His work in our hearts is all the proof we need.

*Prayer Suggestion: Thank your Lord Jesus for having given His life for you and then rising from the grave to make your salvation sure.*

# The Opposite Outcome

Many people take their cues from the society of self-serving individuals. If asked to complete the statement "Whoever exalts himself ..." they might finish the sentence with "shows a healthy self-confidence" or "will have people look up to her" or "will get ahead in the world." When Jesus assures the humble person that God will exalt him, worldly philosophy would change this to mean "Whoever humbles himself has an inferiority complex and will let people step on him."

Our world is full of do-it-yourself achievers of fame and fortune. Some of them do not hesitate to hide their selfish drive under a cloak of religious piety. Religious leaders in Jesus' day made a display of their religion, sought out the seats of honor, and had themselves addressed by honorable titles—not to honor God by the office they held but to exalt themselves.

Jesus gives the scribes, Pharisees, and their imitators something to think about when He declares that all self-seeking efforts are counterproductive. He teaches, "Everyone who exalts himself will be humbled, and he who humbles himself will be exalted" (Luke 14:11).

St. Peter, writing years later, repeats Jesus' admonition with these words: "Humble yourselves, therefore, under God's mighty hand, that He may lift you up in due time" (1 Peter 5:6). Christian humility is achieved through faith in Jesus Christ, who to redeem us humbled Himself to the point of death on the cross. Just as He was lifted up from the grave, so we shall be exalted into heaven to reign with Him forever. Not a bad swap for being humbled now!

*Prayer Suggestion: Ask God to take away from you all pride and arrogance and to adorn you with the precious level of Christlike humility.*

# This Couple Didn't Swing

Today's society keeps pushing to the limits the perimeters of acceptable behavior, especially in marriage. Many condone "open" marriages where two couples exchange partners. Some call these couples "swingers."

If a "swinging couple" meant instead one that moves from place to place, then Aquila and Priscilla could readily qualify. From Rome they moved to Corinth, then to Ephesus, back to Rome, and again back to Ephesus. They first met their fellow tentmaker Paul in Corinth and invited him to make his home with them. From then on, their lives were closely intertwined with this apostle's.

In the current sense of "swinging," Aquila and Priscilla, who probably were childless, knew that a life of double adultery was not for them. This husband and wife team did not take part in the practices mentioned by St. Paul in Romans 13:13: orgies and drunkenness, sexual immorality and debauchery. Instead, they were an active, lively couple—not for their own gratification, but for the Lord. As Christians, they risked their lives for the sake of the Gospel. To them "all the churches of the Gentiles are grateful" (Rom. 16:3).

Very likely, you know at least one Christian couple that has served as a role model in your life. Although you might never have the chance to thank them as publicly as Paul thanked Aquila and Priscilla, can you thank them privately? At the very least, you can thank God for their witness to the presence of Jesus in their lives.

**Prayer Suggestion:** *Thank God for people who, at great personal risk, serve Christ.*

## "Another Counselor" Is Promised

Have you ever tried moving a sofa or long table by yourself? It's difficult because you have to half drag it end by end. Moving it is much easier when another person takes hold of the other end and helps you carry it. That is the picture in the Greek verb that describes how "the Spirit helps us in our weakness" (Rom. 8:26)—literally, "together with us He takes hold of the other end."

The Holy Spirit, whom Jesus promised to send from the Father, is the Counselor—literally, "one who is called to someone's aid," as a mother is called to a sick child's bedside during the night. The Spirit is indeed our helper.

As Counselor, the Spirit consoles. He imparts the comfort, consolation, and peace of the forgiveness of sins.

As Counselor, the Spirit teaches. As Jesus said, "[He] will teach you all things" (John 14:26). The Holy Spirit enlightens, clearing up problems, teaching us that our salvation is in Christ alone.

As Counselor, the Spirit helps us recall. Jesus said, "He will remind you of everything I have said to you" (John 14:26).

Our Lord was soon to leave His disciples through death's door and later to ascend into heaven, but in His place would come "another Counselor," the Holy Spirit. How well for us that He came! We are not left comfortless or as orphans. We have the constant guidance of the Holy Spirit leading us into all truth.

*Prayer Suggestion: Gather your thoughts for a prayer in which you express your gratitude for the Holy Spirit's counsel and comfort.*

# Jesus, Friend of the Family

The famous Walt Disney spent a part of his boyhood on a 48-acre farm near Marceline, Missouri. Apparently he loved his former home and hometown. His feature film *Main Street, U.S.A.* was partly based on his boyhood town.

When so many forces work to tear apart marriage, home, and family, we can be thankful for anything that holds families together. There is, however, no better glue than faith in Jesus, the best friend a family ever had.

From the beginning of His life to its end, Jesus was a positive power for God-pleasing family living. He grew up in Nazareth, where He was an obedient son. He Himself fulfilled the commandment to honor father and mother. At Cana He blessed the marriage estate by His presence and by the performance of His first miracle. When mothers brought young children to Him, He did not turn them away as the disciples suggested, but took them up in His arms and blessed them.

Our Lord was well aware of all the evil influences that corrupt and destroy family life. He knew they came from the sinful heart. To this day He seeks to heal, recreate, renew, and purify the heart. Only the love of Jesus that drove Him to the cross can change hearts of steel and stone, and He does change them through His Word and Holy Spirit.

When Jesus tells His followers to love one another, He wants His own love practiced by the members of the family. He stands behind the words of His apostle St. Paul: "Be kind and compassionate to one another, forgiving each other, just as in Christ God forgave you" (Eph. 4:32).

*Prayer Suggestion: Pray that Jesus may continue to bless you and your family with His loving presence.*

# Man Up a Tree

Zacchaeus, the chief tax collector in Jericho, had climbed into a sycamore tree so he, a man of small stature, could get a better look at Jesus. He was "up a tree" in a spiritual sense as well.

Zacchaeus had accumulated riches through dishonesty. In his own words to Jesus, he implied that he had defrauded the hapless taxpayers. What is more, the people considered him a traitor who cooperated with the hated Romans. Thus they called him "a sinner."

Worst of all, Zacchaeus was in deep trouble with his God, who held him responsible not only for sins against the neighbor but also—and especially—for not loving God and not serving Him with all his heart, soul, and mind.

Many of us are in that kind of predicament today because of unrepented sin against God and others. Perhaps we have not cheated as Zacchaeus did; but as Zacchaeus could, we can easily name our own sins.

There is a way to get down from the tree of trouble. Jesus tells us as He told Zacchaeus, "Come down immediately. I must stay at your house today" (Luke 19:5). He, the Son of Man, who came to seek and save the lost, comes to us. He came not only to Zacchaeus' city but to the Jerichos of the whole world to render obedience in behalf of disobedient humanity and to endure the penalty for sin on the cross.

This is the way things balance out: Jesus Christ went to the tree of the cross to get all people down from the tree of trouble into which their sins had driven them.

**Prayer Suggestion:** *If you are troubled, lay your problems before the Lord and ask for His guidance.*

# When the Spirit Has All of You

Someone has said, "To be full of the Holy Spirit doesn't mean that you have all of Him, but that He has all of you."

The Holy Spirit is true God. Our bodies are rightly called temples in which the Spirit dwells, but none of us can contain Him totally and exclusively because then He could not dwell in anyone else. Rather, to have the Holy Spirit is to have His wisdom, power, love, compassion. Through His work through the Gospel, we have faith in Jesus Christ as the Savior. The Holy Spirit works all good within us.

What a human miracle takes place when the Holy Spirit has all of a person! He took over all of Saul the Pharisee and made him St. Paul the apostle. He took over his heart, his scholarly mind, his energy, his zeal, and gave them a new direction. The Holy Spirit had all of Peter and the other apostles, sending them out to teach, preach, heal, and baptize into the name of the triune God.

He also has all of the hearts, minds, spirits, and bodies of dedicated men and women who today proclaim Christ and bring His love to needy people all over the world.

One might ask, "Does the Holy Spirit have all of me?" Some brush aside this question because they think it means being a religious fanatic. But that is not what is meant when we speak of being filled with the Spirit. To pray, to love the Word of God, to stand on the side of Christ, to please God by doing one's daily work faithfully, to speak a word of kindness and comfort to someone in distress—this is what is meant. It means that the Holy Spirit has all of you!

***Prayer Suggestion:*** *Pray for a greater measure of the Holy Spirit in your life so He may have the full measure of you.*

# Treating People as Persons

The Louvre Art Museum has on display James Whistler's painting entitled "An Arrangement in Grey and Black." Americans know it as "Whistler's Mother."

Whistler's title sounds too impersonal, but that's the way many people see the rest of humanity. Some employers see those under them as an impersonal "work force." Politicians speak of people as "voters." To the commercial world they are "consumers." Some children treat adults as impersonal arrangements of mind and muscle whereby they are cared for and provided with toys.

The term "people" is general, impersonal, nondescript. The term "persons," on the other hand, focuses on individual human beings, each one with a mind, soul, and spirit.

On occasion Jesus addressed large multitudes and fed them. At no time, though, did He lose sight of individuals as persons. At Jacob's well He spoke at length to the Samaritan woman, delivering what many regard as His most beautiful sermon. He also spoke in a parable of a shepherd who left his 99 sheep and went after the lost one. He said the angels of heaven rejoice over one sinner who repents.

Our Lord gave His life for the redemption of all, but He wants each one to regard it as personal, rather than as salvation as mass production. Martin Luther wrote in his explanation of the Creed: "I believe that Jesus Christ ... has redeemed me."

We take a page from Jesus' book when we love people as persons and help them as persons. Then they will deal with us as persons.

***Prayer Suggestion:*** *Thank your Lord for having created you, redeemed you, and sanctified you as a person precious in His sight.*

# A Mother's True Beauty

Helen, the wife of Sparta's King Menelaus, was acclaimed the most beautiful woman of Greece. The Greeks fought the Trojan War to get her back from Troy, where Paris, the son of King Priam, had taken her. In Christopher Marlowe's *Dr. Faustus,* the question is asked concerning Helen, "Was this the face that launched a thousand ships and burned the topless towers of Ilium?"

In May, we honor women with another kind of beauty—the beauty of devotion to maternal duties. We ask, concerning our mother: Is this the face that smiled on us, guided us, and launched us for life's voyage? Are these the hands that served us in a thousand ways and taught us to fold our own hands in prayer? Are these the feet that moved swift and beautiful under the impulse of love? Are these the lips that spoke to us about our Savior's dying love to make us His own? Indeed they are! A mother's sincere devotion far exceeds Helen's beauty because it is the inner beauty of love.

What a wonderful tribute the book of Proverbs gives to the godly mother: "Her children arise and call her blessed; her husband also, and he praises her: 'Many women do noble things, but you surpass them all.' Charm is deceptive, and beauty is fleeting; but a woman who fears the LORD is to be praised. Give her the reward she has earned, and let her works bring her praise at the city gate" (31:28–31).

Having given our mothers such praise, all that remains is that we who are children, young or old, support our words with loving deeds, as our Lord would have it.

***Prayer Suggestion:*** *Thank the Lord for all the blessings He has given you through your mother, especially for teaching you about Christ.*

# Caring for Each Other in Marriage

About a century ago Carry Nation carried on an aggressive temperance campaign. In her zeal she sometimes took the ax to saloon furnishings. It is not too hard to understand this when we remember that her first husband died of alcoholism.

Sometimes even the best we can do in someone's behalf is not enough to solve a serious problem. Only professional help will avail, and sometimes even that will fail. In most instances, however, husbands and wives can help each other in overcoming their difficulties. They can bear one another's burdens. Advice and guidance, when given in love and with proper insight and understanding, are often appreciated. Words spoken in anger, seldom do good.

Husbands and wives are called to forgive. As Christians they are capable of doing this. Here are words well worth noting: "Be kind and compassionate to one another, forgiving each other, just as in Christ God forgave you" (Eph. 4:32).

The realization of God's forgiveness and the change of heart this conviction brings about lays the foundation for Christian loving and caring in marriage. It is not a mere slogan, not an unattainable ideal, to say as St. Paul does that husbands and wives should love one another. He declares, "Live a life of love, just as Christ loved us and gave Himself up for us as a fragrant offering and sacrifice to God" (Eph. 5:2). This love of Christ is not only an example for us, it enables us to follow it.

Partners in marriage who have faith in Jesus Christ as their personal Savior can't help but reflect His love in their daily care for each other.

*Prayer Suggestion: Pray for a better grasp of the love of Christ so you may grow in love for each other.*

# Has the Fire Gone Out?

Many have an interest today in the "baptism of the Holy Spirit" and related subjects. In apostolic times, God bestowed special power in this way. Today, Christian theologians are by no means agreed what the Spirit's baptism is, but one thing is sure: It can diminish the teaching of Jesus that we are to "make disciples of all nations, baptizing them in the name of the Father and of the Son and of the Holy Spirit" (Matt. 28:19). The Baptism of Jesus is the one we need.

According to John the Baptist, Jesus baptizes us "with the Holy Spirit and with fire." Through the Word and water of Baptism, Christ gives us the Holy Spirit for our spiritual rebirth. We are given saving faith and with it the fruits of faith.

The Holy Spirit, active through the Gospel, is like a fire. He warms our hearts so our Christianity is not a lukewarm affair—"neither hot nor cold" as the book of Revelation (3:16) puts it. In kindling faith in us, the Holy Spirit sets us on fire for Jesus Christ.

The fire of which John the Baptist speaks can refer also to God's consuming anger at sin. A baptism of fire in this sense is the fire of divine judgment on those who, through unbelief, quench and smother the Holy Spirit.

Christ's love for us as Savior and Lord continues. Through His Word He desires to impart the Holy Spirit that He may increase our faith, hope, and love. Is our faith like a fire gone out, or is it burning brightly?

*Prayer Suggestion: Pray that the Holy Spirit may, through the Gospel, increase your faith in Christ, granting you a love that in the hymn writer's words may "pure, warm, and changeless be, a living fire."*

# On Saying and Doing

Saying and doing belong together. It does no good to promise a lot of things but not to carry them out. It is a commendation of character when a person's words are as good as his or her bond. We know we can rely on what that person says because deeds will follow.

In the book of Exodus, Pharaoh promised to let the Israelites go, only to change his mind when the plagues subsided. In his play *Green Pastures,* Marc Connelly has Moses upbraid Pharaoh for this, telling him, "You been givin' a lot of say-so and no do-so."

Jesus knew about vacillating human nature—how good intentions often fall short of achievement. He referred to some who piously say "Lord, Lord!" but then fail to fulfill the heavenly Father's will. On another occasion (Matt. 21:28–32) He spoke of two sons whom the father wanted to work in his vineyard. One said very politely, "I will go, Sir," but didn't go. The other promised nothing; in fact, he declared his unwillingness to go. But he proved better than his word. He went after all and did what the father wanted.

There is another Son whom the heavenly Father sent to work in the vineyard of this world. He is Jesus Christ, who not only said He would go to serve and to give His life for all sinners, but also went and did it. Christians, who by adoption are the sons and daughters of God, let their family resemblance show when they keep their promises.

There is a time to speak, and there is a time to do. God grant us the wisdom and ability to do both.

***Prayer Suggestion:*** *Ask for the help of the Holy Spirit to speak and do what pleases God and helps people.*

# Thorns and Other Troubles

In a museum in Rome sits a copy of a Greek statue dating back to the fifth century before Christ. Called "Boy with the Thorn," it shows a seated boy picking a thorn out of his foot.

The apostle Paul had a far more painful affliction that he called a thorn in the flesh (2 Cor. 12:7–10). Just what that thorn was we don't know—perhaps it was a physical ailment causing him a great deal of distress. It tended to keep him humble amid the many glorious revelations he had received from God.

Perhaps you suffer from a thorn in the flesh—something far more painful than a splinter or thorn in the foot. A mere thorn can be removed, a bandage applied, and you are ready to go. But a thorn in the flesh like St. Paul's is far worse. It causes anguish of body and mind. It is a special burden to bear, that festers and causes you suffering.

"Why me?" you may ask. "Why has God permitted this to come to me?" Could it be that it is to keep you humble, to compel you to keep your feet on the ground after some exhilarating experience, to draw you closer to Christ, who is our good physician and dearest friend? If so, the thorn in the flesh is fulfilling a wholesome purpose.

When life brings difficulties of any kind, we always have access to the Lord in prayer, asking Him to remove them, if that is His will, or to help us cope with them. Jesus Christ knew a lot about thorns. On His head He bore a crown of thorns when He suffered on our behalf. He will not turn us away. He will help, and He will heal.

*Prayer Suggestion: Ask God to extract the thorn bothering you, or if it is to stay, to enable you to live with it to His glory.*

# A Firm Foundation for Life

Inscribed in large letters on the facade of the Nelson Art Gallery in Kansas City, Missouri, is this verse:

As all nature's thousand changes
but one changeless God proclaim,
So in art's wide kingdom ranges
one sole meaning still the same.
This is truth's eternal reason
which from beauty takes its dress
And serene through time and season
stands for aye in loveliness.

The words reflect what David wrote long ago in Psalm 19:1, "The heavens declare the glory of God, the skies proclaim the work of His hands."

Nature, of course, has a thousand changes, as the poet said. However, behind the changing scenes of life stands our changeless God. God's wisdom and power revealed in the universe abide, and so does His steadfast love. The Word, which proclaims God's love, is abiding, steadfast, firm, and sure. God stands behind all His promises, including the greatest of them all: "God so loved the world that He gave His one and only Son, that whoever believes in Him shall not perish but have eternal life" (John 3:16).

God's changeless love gives us something to build on. God's truths as Jesus taught them are a sure foundation for life. The rains, storms, winds, floods of time cannot destroy it.

*Prayer Suggestion: Ask Jesus, who is the same yesterday, today, and forever, to abide in your heart.*

# The How and When of Christian Forgiveness

While visiting the United States in 1959, the Russian Communist leader Nikita Khrushchev said in a speech in San Francisco, "Christian teaching tells us to be forgiving to others if they understand that they have trespassed." For a professed atheist, he made a point many of us overlook: Only those who recognize their wrongdoing are to be forgiven.

"To repent" means to be contrite and sorrowful for sins committed, and then to trust God's forgiveness for the sake of Jesus Christ, who died for sin. God does not throw His love and forgiveness at people. It goes only to those who own up to their sinfulness and look to God for help.

As God forgives, so we are to forgive those who trespass against us. None of us wants to hold a grudge; it hurts us more than the person against whom it is directed. That's why Jesus taught us to pray: "Forgive us our trespasses as we forgive those who trespass against us."

When it comes to forgiving the neighbor—the brother or sister—a mutual basis ought to exist. Erring brothers or sisters are not apt to change their ways unless they recognize their errors. To gloss over their sins by offering them unasked-for forgiveness does not lead to repentance. Instead, Jesus said, "If your brother sins against you, go and show him his fault, just between the two of you" (Matt. 18:15). Khrushchev was right: Forgive others "if they understand that they have trespassed." Then, "Be kind and compassionate to one another, forgiving each other, just as in Christ God forgave you" (Eph. 4:32).

*Prayer Suggestion: Pray for courage and strength to forgive those who repent of their wrongdoing.*

# When Two Contradictory Voices Speak

When two persons in a room speak to you at the same time, you may have trouble understanding both of them. A more difficult problem arises when, on the moral and spiritual level of life, two voices bid for your attention, especially when they are contradictory, one good and one evil, but they both sound right. One voice calls you to the good life through sacrifice; the other calls you to the good life without pain.

There is consolation in knowing that contradictory voices spoke also to Jesus. At His Baptism the voice of the heavenly Father was heard to say: "This is My Son, whom I love" (Matt. 3:17). Then, when the Spirit led Him into the wilderness, another voice sought to raise doubt by saying: "If You are the Son of God … Don't You have just a little doubt?"

Some might think that, for Jesus, the voice was no problem. Jesus, after all, was the holy Son of God and always knew right from wrong. True, but He had become a human being, and as such He was in all points tempted as we are.

What did Jesus do? He clung to the voice of God—the voice that spoke to Him at His Baptism, and the voice that spoke to Him in the Holy Scripture. He met every temptation of the devil with the "It is written" of God's Word. He heeded this voice at all times, even at the end when He was obedient unto death, even death on a cross for our salvation.

That is also what we can do when the voice of evil tries to outshout the voice of good. We follow God's Word because we know He will lead us aright.

*Prayer Suggestion: Pray that the voice of Jesus Christ, your Good Shepherd and dearest friend, will at all times prevail in your heart.*

# Duel in the Desert

There is really no place in this world where we can say that we are absolutely safe from the devil's temptations.

We all know the usual worldly props the devil uses for his temptations—bars, bright lights, expensive goods of all kinds, throbbing music. Undoubtedly that was the bait he held out to the prodigal son of Jesus' parable. We tell ourselves if we stay away from such places, we are safe. But are we?

The devil can tempt people also when all the worldly glitter and glamour is absent—when there are only barrenness and loneliness, bleak rocks and sand, thorns and thistles. This was the experience of Jesus when He was in the wilderness for 40 days, tempted by the devil. There Satan made his first assault by saying: "If You are the Son of God, tell these stones to become bread."

In his temptations the devil tries to appeal to human desires for exotic books and drinks, for honor and power, for running foolish risks to avoid unpleasantries. What Satan did not figure on was that Jesus would not succumb to his overtures. Jesus adhered to God's Word. That is also how we can defeat the devil.

This was not our Lord's last duel with His prime opponent. The Gospel account says that the devil "left him until an opportune time" (Luke 4:13). The final showdown came in the encounter on Calvary's cross. There Jesus triumphed totally. On Calvary Jesus won a great victory—enabling us to overcome Satan also.

*Prayer Suggestion: Pray that in the hour of trial and temptation Jesus Christ may plead for you and give you the strength to overcome your opposition.*

# Designed for Life

The human body represents a myriad of miracles. It consists of 206 bones, 639 muscles, four million pain sensors in the skin, 750 million air sacs in the lungs, 16 billion nerve cells, 30 trillion cells in all. The body is designed for living.

Not only the body but the total person, inclusive of mind, spirit, and soul, is designed for life. God gave us minds to think. He gave us emotions so we can feel and love and appreciate beauty. He gave us a spirit so we can know our Creator, contemplate His wisdom everywhere evident in the universe, and sense the love He has for us. In that love He sent His Son into our world to give His life for a fallen humankind and to raise it up for the newness of life in Him. This Son is Jesus Christ, who calls Himself the Life and who imparts life to all who believe in Him. He gives us spiritual life that enables us as Christians to live according to the life of Christ. God also has given us an immortal soul—a soul that with the resurrected body shall have eternal life.

Some ask the age-old question, "If a person dies, will he or she live again, or do we exist only so long as we have physical life?" The answer is, "The human being is designed for life, being fearfully and wonderfully made in every respect—be that physical, mental, spiritual—so we may praise our Maker and live to His glory in this life and in the life to come."

We say with St. Paul: "The life I live in the body, I live by faith in the Son of God, who loved me and gave Himself for me" (Gal. 2:20).

**Prayer Suggestion:** *Pray to Christ, asking Him to come and live in you so you may live on all levels of life as a total person.*

# God's People Are Like Rivers

The Mississippi River starts with a trickle in the north woods of Minnesota, then heads south on a 2,562-mile journey to the Gulf of Mexico. It gradually increases in size and volume and finally becomes, as the song says, "Old Man River."

Human beings are something like rivers in that they have a beginning, reach maturity, and finally attain old age. As sinners they can—and often do—go on rampages and cause destructive floods with their riots and revolutions. But when properly trained and guided, they can be a force for good, bringing fruitfulness to the land.

There is a special way in which people can become streams for good, and that comes about when they receive the water of life given by Jesus Christ. This is the water of salvation flowing from Christ, the Fountain of life. Time and again the Holy Scripture invites us to come and drink of this water free and without charge. Many accept this invitation.

When we drink from Christ, something wonderful happens. The Savior says, "Whoever drinks the water I give him will never thirst. Indeed, the water I give him will become in him a spring of water welling up to eternal life" (John 4:14). Elsewhere He declares, "Whoever believes in Me, as the Scripture has said, streams of living water will flow from within him" (John 7:38).

The psalmist tells God,"You give them drink from Your river of delights" (36:8). Then those who have received of God's grace become rivers of blessings in this world.

*Prayer Suggestion: Ask God to quench your spiritual thirst with the water of His Word and to make you a river of His living water for others.*

# Lambs Need a Shepherd

Just about everywhere in the Bible we read about sheep—how, for example, King David in his youth took care of his father's sheep and later wrote Psalm 23 about how the Lord takes care of His sheep. Our Scripture reading is another beautiful verse asserting God's loving care: "He tends His flock like a shepherd: He gathers the lambs in His arms and carries them close to His heart; He gently leads those that have young."

The dependence of sheep on their shepherd is a true analogy of our dependence as people on God. Isaiah declares, "We all, like sheep, have gone astray [in sin], … the LORD has laid on Him [the Messiah] the iniquity of us all" (Is. 53:6).

As sheep depict our dependence on God, so they also remind us of the measure God has taken for our salvation. Lambs were sacrificed in the Old Testament to take away sin, which pointed to Jesus Christ, the true Lamb of God offered up for the sins of all humankind. He is the Passover Lamb. St. Peter asserts, "You were redeemed … with the precious blood of Christ, a lamb without blemish or defect" (1 Peter 1:19).

Now that Christ has purchased us and made us His own, He takes very good care of us. He guides us in the paths of righteousness for His name's sake; He shields us from our enemies; He bestows on us goodness and mercy all the days of our life. In thankfulness we obey His voice, serve Him, and give Him His due. With sheep, that would be wool. With people, it is many more things—our talents, our possessions. But the best return is our heart—that's the greatest gift.

*Prayer Suggestion: Pray that Jesus the Good Shepherd may continue to lead you into the green pastures of His Word for your spiritual nourishment.*

# Lion: Symbol of a King

Lions made a deep impression on biblical writers, who mention them some 80 times. It is not always with admiration, for lions can be destructive, as St. Peter declares, "Your enemy the devil prowls around like a roaring lion looking for someone to devour" (1 Peter 5:8).

Most generally lions are cited for their strength. The writer of Proverbs says that "a lion [is] mighty among beasts" (30:30). The same writer states, "The wicked man flees though no one pursues, but the righteous are as bold as a lion" (28:1).

The strength and courage of lions is celebrated in biblical prophecies of the coming Messiah. When Jacob blessed his son Judah, he said, "You are a lion's cub … Like a lion he crouches and lies down" (Gen. 49:9). In consequence the tribe of Judah bore a lion on its banners as a symbol of royal power.

Jacob was speaking of one greater than King David or other of his descendants. When in Genesis 49:10 he refers to the scepter that would not depart from Judah until the Great Ruler had come, he prophesied of Christ. On the basis of this prophecy the book of Revelation calls Christ "the Lion of the tribe of Judah, the Root of Jesse." This is Jesus, whose mother was of the house and lineage of David.

Our Lord, the conquering Lion, broke the power of sin, death, and devil. He utterly destroyed Satan's kingdom and set up His own, a kingdom of grace and love into which He transfers all who believe in Him as their Savior. He wants us to live in peace—peace with God and peace with one another.

*Prayer Suggestion: Pray that Jesus, the Lion of the tribe of Judah, may give you of His strength to meet life's every crisis.*

# Camel: For Dependable Travel

According to some, the ungraceful camel looks like an animal put together by a committee. Yet camels are the dependable "cargo ships" of the desert, "freight trains" on legs. A camel caravan en route to Egypt carried "spices, balm and myrrh," and to this was added a slave, Joseph, when his brothers sold him to the Midianites (Gen. 37:25).

Camels enter into many Bible stories. With 10 camels Abraham's head servant set out for the former homeland to find a wife for Isaac; he found Rebekah.

Our Lord referred to camels in His teachings. He said, for example, "It is easier for a camel to go through the eye of a needle than for a rich man to enter the kingdom of God" (Matt. 19:24). He also said that the religious nitpickers would "strain out a gnat but swallow a camel" (Matt. 23:24).

Isaiah (60:6) had foretold in a messianic prophecy, "Herds of camels will cover your land … all from Sheba will come, bearing gold and incense." This prophecy began to be fulfilled when the Wise Men of the East came to Jerusalem, then to Bethlehem, to worship Christ, the newborn King.

Camels were the means to bring these men to Christ. The means that brings us to Christ today is the Word—the Word of Christ and about Christ—the Gospel. This Gospel tells us that God so loved the whole human race that He gave His Son, Jesus Christ, into death for their salvation. It is also the means that brings us to Christ as our Savior. As the Middle Easterners trusted their camels to get them there, we can trust the Word to bring us to Christ, our heavenly King.

*Prayer Suggestion: Ask that God the Holy Spirit may open your heart and mind to the Word of God that brings you to Christ.*

# Deer: Like a Thirsty Soul

Swiftness of foot and gracefulness are the characteristics of a deer. The writer of Proverbs (6:5) has this advice for a young man about to get into trouble: "Free yourself, like a gazelle from the hand of the hunter."

How could Isaiah describe the great joy of people who, long afflicted by sin and its consequences, were to be healed by the promised Savior? He could think of no better example than the agile, nimble jumping of a deer: "Then will the lame leap like a deer" (Is. 35:6). This prophecy was fulfilled when Jesus healed the sick and lame. Imagine the spring in the step of the man who, after 38 years of waiting at the pool of Bethesda (John 12), was healed by Jesus and now could walk!

But how did this man and many others feel before Christ's help came to them? Like the psalmist, who said, "As the deer pants for streams of water, so my soul pants for You, O God. My soul thirsts for God, for the living God" (Ps. 42:1–2).

People, too, are pursued and harassed by their enemies, especially by the enemies of the soul, the greatest of these being the devil. It causes them to have soul thirst for God, for the living water of His Word, for Jesus Christ, who not only gives the water of life but is Himself this Water. St. Augustine said, "Thou has made us unto Thyself, and our hearts are restless until they rest in Thee."

The Gospel of Christ's redemption renews and refreshes people. It gives them life through the merits of Him who gave His life for their salvation.

*Prayer Suggestion: Ask that the Lord Jesus may quench your soul thirst with the water of life—with the Gospel.*

# Donkey: The Poor Man's Friend

Donkeys were domesticated long ago. The first mention of such beasts of burden occurs in Genesis (22:3), where Abraham saddled a donkey so he and his son Isaac could begin their journey to the land of Moriah, where Isaac was to be sacrificed.

Donkeys are usually the property of the poor who have to work hard to make a living. The Bible considers it a most dastardly deed to steal them from their needy owners, for the wicked "drive away the orphan's donkey and take the widow's ox in pledge" (Job 24:3).

A donkey was once Jesus' conveyance when He entered Jerusalem for the last time. He was the one who once said that He had less than the birds with their nests and the foxes with their holes, for He was homeless.

Our Lord had come to begin His suffering during this last week of His life—Holy Week. On Good Friday of that week He was crucified. Abraham's son, Isaac, was spared the last moment, but God's Son, Jesus Christ, was not. God delivered Him up for us all that He might be sacrificed for the sin of all.

Like Isaac, Jesus rode on a donkey. For Jesus it was a mark of humility to be so conveyed, as had been foretold: "Your King comes to you, righteous and having salvation, gentle and riding on a donkey, on a colt, the foal of a donkey" (Zech. 9:9).

A donkey was a true "Christopher," that is, a Christ-bearer. The two went well together: a humble animal and a humble Savior. We, too, can be burden-bearers in Christ's behalf, serving Him gladly and by doing His work.

*Prayer Suggestion: Ask God for a humble spirit and for the willingness to serve Christ and the least of His brothers and sisters.*

# The Ox: A Sacrificial Substitute for Man

Because oxen are strong and enduring, they have served people in many ways, doing their work for them. Because cattle have served so well, the adherents of some religions regard them as sacred. Hence the expression "holy cow." The ancient Egyptians worshiped Apis, the sacred bull. Perhaps the Israelites en route to the Promised Land imitated this idolatry when they worshiped the golden calf (Ex. 32:4).

In another much different way, oxen played a part in Old Testament religion. They were offered as sacrifices in atonement for the sins of people and were in a sense substitutes for those sins. God was pleased with these sacrifices when brought in the right spirit, as David declares in a psalm, "Then there will be righteous sacrifices, whole burnt offerings to delight You; then bulls will be offered on Your altar" (Ps. 51:19).

But the shedding of animal blood could not itself appease the wrath of God. Only the blood of Jesus Christ could—and did—atone for sin. It was to this atonement that the Old Testament sacrifices pointed. The writer of the letter to the Hebrews declares that Jesus "did not enter by means of the blood of goats and calves; but He entered the Most Holy Place once for all by His own blood, having obtained eternal redemption" (9:12).

This is the Gospel—and what good news it is! St. John writes, "The blood of Jesus, His Son, purifies us from all sin" (1 John 1:7).

***Prayer Suggestion:*** *Speak a prayer of thanksgiving to Jesus Christ for having sacrificed Himself for your benefit.*

# Law, Order, and Freedom

That crime has been on the increase in many communities is not all that new of a revelation. Citizens rightfully demand that law and order be maintained so they may, in St. Paul's words, "live peaceful and quiet lives" (1 Tim. 2:2). The demand is accompanied, of course, by concern for justice, human rights, and rightful freedom.

What is good for a secular community goes also for God's kingdom, the church. God's Law has its place, good order is necessary, and freedom under the Gospel is a guarantee.

We are saved through faith in Jesus Christ and His redeeming merits—not by doing the deeds of the Law. We are "justified freely by [God's] grace through the redemption that came by Christ Jesus," writes St. Paul (Rom. 3:24).

What happens now to the Law? May we disregard it, even transgress it? The apostle Paul writes, "Do we, then, nullify the Law by this faith?" His answer: "Not at all! Rather, we uphold the Law" (Rom. 3:31). The Law is still needed to condemn sin and to inform Christians what the good, acceptable, and perfect will of God is.

If Christians were 100 percent perfect and totally Christlike, such guidance from the Law would be unnecessary. But such perfect Christians we do not find on this side of heaven.

Freedom under the Gospel? Yes. Law and order? Again, yes, for in His church God wants everything "in a fitting and orderly way" (1 Cor. 14:40) because we love the Lord.

*Prayer Suggestion: Pray that God would keep you from abusing your freedom under the Gospel, showing you its right use for His glory and the good of people.*

# Knowing the Love of God

Our industrial society has turned into an information society. In his book *Megatrends* John Naisbitt states that 90 percent of newly created jobs are computer-related, having to do with the processing of knowledge. The head rather than the hands is now the focus of skills.

The Christian church is not afraid of true science in any field (science, as distinguished from theories and hypotheses). From time immemorial Christians have joined in the general prayer that God would give success to all pure arts and useful knowledge and crown them with His blessings. If computer data add to the skills of the human race in solving its problems, in combating poverty and sickness, in releasing people from drudgery so they have more time for one another, then the church thanks God for them. What is more, we will use all the skills of communication to proclaim the Gospel of God's love in Christ.

Some knowledge pertains to life in this world; if it is helpful, it should be furthered. But there is another knowledge, a knowledge of the life in Christ. It not only makes life in this world more meaningful, but it also prepares us for life in the world to come. It is the knowledge of the Gospel that God loved the world and gave His only Son, Jesus Christ, to be its Savior from sin and the fear of death.

The Word of God not only conveys this knowledge, but it is also the means through which the Holy Spirit persuades and convinces us that it is the truth, granting us reliance on it.

*Prayer Suggestion: Thank God for making His love in Christ known to you, and pray that He may reveal it to others through you.*

# Recognizing Prophets by Their Fruit

In our day, as ever in the past, there have been those whose teaching and preaching differs widely from the truth revealed in God's Word. Because of the great number and wide variety of such prophets, some people are led to believe that this is what we should expect. They think that Christian denominations are so diverse in their beliefs and the Bible so imprecise that every interpretation is equally as true as the other.

But this is a delusion. False prophets are no more the product of the Christian church and of the Holy Scripture than are counterfeit bills the product of a United States mint.

Our Lord, Himself the true Prophet, makes it very clear that there are prophets who teach contrary to His Word and whom we can know as such. "By their fruit you will recognize them," He said (Matt. 7:20). What a prophet teaches and preaches and the kind of life he lives and advocates—that is his fruit. When the fruit of a prophet's lips is the true and pure Gospel, then we know he is a true prophet. Always we must compare his utterance and action with God's Word.

Jesus Christ, who bears witness to the Holy Scripture (John 10:35) and to whom the Holy Scripture testifies (John 5:39), must be the heart and center of all our teaching. "Anyone who runs ahead and does not continue in the teaching of Christ does not have God," writes the apostle (2 John 9). When we abide in the biblical teachings of Christ and about Christ—that He was born of a virgin, suffered and died for our sins, and rose again—we have Him as our Savior and God as our Father.

*Prayer Suggestion: Pray that the Holy Spirit may lead you deeper into the Holy Scriptures, which bear true witness of Christ.*

# Remembering Our Loved Ones

People in ancient Rome and elsewhere had a seemingly strange custom. Every year they would observe a memorial day for departed family members or friends by bringing food and eating it near their tombs, either banquet or picnic-style. It was like a family reunion.

Every custom can be abused, as was also this one. Early Christians, who also did this, gradually drifted into the cult of worshiping the saints and martyrs whose graves they visited.

There is a right way of remembering loved ones no longer with us. If we're thinking of our Christian parents, an excellent way of honoring them is to continue to live as they taught us by word and example. The same is true of all others who taught us the Word of God—pastors and teachers for example. In Hebrews 11:7 it is written, "Remember your leaders, who spoke the word of God to you. Consider the outcome of their way of life and imitate their faith"—and not just imitate it after the fashion of actors, mimics, and copy cats, but by truly living the faith as your spiritual leaders lived it. People pass on, but the faith they inculcated lives on, for it is not people but our Lord who lives on. The writer says in the very next verse: "Jesus Christ is the same yesterday and today and forever."

Jesus Christ, once crucified, dead, and buried, rose from the dead and is our living Lord. In Him, we, whether living or dead, have our fellowship. Faith in His redemption and His promise of eternal life is the bond that unites us to Him and to one another.

**Prayer Suggestion:** *Say a prayer of thanks for all the good that God has sent your way through parents and other Christians.*

# The Prophet Foretells

While occupying the White House, President Eisenhower on several occasions denounced so-called experts in political and economic circles who saw only bad days ahead. In our religious world, the "bad news" prophets say youth is corrupt, the church is doomed, mission work is useless, and God is as much as dead.

Jesus was the Prophet, and as such He did not only tell the Gospel but also foretold future events. He was a truthful prophet, not one of unnecessary doom and gloom.

As God, Jesus knew all things and could foretell. At the same time, while in the state of humiliation, He as man did not always use the powers of His divine nature, so He could truthfully say that the Son didn't know the hour and day when He shall return to judgment. This does not take anything away from the fact that Jesus Christ is the Prophet who foretells.

Toward the end of His ministry, Jesus returned to Jerusalem and wept over it because its inhabitants, especially its spiritual leaders, persisted in unbelief. For this, He declared, they would be punished. What He foretold of the fall of the city came to pass in the year A.D. 70, when the Roman legions leveled the city. Truly, not one stone was left upon another in it.

As our Lord foretold the results of the sin of unbelief, so He also foretold the salvation from sin through His atoning work. He told His disciples that He would be captured, crucified, and "on the third day He will rise again" (Luke 18:33). Exactly as He foretold, so it came to pass. We thank God for this.

*Prayer Suggestion: Thank the Lord Jesus for not only warning us but also for promising deliverance from every evil.*

# Surprises

Many find Jesus' words in the reading from Luke's gospel full of surprises. Should not Jesus, in order to attract people, lower the threshold and make Christianity easy? Should He not stand at the main entrance and say, "Come right in and be comfortable; no great effort is required of you to be a Christian"? Instead He says this: "Make every effort to enter through the narrow door" (Luke 13:24).

Some expect Jesus, the Lord of love, to say, "Come to Me anytime—whenever you feel like it; My door is always open." But the Savior does not misrepresent Himself as always at our beck and call, as one unconcerned whether we come to Him today, tomorrow, or the next day. He tells us that if we spurn His grace, thinking we can come to Him at times convenient for us, He will say, "I don't know you."

A third surprise is that the ones to be seated at the table of grace in Christ's kingdom are not necessarily the ones we might logically expect—those who took His acceptance of them for granted because of longstanding membership in His church. If they lack faith and love, they will be on the outside looking in, while strangers from east, west, north, and south will fill the places.

Our Lord's words of warning take nothing away from His promises of salvation to those who rely on Him, their Savior: "Come to Me ... I will give you rest" (Matt. 11:28); "Whoever believes and is baptized will be saved" (Mark 16:16); "My peace I give you" (John 14:27). Jesus invites you and me—sinners that we are. That is the greatest surprise of all.

*Prayer Suggestion: Ask the Lord Jesus for courage and strength to follow Him wherever He leads you.*

# Praying Towns

Around the middle of the 17th century, John Eliot, the apostle to the Massachusetts Indians, established over 20 communities in which the natives could live, work, go to school, and worship. These communities were nicknamed "praying towns." They didn't last.

While it would be rare today to find praying towns, that is, towns in which everybody prayed, we do have communities in which people pray. Through Jeremiah, God said to the Israelites transported to Babylon, "Seek the peace and prosperity of the city to which I have carried you into exile. Pray to the LORD for it" (Jer. 29:7). There are many places in a town where prayer can be made—in the home, in places where we work, and especially in church.

Righteousness exalts a nation and all its communities. So does prayer, worship, and learning the Word of God, for they are the basis of righteousness. Of course, God doesn't expect that we do nothing but pray, for we also have work to do. Yet we can always take the time to pray. For this we have the example of Jesus, who amid all the work He had to do prayed regularly.

By faithfully doing all His work—the work of atoning for our sins and making peace with God—Jesus established us as God's children, who may with all boldness and confidence pray to our heavenly Father in our towns or wherever we live.

*Prayer Suggestion: Pray for your town, city, or community, asking God to bring the people to the knowledge of the truth revealed in Christ Jesus.*

# Are You Getting the Right Food?

A Canadian propeller-driven cargo plane crashed near the St. Louis airport because an attendant had filled it with the wrong fuel—jet fuel instead of high-octane gasoline.

Human beings are not machines, but they, too, can suffer from the wrong food and fuel. This is especially true of the improper soul foods. Isaiah (55:2) asks, "Why spend money on what is not bread?" People today spend money on worthless religions, on religious cults, on remedies that cannot heal sick souls. Neither can anyone nourish his inner spiritual life with foods or materials meant for the body. As Psalm 42:1 declares, "As the deer pants for streams of water, so my soul pants for You, O God." The thirst for God cannot be satisfied with physical drink—strong, weak, or other.

St. Peter writes, "Like newborn babies, crave pure spiritual milk, so that by it you may grow up in your salvation" (1 Peter 2:2). This is the milk of God's Word. The ABCs of God's Word are the right food for children attending Sunday school and for beginners.

Christians should not want to stay babies forever. They should mature, and for this, says another writer of the Bible, they need solid food (Heb. 5:11–6:1). This can be obtained through more in-depth reading, through attending adult Bible classes, and the like.

Jesus Christ is the Bread of Life. He it is who laid down His life so we might live. When we believe in Him as our Savior, we are well nourished.

*Prayer Suggestion: Pray that God may guide you in finding the right spiritual nourishment in Jesus Christ.*

# Salvation Is Free

The name of some rugged hills in Italy, translated into English, is "Milk Mountains." No ready-to-drink milk flows from them; they are so named because the grassland is good for milk cows.

Some people seem to think that you can have milk without milking the cows, that nature's—and society's—bounty is so great that we need not work for food and drink, that everything is free, there for the taking.

To the children of Israel, God promised a land of abundance. In the new homeland there was no more manna from heaven. The people had to work, struggle, and fight for what they needed.

Because we must work manually and mentally for our daily bread, some draw the false conclusion that we must work also for the Bread of Life that brings salvation. This is not so. All that the soul—the total person, in fact—craves is peace with God, the forgiveness of sins through Christ's atonement; and for this we do not have to work.

If this sounds too good to be true, it is because this is the true nature of the Gospel—beyond human comprehension but nevertheless God's bona fide offer. His golden words for you are, "By grace you have been saved, through faith—and this not from yourselves, it is the gift of God—not by works, so that no one can boast" (Eph. 2:8–9). We can always take God at His word. His promises are guaranteed by the death and resurrection of Jesus Christ.

*Prayer Suggestion: Pray that you may live a life of thankfulness for your free and full salvation in Christ.*

# Total Discipleship

A New York City play director, Jose Quintero, said to his drama students, "The theater has to be more than a career; it has to be an obsession. Theater requires your complete and total preoccupation. If you enter it, it is for life."

Jesus, the divine director of the drama of life, likewise calls for total commitment. He says, "Anyone who does not carry his cross and follow Me cannot be My disciple" (Luke 14:27). He disapproves a Sunday-only Christianity, a part-time discipleship. He wants it all.

Our Lord does not say that one has to spend all hours of the day and night in prayer, or that discipleship means forsaking one's home and vocation to be a missionary. True, He does call some for full-time church ministries, but for most Christians total discipleship means staying in one's vocation and serving Christ in faithful daily work. He calls on all His followers to be the salt of the earth and the light of the world. Total discipleship consists in worshiping the Lord and in working and witnessing for Him.

This is not hard, for our hearts are filled with love and gratitude to Jesus. In all He said and did—all the way to the cross—He made Himself a sacrifice for our good. Our response is to follow Him all the way. It is not hard. Our Lord declares, in inviting us to come to Him, "Take My yoke upon you and learn from Me, for I am gentle and humble in heart, and you will find rest for your souls. For My yoke is easy and My burden is light" (Matt. 11:29–30).

**Prayer Suggestion:** *Pray for the Holy Spirit's power to make you a totally committed disciple of Jesus.*

# God Has the Last Word

Jonathan Edwards was a prominent Puritan minister and author in Northampton, Massachusetts, in the 18th century. After 23 years of service, the church dismissed him. He became desperately poor and had to do his writing on scraps of paper. Many years later the congregation, then aware of his prominence, put up a memorial tablet in the church. On it, the words of God to Malachi were quoted: "The law of truth was in his mouth ... He walked with me in peace and equity" (2:6 KJV). This was a fine tribute, but it came many years too late.

Much more the victim of misunderstanding and mistreatment was Jesus Christ. Many of His contemporaries held Him in contempt. But the heavenly Father did not think as many humans did. The apostle Peter told an audience in Jerusalem that Jesus, who was crucified, was honored by God, who raised Him from the dead.

During His life on earth Jesus went about doing good and preaching the Good News of the forgiveness of sins. But the majority rejected Him and stood by when He was nailed to the cross. But His Father had the last word. He made Him sit at His own right hand.

There is a lesson here for our own lives. People sometimes put us down, or, as in the case of Jonathan Edwards, put us out or fire us, perhaps wrongfully. We can rest assured that the last word has not been spoken when people act in error or indiscretion. God will have His say. He knows the truth, and He will bring it to light. We can depend on that.

*Prayer Suggestion: Pray for courage to say and do what is right, not according to what people think but according to what God says in His Word.*

# A Change for the Better

Lorraine Hansberry's play "A Raisin in the Sun" drama-tized problems that an African-American family encounters as it leaves the ghetto for another neighborhood. It underscores that changes are often accompanied by difficulties.

People in apostolic times experienced culture shock when they converted from paganism to Christianity. Many were per-secuted as their neighbors, even the government, turned on them.

One who found that change brought trouble was St. Paul. When he became a Christian, he had not only Christ's enemies on his back but also some of Christ's followers. These fellow Christians could not believe that so great a persecutor could become so true a proclaimer of the Christian Gospel.

Yet St. Paul would be the first to say that becoming a Christian was a change for the better. As he told other converts such as the Roman Christians, "When you were slaves to sin … what benefit did you reap at that time from the things you are now ashamed of? Those things result in death! But now that you have been set free from sin and have become slaves to God, the benefit you reap leads to holiness, and the result is eternal life. For the wages of sin is death, but the gift of God is eternal life in Christ Jesus our Lord" (6:20–23).

So it is in our lives because Jesus Christ has become the main part in it. What a change it is when we have faith in Jesus Christ, who is our Redeemer, Reconciler, and Friend! Nothing can compare with the greatest of God's gifts: eternal life.

*Prayer Suggestion: Lord Jesus, You changed my life completely when You gave me faith. In thankfulness I now … (finish the prayer).*

# It All Starts with Right Thinking

"No Parking" signs are so common that to emphasize the necessity of keeping an area clear, some have devised a new sign: "Don't even think about parking here!"

Proverbs 23:7 (NKJV) declares, "As [a person] thinks in his heart, so is he"; and we might add, "so does he." Many a time a motorist makes a wrong turn because he mistakenly thinks his destination lies in that direction. It has been said that a golfer who swings wrongly is thinking wrongly.

Wrong thoughts and desires beget wrong deeds—how true in people's spiritual lives! Jesus begins a statement by saying, "out of the heart come evil thoughts" (Matt. 15:19), and He then enumerates the evil actions that follow. In his letter to the Romans, St. Paul declares that "although they knew God, they neither glorified Him as God nor gave thanks to Him, but their thinking became futile and their foolish hearts were darkened" (1:21). Then follows a list of perverse deeds.

The growth of sin from heart to hands, from wrong desires to wrong deeds, is traced by St. James (1:14–15): "Each one is tempted when, by his own evil desire, he is dragged away and enticed. Then, after desire has conceived, it gives birth to sin; and sin, when it is full-grown, gives birth to death."

There is, of course, a right side to this coin. It says that right thoughts lead to right words and works. Right thoughts are the products of the Holy Spirit's work in our hearts and minds. He has given us faith in Jesus Christ as the Redeemer from sin and has given us new life in Him.

*Prayer Suggestion: Pray that the Holy Spirit may through the Gospel create a clean heart in you and renew a right spirit within you.*

# The Portrait of a Christian

James Carroll Beckwith, born in Hannibal, Missouri, did with his brush what Mark Twain, his contemporary and fellow townsman, did with his pen: sketch human nature. Beckwith was a well-known portrait painter.

Portrait painting is not in great demand today. Most people who want pictures of themselves or loved ones simply have a photo taken. Quick, easy, and a lot cheaper.

A new age always requires new skills. The expertise of a century ago, be it glassblowing, carriage-making, or portrait-painting, gives way to the new. In fact, things change so rapidly and basically in our computer age that a person may have to train for several crafts in a lifetime.

While portrait painting is to some extent not what it once was, one thing is sure: The moral and spiritual portrait of human beings is basically the same as ever. The writers of the Bible, inspired and moved by the Holy Spirit, give us true portraits of people in all ages. They show the warts, wrinkles, and imperfections of sin. Sin cannot be ignored, painted over, or removed by face-lifts. It is deeply ingrained in human nature.

In the Word of God, however, we see another portrait—that of the sinless Christ. He redeemed us from the slavery of sin by His perfect life, atoning death, and glorious resurrection. Through the Holy Spirit He renews us in His image, and what a beautiful portrait that is—the portrait of a born-anew person who is Christlike in words and deeds!

*Prayer Suggestion: Pray that the Holy Spirit may renew Christ's likeness in you through the Gospel.*

# The Message of Clouds

Clouds play a part in our lives—cirrus, cumulus, nimbus, stratus. In the Bible, clouds represent various truths about human beings and about God.

As clouds are always shifting, so do people change and finally pass away. Job (7:9) declares, "As a cloud vanishes and is gone, so he who goes down to the grave does not return." False prophets and teachers, writes St. Jude (v. 12), are "shepherds who feed only themselves. They are clouds without rain, blown along by the wind."

The Bible speaks of clouds also in connection with God, who, in the hymnist's words, "gives freest courses to clouds, and air, and wind." He will also find a way that distressed people can follow. According to Psalm 104:3, clouds are God's transports: "He makes the clouds His chariot."

Clouds played a part in the life and ministry of Jesus. In the prophecy of Daniel (7:13), Christ was spoken of as the Son of Man "coming with the clouds of heaven." When our Lord's work of redemption was finished, as attested by the resurrection, He ascended into heaven, the disciples watching Him until "a cloud hid Him from their sight" (Acts 1:9).

In His last words Jesus called on His disciples to be witnesses. So faithful were they in their work that before the close of the first century the writer of the epistle to the Hebrews could say, "We are surrounded by such a great cloud of witnesses" (12:1). You and I are today a part of that cloud.

**Prayer Suggestion:** *Pray that Christ may bring you to His Father's house, where no clouds hide His glory.*

# Rich Man, Poor Man

Rich people, poor people—their contrasting lots in life have been discussed in sociology classes, in church circles, in the columns of newspapers. One could write a book on the subject, and Irwin Shaw has done just that in *Rich Man, Poor Man*, a novel serialized on television.

As far as happiness is concerned, people of plenty and people of poverty are not always far apart. Wealth is no guarantee of contentment, nor are poor people always unhappy. In 1976, Howard Hughes, one of the world's wealthiest men, died in the United States. It was then revealed how he had lived, much like a poor hermit in the woods: social isolation, suspicion, unmet personal needs.

Rich man, poor man—in Christ's parable they differed greatly in the outward circumstances of life. Yet they also had much in common. Both were sinners, and both had to keep their rendezvous with death. They also had in common the salvation procured for them by Jesus Christ, who went to the cross for sinners rich and poor. Although the rich man rejected this salvation, this took nothing away from the fact it had been gained also for him.

Abraham, a wealthy man, "believed the Lord, and He credited it to him as righteousness" (Gen. 15:6). By faith clothed in the righteousness of the Redeemer, Abraham was saved. And that is also the way poor Lazarus and those a little better off financially are saved.

***Prayer Suggestion:*** *Ask the Holy Spirit to lead you closer to Jesus Christ, in whom is found the riches of the soul and true happiness.*

# The Story of Two Cities: Nain and Cana

Nain and Cana were two towns located only a few miles from Jesus' hometown, Nazareth. Nain (meaning "beauty") lay in a fertile valley, while Cana was situated in steep hill country. The first was easy to reach, while the latter required hill climbing. They were the scenes of two biblical events: a funeral in Nain (Luke 7:11–17) and a wedding in Cana (John 2:1–11). In Nain Jesus raised the widow's son, while in Cana He performed the first of His miracles, changing water into wine.

One can draw conclusions from the two towns and the events occurring there. The sorrowful procession in Nain teaches us that death is no respecter of persons and places. Death takes people in the flower of youth, and it comes to beautiful places, without invitation or effort on the part of people. The wedding in Cana tells a different story. It speaks of the joy of a marriage ceremony and reception. But marriage is not all fun and games. It requires effort to make it work.

These are two vignettes of life. They deal with realities. We don't have to ask death to be our guest. On the other hand, we do have to make a concerted effort to make marriage what God intended it to be: a lifelong union of a man and a woman for mutual assistance and for the orderly propagation of the human family. It requires sacrificial love.

Nain reminds us that Jesus Christ overcame death by His own death on the cross. Cana brings to our remembrance that He is our friend and provider, indeed the Bridegroom and Savior, who loved us and gave Himself up for us.

***Prayer Suggestion:*** *Pray that Jesus may bless your marriage, family, and home with His presence.*

# Building a Better Community

The Nauvoo, Illinois, community, after the Mormons abandoned it in 1846, was taken over by a socialistic group, the Icarians. The leader was a Frenchman, Etienne Cabet, who during his exile in London had studied the writings of Robert Owen. He envisioned a utopia, a perfect communistic society. But it failed, and by the 1890s the rest of the Icarian communities in Missouri, Iowa, and California were abandoned.

Among the reasons that can be cited for these failures is the fact that imperfect people—people burdened with the sins of greed, lust, laziness, and the like—cannot create a perfect society. After the fall of Adam and Eve, it is impossible to organize gardens of Eden where wealth is equally distributed, perfect justice prevails, love is fully practiced, and all uphold their end in a common life.

Someone has said, "There can be no Christian community unless there is first of all a community of Christians." From the Christian perspective, a rebirth is necessary, for everyone is by nature sinful, alienated from God, self-centered, full of misdirected drives, prone to evil. The change comes with conversion. The convert is given a new heart, a heart that relies on Jesus Christ for salvation and peace with God, a heart that loves God and fellow human beings.

The new relationship in which converted people stand before God and one another expresses itself in greatly improved community living. Things are much better where and when Christians practice their faith.

*Prayer Suggestion: Ask God to show you how you can help to improve life in your neighborhood.*

# Blessed Be the Holy Trinity!

We are well past Christmas and Easter, festivals focusing on Jesus Christ and His work for our salvation. During these summer months we dare not forget Christ's work nor the important works of God the Father and God the Holy Spirit.

St. John wrote in his first epistle, "No one who denies the Son has the Father; whoever acknowledges the Son has the Father also" (2:23). He might have added, "And the Holy Spirit," for it is the Spirit who leads us to faith in Jesus as Savior and friend, as St. Paul has written: "No one can say, 'Jesus is Lord,' except by the Holy Spirit" (1 Cor. 12:3).

Those who by faith have Jesus in their hearts as the one who by His obedient life, His suffering, death, and resurrection reconciled all sinners to God, have also the Father and the Holy Spirit. The opposite is also true. Those who deny the Father and the Spirit deny also the Son, Jesus Christ.

We are blessed by Jesus and by the Father. Listen to the opening words of St. Peter in his first epistle (1:3): "Praise be to the God and Father of our Lord Jesus Christ! In His great mercy He has given us new birth into a living hope through the resurrection of Jesus Christ from the dead."

And we are richly blessed by the Holy Spirit because He gives us faith and all its fruits, as St. Paul tells the Galatians (5:22–23), "The fruit of the Spirit is love, joy, peace, patience, kindness, goodness, faithfulness, gentleness and self-control."

Blessed be the Holy Trinity—God the Father, God the Son, and God the Holy Spirit, three in one and one in three!

*Prayer Suggestion: Pray that the Holy Spirit may through the Word lead you into all truth.*

# It Is Summer When They Smile

In a poem called "Krinken," Eugene Field, the children's poet, wrote, "Krinken was a little child; It was summer when he smiled."

Little children frequently bring warmth and joy into the lives of their parents. This makes it all the harder to understand why child abuse is ever committed. In anger or exasperation, some parents have done great physical harm to their little ones, to say nothing of damaging them emotionally. Children, too, are sinful, and can cause frustration. But this does not justify the use of violence to correct them.

Parents, teachers, and those who deal with children ought to remain mindful of the love Jesus showed to little children. On one occasion, when mothers brought infants to be blessed by Him, Jesus said, "The kingdom of God belongs to such as these" (Mark 10:14). The account goes on, "He took the children in His arms, put His hands on them and blessed them" (Mark 10:16).

Our Lord continues to bless little children who are brought to Him. The Bible tells them that God so loved them that He gave His own Son, Jesus Christ, into death and then called Him out of the grave alive again for their salvation.

Child abuse—how dreadful! Proper, tender care of little ones—how wonderful and rewarding it is! They not only receive love but also give it. Little wonder that Jesus said, "Whoever welcomes one of these little children in My name welcomes Me" (Mark 9:37).

*Prayer Suggestion: Pray for a faith that takes Jesus at His Word so like believing children, you may have a place in God's kingdom.*

# On Staying Fresh and Green

In 1961 Anna Mary Robertson Moses, better known as Grandma Moses, died at age 101. What is remarkable is that she took up painting at age 80 and became famous for her folk art. She depicted scenes in upstate New York—harvesting, "sugaring-off" times, sleigh rides, and the like. Grandma Moses' late blooming inspires us to search our lives for talents and opportunities.

In the Bible, the original Moses was also 80 years old when he began a new career, when God called him to lead His people out of Egypt. Moses did so; he led them wisely and well for the next 40 years—as long as God wanted him to. At age 120, Moses delivered a long farewell speech (found in the book of Deuteronomy), and then climbed Mount Nebo from where God took him to heaven. Even then "his eyes were not weak nor his strength gone" (Deut. 34:7).

Moses, of course, was particularly favored with long life because God had important work for him to do. Very likely, none of us will attain his age, and very few of us the 101 years of Grandma Moses. We may not be qualified to lead a nation, nor have the skill to wield an artist's paintbrush. But all of us can find ways and means to serve God and other people with hearts and hands and voices.

We recognize the love, compassion, and uprightness of God, for in Christ Jesus He made us His own, reconciling us to Himself through the death of His Son and making us the heirs of eternal life.

*Prayer Suggestion: Ask God, for Jesus' sake, to bring the freshness of faith into your life and make you fruitful so long as life is yours.*

# The Whole World in His Hands

Various theories have been propounded as to what might happen to our world if we put too many fine particles into the air. Too much carbon dioxide, some say, keeps the heat on the earth, causing the so-called "greenhouse effect." Others claim that we are creating a "shield effect": the stuff in the air will screen out the sunlight; nothing will grow; people will starve and freeze to death.

What about this? To be sure, we ought to be more careful as to what we do to God's earth. It is not ours to do with as we please. The psalmist declares, "The earth is the LORD's, and everything in it" (Ps. 24:1). God is the owner; we are only the stewards, the caretakers.

A greater truth to keep in mind is that, despite human foolishness and wickedness, God is still in control over the world and the people in it. It is He who makes the final determination of this created world.

God's power, concern, and love extend especially to the beings He once made in His image: the people who through faith in Christ's redeeming, renewing, life-giving merit have become God's children. God is not far away from us. St. Paul told the would-be philosophers in Athens, "In [God] we live and move and have our being" (Acts 17:28).

The assurance of God's care is stated in the simple terms of the old spiritual, "He's Got the Whole World in His Hands."

How great is God's love!

*Prayer Suggestion: Say thanks to God for His assurance that He cares for you like a father for his children.*

# Making a New Start

*Medea*, a play written by dramatist Euripides some 2,500 years ago, features the eternal triangle: Medea's husband, Jason, falls in love with a younger woman. This so angers Medea that she murders Jason's two children and her youthful rival.

Human nature today is what it always was: marked by love and hatred, joy and sorrow, sympathy and insensitivity, ambition and the lack of it. As in times past, so today. Some people are diligent, while others think the world owes them a living.

There is an unevenness in human behavior, and this has always been so. At the same time, all people have a common denominator, a common trait. There has never been an exception to that. What is it? The psalmist declares, "They are a people whose hearts go astray" (Ps. 95:10). To emphasize that believers also have this common fault still in them, the prophet Isaiah writes, "We all, like sheep, have gone astray" (53:6). Isaiah is talking about sin, a straying from God's guidelines for true goodness and righteousness.

We are probably right in saying that moral straying is more pronounced in one age than another. But it has always been there because human nature hasn't changed basically.

There is only one way out: conversion, regeneration, the new birth, the coming to faith in Jesus Christ as personal Savior. Through the Gospel the Holy Spirit brings us to Christ and makes us a new creation in Him. Now we walk in the newness of life. What a pleasant journey!

**Prayer Suggestion:** *Pray for God's help to break the old molds and to live your life anew in Jesus Christ.*

# Our Father Lives

In her book *Changing,* Liv Ullmann, a Norwegian actress, writes, "The void that Papa's death left in me became a kind of a cavity, into which later experiences were to be laid."

Ullmann is not alone. The death of a dear one always affects the members of the family and shapes their lives for good or ill.

It is different with our heavenly Father, who in distinction to human fathers has immortality. God is eternal, from everlasting to everlasting, without beginning and end. Death will never take Him away from us.

Yet we sometimes act as if God were dead. We are no different from the man who worried a lot because his business was failing. He said for him God was dead. So his wife pretended a great and deep sadness. When her husband asked about it, she told him about a dream. In it she supposedly saw God with silver-white hair lying in a coffin, angels weeping as they looked on. The husband assured her that her dream was impossible, for God cannot die, and God cannot lie, for He is faithful. While he was still speaking, he realized his error— and thanked his wife for the lesson.

God alone has immortality. He has eternal life in Himself. What is more, He shares this endless life with us, His children. Jesus Christ, His Son, went into death for us and thereby "has destroyed death and has brought life and immortality to light through the Gospel" (2 Tim. 1:10). God promised that whoever believes in Christ shall not perish but have eternal life. God is alive, and He wants you to live in Him through Christ.

***Prayer Suggestion:*** *Pray that God may open His Word to you, assuring you that He is alive and wants to enter your life.*

# In the World but Not of the World

A Houston, Texas, boy lived his 12 years in a plastic bubble because he had been born without immunity from disease germs.

Can the life of faith be lived in such a protected environment? Can we devise some kind of a spiritual bubble where we are safe from the germs of sin, evil examples, the devil's temptations, the world's greed, profanity, pornography?

If Christians were to withdraw from the world, they could not be the salt of the earth and the light of the world that Jesus wants them to be. Faith cannot flourish in isolation.

In His High Priestly Prayer (John 17), Jesus asked this of the heavenly Father in behalf of His followers: "My prayer is not that You take them out of the world but that You protect them from the evil one" (17:15). In the world but not of the world, not removed from the devil's temptations but enabled to resist them—this is what Jesus asked.

Faith in Jesus Christ has built-in immunity power, which makes flight from the world unnecessary. St. Paul tells us to "take up the shield of faith, with which you can extinguish all the flaming arrows of the evil one" (Eph. 6:16). Faith has this power, not because the Christian is strong but because Jesus Christ is mighty. He overcame the evils of the world. He defeated the evil one from whom they proceed. Our Lord's "It is finished!" (John 19:30) on the cross announced the fulfillment of redemption, and His resurrection sealed it.

We don't need a protective bubble to survive; we are sustained by believing in the victorious Christ.

*Prayer Suggestion: Ask God to strengthen your faith in Jesus Christ so you can prevail over evil and grow in grace.*

# The Pursuit of Peace

While General Lew Wallace was writing his book *Ben Hur*, United States President Rutherford B. Hayes ordered him to put down a violent feud in Lincoln County, New Mexico, in which the outlaw Billy the Kid was involved.

Many other people who are pursuing peaceful pursuits also have been interrupted by outbreaks of violence. Abraham had to pull his 318 servants off their peacetime work to rescue Lot, a prisoner of war. Jesus was in the Garden of Gethsemane praying when an armed band came to arrest Him.

Life today is full of peace-disturbing happenings such as burglaries, break-ins, family feuds, racial disturbances, to say nothing of unrest in the world at large.

It is necessary that we do what we can to promote peace, lest violence increase. "Live at peace with everyone" (Rom. 12:18), the apostle tells us. Note that peace is not isolated; it goes together with righteousness, faith, and love. When St. Peter tells us "Whoever would love life and see good days … he must seek peace and pursue it" (1 Peter 3:10–11), he speaks of the context in which peace occurs: the seeking of unity, the keeping of one's tongue from speaking evil, the turning from evil to that which is right.

Before us we have the example of our heavenly Father, who is a God of unity and reconciliation. He enables us, who in Christ are forgiven and at peace with Him, to pursue peaceful relations with others—in the family, in the church, in the community, at work.

*Prayer Suggestion: Pray that God's peace in Christ may be yours so you, too, can be a peacemaker and a peacekeeper.*

# Honor, Not Humiliation!

Woody Herman, who in his 70s was still leading orchestras and instructing young musicians, spoke of old age as "a series of humiliations." He was referring to the usual ailments of advancing years.

Some people are fired from their jobs or otherwise put down for no other reason except their age.

It is not to God's liking when people are subjected to "a series of humiliations." "Do not despise your mother when she is old," God tells us through the writer of Proverbs (23:22). Again, through Moses: "Rise in the presence of the aged, show respect for the elderly and revere your God" (Lev. 19:32). Parents, in their prime or in their later years, are God's representatives to their children.

Instead of humiliation—honor! God's commandment directs us to honor father and mother. This includes helping them bear the burdens of old age; keeping in touch by visits, phone calls, and letters; helping them shop; picking them up for church; and rendering other services.

We do this for the sake of Jesus Christ, who for our salvation endured "a series of humiliations." He suffered many indignities. The Bible says of Him, "In His humiliation He was deprived of justice … His life was taken from the earth" (Acts 8:33). The amazing thing is that our Lord endured all this of His own free will.

When this mind is in us, we are able to bear up under life's indignities; we will honor others instead of humiliating them.

*Prayer Suggestion: Ask God to make you equal to life's challenges, including the experiences of old age.*

# Toxic or Tonic?

The yellow-flowered plant St. John's wort is named in honor of John the Baptist. In ancient England, on the eve of John's birthday, June 24, it was picked as protection against evil spirits and for medicinal purposes. But it also had an opposite effect on the cattle that ate it; it was noxious to them.

What John the Baptist offered to the people around him, like the offering of the plant named after him, was both a toxin and a tonic. First, he proclaimed the Law in all its sharpness. His message of judgment and repentance was poison to those who didn't want to repent. They were now worse off.

But John preached also the Gospel, and this was a tonic for sin-sick souls. His message was: "Look, the Lamb of God, who takes away the sin of the world!" (John 1:29). He testified that Jesus the Christ was to be offered up for the sins of all people. Christ is still proclaimed to us as the Good Physician whose blood cleanses, whose Word heals troubled hearts, whose comforting presence is a tonic to life-weary persons.

To some people, Christ is not a tonic but a toxin. Jesus is like the sun that, at the same time, melts wax but hardens clay. He is for some a stone of stumbling and a rock of offense, while He really wants to be the Rock of Ages on which people can build their lives.

That is what Jesus Christ wants to be in everyone's life: a tonic, a spiritual treat, a lifesaver.

*Prayer Suggestion: Pray that the Word of Christ, your Savior, may have a healing effect on you as a total person—on your heart, mind, and body.*

# Weapons with Which to Win

When in the fourth century the Huns were ravaging Europe, Ursula, a holy woman in England, is said to have raised an army of 11,000 virgins to fight them. All were slaughtered at Cologne, Germany. The Virgin Islands were named in their honor.

History knows of other uneven fights, and so does the Bible—Samson versus the Philistines, David versus Goliath, Peter in Gethsemane versus the mob that came to arrest Jesus. No contest, however, is as unevenly matched as when human beings try to overcome their greatest enemy, Satan. As St. Paul wrote, "Our struggle is not against flesh and blood, but against the rulers, against the authorities, against the powers of this dark world and against the spiritual forces of evil in the heavenly realms" (Eph. 6:12).

While Satan is a spiritual opponent, his temptations are very materialistic and sensual: the love of money, greed, sexual immorality, drink and drugs, dirty gossip.

To stand against the wiles of the devil, we need weapons other than those used in human combat. We need spiritual weapons, and St. Paul tells us what they are: the belt of truth, the breastplate of righteousness, the footgear of the Gospel of peace, the shield of faith, the helmet of salvation, the sword of the Spirit, which is the Word of God (Eph. 6:14–17).

With spiritual weapons we can prevail because Jesus Christ has won the major battle against the devil with His death and triumphant resurrection.

*Prayer Suggestion: Pray for strength and skill not only to understand evil but also to grow in grace and all that is good.*

# The Peace Weapon God Has Given Us

In a house in St. Joseph, Missouri, Jesse James and the two Ford brothers were discussing their next bank robbery. In the house, the framed wall motto "God Bless This House" was hanging askew. As Jesse James got up to straighten it, Bob Ford shot him to death.

"The accomplice of a thief is his own enemy," declares the Bible (Prov. 29:24). What is more, he may sooner or later lose his life, sometimes at the hands of a so-called friend. There is no honor among thieves.

Under ordinary circumstances—and apart from self-defense—weapons that kill human beings are not for Christians. In the Garden of Gethsemane, Peter drew his sword to fight off the armed posse come to arrest Jesus. But the Lord restrained him: "Put your sword back into its place ... for all who draw the sword will die by the sword" (Matt. 26:52).

No one knew better than Jesus the true nature of human beings. He knew that from the heart proceed all kinds of sins, including murder by word and deed. He also knew that the sword cannot be used to convert sinners. A Christianity by compulsion is no Christianity at all. That's why He appeals to all people with His love, as declared in the Gospel. Only the Gospel, as God's peace weapon, can turn people around and make them the children of God.

Instead of homes where not only wall mottoes but morals are crooked, we can have homes where love and peace prevail.

***Prayer Suggestion:*** *Pray that Christ's peace may prevail in your heart and home.*

# The One Door

An historic church near Hamburg, Germany, has two doors: one entrance for the men and one for the women. It was at one time customary there for men and women to sit on opposite sides of the church. There is a different reason for the two entrances to a car factory in Belfast, Northern Ireland. Because of hostile feelings, one door is for Protestant workers and the other for Roman Catholics.

Whatever reasons, good or bad, people have for separate doors, Jesus Christ is the one and only door to eternal life. In the Good Shepherd chapter (John 10), our Lord declares, "I tell you the truth, I am the gate for the sheep … whoever enters through Me will be saved" (vv. 7, 9). Again, in John 14:6, He says, "I am the Way and the Truth and the Life," adding that He is the only way or door to the heavenly Father and His house of many mansions.

Christ is the one door, the one gate of salvation for both men and women, however they may sit in church. As St. Paul teaches in Galatians 3:27–28, "All of you who were baptized into Christ have clothed yourselves with Christ. There is neither … male nor female, for you are all one in Christ Jesus."

Jesus Christ is the one Savior, the one door for you and for me. There are not two doors to eternal life, one labeled "Faith" and the other "Good Works" or "Human Virtues." Only faith in Christ saves. So we enter the "Faith" door, convinced that only trust in the redeeming merits of Christ opens the door to heaven.

*Prayer Suggestion: Pray that more and more people will come to know Jesus Christ as the door to peace and salvation.*

# Abiding Love

Human love sometimes grows lukewarm, even cold. Yet, of all human emotions, love is apt to last the longest.

Even more lasting than romantic love—called *eros* in Greek—is love flowing from the Christian's faith in the love of God. The Greek New Testament calls it *agape.* The apostle Paul extols it in 1 Corinthians 13. He speaks of love as giving validity to phenomena that would otherwise be passing—speech in superhuman and angelic tongues, prophecy, the understanding of mysteries, knowledge, heroic faith, works of charity, and self-sacrifice. He boils everything down to these three abiding virtues: faithfulness, hope, and love, adding, "But the greatest of these is love."

Much of what we hold in the Christian faith must await eternal life in heaven before it comes to fruition and completeness. Our knowledge is imperfect; some of the truths we hold in faith don't make sense because they surpass human understanding. With love it's different. It always makes sense; it doesn't have to be put away on a shelf as we await further enlightenment. It is always in place, always applicable, always understandable in life's here and now. How thankful we are that love abides!

Such love inheres in the love of God and in that great gift He gave: His Son, Jesus Christ. Believing in Him, we have eternal life. What is more, from that love springs our love to Him and to one another—abiding love.

*Prayer Suggestion: Pray for a greater measure of Christian love in your heart, and pray that it may abide.*

# By Grace, Saved to Serve

In everyday life we have to pay for the things we procure through purchase, even when we use credit cards. How is it with spiritual blessings? Can we pay for them by rendering something in return?

The Scripture teaches most clearly that salvation, forgiveness, and peace with God are given by divine grace, through faith, for the sake of Jesus Christ, who in our stead went to the cross to suffer and die for every person's sin. The Scripture teaches that "By grace you have been saved, through faith and this is not from yourselves, it is the gift of God—not by works, so that no one can boast" (Eph. 2:8–9).

If salvation, totally or in part, depended on what we did or did not do, we could not be sure of doing enough to satisfy a just and holy God.

So what does it all add up to? Does our reliance on Christ's work which cost Him His life make for "cheap grace"? Can one say, "Thank You, God, for saving me," and then go about the regular business of serving only him/herself? Indeed not, for that would mean that we are still spiritually dead.

Those who are alive in Christ consider that they were not only saved from something but also for something—for serving Jesus and all His brothers and sisters with holy, helpful lives of love because He first loved us. Saved by grace, yes—but saved to serve!

*Prayer Suggestion: Ask God to show you how you can serve Him in gratitude for full and free salvation in Christ.*

# Recruited to Serve

When harvest time comes, crews of workers have to be recruited to bring home the grain and fruits of the earth. Jesus spoke of the need for spiritual harvesters. He told us to pray God to "send out workers into His harvest field" (Matt. 9:38).

What was a critical situation in our Lord's time is much more pressing and urgent now. Humankind has multiplied itself many times over, and with the population explosion has come also an alarming increase of sin. Many laborers are needed to bring in the sheaves of immortal souls, whom Christ purchased with His blood.

As in days of old, God still extends special calls to certain persons to be His missionaries, doing this mainly through congregations and groups of congregations forming church bodies. God is still recruiting men and women for full-time work, saying, "Whom shall I send? And who will go for Us?" (Is. 6:8).

But God does more. He recruits every Christian, regardless of what his or her vocation and station in life may be, to be a witness and worker for Him. Yes, every Christian is recruited to "declare the praises of Him who called you out of darkness into His wonderful light" (1 Peter 2:9).

Through the Gospel made alive in Christ, we received a new heart, a new mind, new powers, a new motivation. We are capable of being Christ's spokespeople and all-around disciples wherever there are mission fields ready for the harvest. Usually that is right in our own backyard.

*Prayer Suggestion: Pray the Lord of the harvest to send out laborers into His harvest.*

# Beauty in God's World

A writer in the *Kansas City Times*, having referred to the "woe that abounds on this gloomy globe," went on to mention pleasant things: "The gold of the sun, the silver of the moon, the diamond stars, the wings of a bird, the face of a babe, the joy of lovers, the good of the selfless. These are round about us if we but see."

The writer of Ecclesiastes states, "[God] has made everything beautiful in its time" (3:11). In the beginning God created a perfect world. Then came sin to tarnish the beauty of the earth. But even after the fall, we still have a beautiful world of blue skies, green meadows, snow-capped mountains, red sunsets. What is more, we ought to keep our air, land, and water free from pollution so we and people coming after us can enjoy God's creation.

God has blessed us with love and friendship, poetry and prose, good books and good music, laughter and good times at birthdays, weddings, and other occasions.

God did something even more beautiful "when the time had fully come," as St. Paul declared in Galatians 4:4. He sent His Son as Deliverer from sin and death so whoever believes in Him will find new meaning and new beauty in this life and eternal life in the world to come. So now we have good reason to look away from what the writer called the abundant woe on this gloomy globe and focus our attention on the world God loved so greatly. Having experienced this love, we are in a position to pass it on to others.

*Prayer Suggestion: Pray that God may open your eyes to all the good He has brought into your life, especially the gift of His Son, Jesus.*

# Your Roots and Fruits

People are like trees in that without roots, they cannot bear fruit. While the roots of character are of utmost importance, it matters little in what place they first grew.

In the long run, it is not important where you came from, but where you are now and where you are going—what you are now doing with life's opportunities: That is all-important.

When God called Gideon to save His people from the invaders, he said: "But Lord, how can I save Israel? My clan is the weakest in Manasseh, and I am the least in my family" (Judges 6:15). God was with him in his great work; it didn't matter where he came from.

When God needed a prophet to assist and later succeed Elijah, He chose a farmer, a man plowing with oxen: Elisha. When Jesus needed 12 apostles, He went to fishermen and the like. Because they had the roots of faith, they bore fruit, and it made no difference from what town they came.

Jesus Himself was born in Bethlehem, which the prophet Micah calls "least among the rulers of Judah" (Matt. 2:6). Later He lived in Nazareth; and when Philip spoke to Nathanael about Him, the latter said, "Nazareth! Can anything good come from there?" (John 1:46). Yes, it could, for Jesus, the Son of God, gave His life on the cross for the salvation of all.

So when someone asks where your roots are, don't think of where you were born, but where they are now and whether you are bearing fruit.

*Prayer Suggestion:* Ask God to make His Word and Spirit fruitful in you.

# Beginning Our Work with Prayer

In the graveyard at Old Mines, Missouri, where lead mining began as early as 1726, you will find this headstone inscription: "Henry B. Murphy, died February 28, 1859, from injuries received from the explosion of the steamer Princess."

Some occupations are hazardous. Jesus once spoke of 18 persons, probably workmen, who were killed when the tower of Siloam fell on them (Luke 13:1–5). No occupation is absolutely safe. Even the shepherds of Jesus' day had to face the threats of wolves, thieves, and robbers.

Some encourage everyone to get out of high-risk jobs. But if everyone did that, who would mine our coal, fly our planes, serve as police officers? Still, in every job, we can be careful, anticipating potential dangers and taking precautions accordingly. Further, it helps to reduce accidents when we learn our jobs thoroughly and get enough rest at night.

Most of all, it helps when we begin our work with prayer. "Lord Jesus, let the holy angels be with me today, guarding me in all my ways. Keep me from falling into any kind of danger, either by my own neglect or from other causes. Keep me aware of the safety of my fellow workers. Remove from my heart and mind all distractions and conflicts I bring with me from home. Give me inner peace, knowing that through Your redeeming merit I am at peace with God. Enable me to do my best at work, bringing to my tasks not only courage but also due caution. I put myself into Your hands, Lord Jesus!"

It certainly makes a difference when by prayer we put things into perspective. It makes for safety.

**Prayer Suggestion:** *Pray that God may keep you alert to potential dangers at work and at home.*

# Freedom for Something

Independence Day in the United States celebrates the signing of the Declaration of Independence in 1776. Among the tyrannies from which the colonists declared themselves free were commercial exploitation, arbitrary government by remote control, taxation without representation, and the like.

Independent nationhood, of course, implies also freedom for something—freedom for a country to determine its own affairs, freedom for the citizens to make a decent living, to educate their children, to pursue happiness, and to worship God.

Freedom's fight for something continues today. Citizen groups work for civil rights. It is good when people come out of the shells of indifference—or the "I don't want to be involved" spirit—and show concern for what is socially, politically, and morally right.

As Christians we are the beneficiaries of another freedom, the freedom from the curse of the Law, the power of sin, the fear of death. This freedom Jesus Christ gained for us at great cost to Himself—it cost Him His life.

Thanks to Christ's work of redemption, we are freed for something: free to hear and follow His Word, free to serve Him. He tells us, "If you hold to My teaching, you are really My disciples. Then you will know the truth, and the truth will set you free" (John 8:31–32). And with this freedom goes responsibility, as St. Paul tells us: "It is for freedom that Christ has set us free. Stand firm, then, and do not let yourselves be burdened again by a yoke of slavery" (Gal. 5:1).

*Prayer Suggestion: Give thanks for the freedom we enjoy in our country, and ask God to keep us from neglecting or abusing it.*

# Freedom with Resposibility

Following the signing of the Declaration of Independence, the colonies of the new world, later becoming the United States of America, have enjoyed more than two centuries of free nationhood. The Scripture words on the Liberty Bell need to be emphasized today: "Proclaim liberty throughout all the land unto all the inhabitants thereof " (Lev. 25:10 KJV).

Freedom can be lost when the citizens become careless, unthinking, and selfish. We give away what our forefathers won when we think only of freedom from something and not of freedom for something—freedom for participating in democracy.

Freedom is endangered when people fail to exercise the responsibility that always goes with it. One who enjoys freedom must never forget that others have freedom too. Dr. John H. Knowles, former president of the Rockefeller Foundation, has well said, "The cost of sloth, gluttony, alcoholic overuse, reckless driving, sexual intemperance … is now regarded by many as a national, not an individual responsibility. These abuses are justified on the ground of individual freedom, but what happens then is that one man's freedom in health abuse is another's shackle in taxes and insurance premiums."

Freedom is a sacred trust. It has its roots in our freedom before God, our Creator and Redeemer. Christ has freed us from sin, setting us free to serve Him. He declares, "If you hold to My teaching, you are really My disciples. Then you will know the truth, and the truth will set you free" (John 8:31–32).

*Prayer Suggestion: Pray that God may bless our land and all nations of the world with true freedom and with the wisdom to use it rightly.*

# Follow God's Instruction!

In an emergency a person can rise to heroic heights. For example, when the pilot of a private plane died of a heart attack, a 78-year-old woman without flying experience was able to land the craft by following instructions from the ground. Someone quoted the odds for such an achievement as 20,000 to 1.

When people lack the wisdom, skill, and strength to fulfill a difficult task, it is all the more important to follow the instructions of another.

Following instruction is especially necessary in our spiritual lives. After the human race fell into sin, it became impossible for anyone to attain God's standards for right living.

God comes to the rescue. By means of His Word, He makes us wise unto salvation through faith in Jesus Christ, who did for us what we were unable to do: He gave His life so we might have eternal life. Faith enables us to lead a God-pleasing life and be blessed or happy in doing so. Guidance for this comes from God's Word. Psalm 119:9 asks, "How can a young man keep his way pure?" The answer: "By living according to Your Word." Likewise St. Paul said in 2 Timothy 3:16, "All Scripture is God-breathed and is useful for teaching, rebuking, correcting and training in righteousness."

It is wise to realize that we are in God's hands. When we follow His instructions, we can accomplish what is beyond ordinary human competence and find happiness.

**Prayer Suggestion:** *Pray that through the Word the Holy Spirit may guide you to a fruitful life.*

# The Power of God's Word

A theologian used language people can understand when he wrote, "The word of God is never an idle thing in a Christian's life, like some bowl of soggy Rice Krispies that has lost its snap, crackle, and pop."

The Word of God in Holy Scripture is good spiritual nourishment. It has good taste, which Psalm 19:10 calls sweeter than honey. The prophet Jeremiah ingested the Word and wrote, "Your words ... were my joy and my heart's delight" (Jer. 15:16). The Word is appetizing and zestful.

What is more, God's Word is energetic, and it imparts energy. In Hebrews 4:12 we read, "The Word of God is living and active. Sharper than any double-edged sword." The law of God is certainly like the sword as it penetrates to the sinful, spiritually sick heart like a surgeon's knife. God's purpose in using this knife is to expose sin so healing may follow.

The Law is strong, but the Gospel is even more powerful. It is the sword of the Holy Spirit, the medium He uses to lead us to Jesus Christ, the physician and healer of souls. Balm for the wounds of sin, sorrow, grief, and worry is the Good News that our Savior has atoned for our wrongdoing and that, believing in Him, we have forgiveness and peace with God.

Truly the Gospel "is the power of God for the salvation of everyone who believes," as St. Paul writes in his letter to the Romans (1:16). Plug in to its power!

*Prayer Suggestion: Ask the Holy Spirit to release the power of God's Word in your life so you may become more and more like Jesus.*

# Learning God's Word Brings Rewards

Some people have to go to great effort to obtain an education. In *Yentl, the Yeshiva Boy,* Isaac B. Singer tells the story of a rabbi's daughter who disguised herself as a boy so she could attend the yeshiva, or school. Other young people have made great sacrifices to go to college. They saved their money, left home, and did odd jobs when not going to classes. To these young people belongs the future.

A broad-based education includes spiritual learning, a learning of the Word of God. This too takes effort as you read your Bible regularly, attend study groups, and the like. The source of spiritual knowledge as the basis of faith is the Holy Scripture. In it you find testimonies to Jesus Christ, the Son of God who came to earth to reconcile humankind to God by assuming the consequences of its sins.

Learning the Bible, the "Jesus Book," brings great rewards. The apostle Paul tells us that the truth of the Bible was written for our instruction, "that through endurance and the encouragement of the Scriptures we might have hope" (Rom. 15:4).

Who of us doesn't need encouragement, hope, the upward look of faith, and spiritual support when the burdens of life descend on us? We have trouble in the family, perhaps; we lose jobs; we experience sickness and death in the home; we are entrapped in all kinds of unpleasant situations. However, a change can occur when we listen to what God has to tell us, get to know Jesus Christ better, and turn to God in prayer.

*Prayer Suggestion: Ask God the Holy Spirit to guide you in learning God's Word in the Scriptures so by faith in Christ you may have hope.*

# Saved by a Child

Often parents save their toddlers from physical harm. Sometimes the roles are reversed as children save their parents.

"You forgot this," said a 3-year-old son of a Maplewood, Missouri, policeman as the latter was getting ready to go on duty. He was bringing his father's bullet-proof vest. Later that evening, as the policeman was interrupting a burglary, he was shot—but the vest saved his life.

"A little child will lead them," wrote Isaiah in a prophecy of the Messiah's rule of peace (Is. 11:6). The Lord Jesus likewise had good things to say about children, about those who believed in Him implicitly. He said adults should learn from them and believe as they did if they wanted to enter the kingdom of heaven.

"Saved by a child" applies especially to our salvation in and by Jesus Christ. Isaiah prophesied of Him when he announced, "To us a Child is born, to us a Son is given" (Is. 9:6). When Jesus was born in Bethlehem, the angel said to the shepherds, "Today in the town of David a Savior has been born to you; He is Christ the Lord" (Luke 2:11). This Child, the Son of God, grew up to lead an obedient life in our behalf and on the cross to bear the consequences of our sins. Only in Him do we find forgiveness and peace with God.

*Prayer Suggestion: Ask God to bless you with childlike humility and with a strong faith in His Son, our Savior Jesus Christ.*

# How Good Is Your Reputation?

A good reputation is an asset. The manuscript of novelist William Kennedy's best-seller *Ironweed* was turned down by 13 publishers. But after he had established his reputation, publishers would buy his manuscripts before they were written.

A good reputation is important. The apostle Peter writes, "Live such good lives among the pagans that, though they accuse you of doing wrong, they may see your good deeds and glorify God" (1 Peter 2:12). This tells us why God's people look to their reputation and try to keep it good, true, and honest: to glorify God, to be walking exemplars of the God they serve.

Our reputation should stand for what we really are, not for what people think we are. More is involved than a surface glitter, more than a show of uprightness. Reality is the key word here. In a recent commercial one workman doing sloppy work tells another, "Why be so careful? Who'll ever know?" The other replies, "We would know it." And to that we have to add, God would know it.

A good reputation based on true virtue is not an accident; it is nothing automatic. It comes as a fruit of faith in Jesus Christ, who changed things around in our hearts and lives when He "made Himself of no reputation, and took upon Him the form of a servant, and … became obedient unto death, even the death of the cross" (Phil. 2:7–8 KJV).

Be like Christ, and your good reputation will be established.

***Prayer Suggestion:*** *Pray that people may think well of you because all is well in your heart, thanks to Christ's presence.*

# Seeking and Finding

Sometimes a discovery is made entirely by accident, but most often discovery comes to one who has been looking.

We are told that Charles Goodyear by accident discovered that rubber mixed with sulphur becomes less gummy in summer and less brittle in winter—a necessary quality for rubber tires. Goodyear was a finder because he had been looking.

So it is also in one's spiritual quest. Jesus said, "Seek and you will find" (Matt. 7:7). Yes, one can stumble across a great find, as did the man in another of Jesus' parables who accidently found a treasure in a field. But the successful finders are usually those who have been looking and searching for treasures.

The Bible, as the Word of God, is full of spiritual treasures, full of truths about our present and future life. The psalmist finds God's ordinances to be "sure and altogether righteous. They are more precious than gold, than much pure gold" (Ps. 19:9–10).

The greatest treasure of all found in the Holy Scriptures is our Lord and Savior Jesus Christ. He is the heart and center of divine revelation. To Him the written Word bears witness as the Son of God, as the promised Messiah, as the Redeemer who went to the cross, died, and rose again for our salvation.

To come upon this treasure in the Bible, we need to search the Scriptures! Read them daily and study them diligently.

Remember: Discoveries, also the pleasant and unexpected ones, come to those who are looking.

*Prayer Suggestion: Pray that your study of Holy Scripture may enrich you by strengthening your personal relationship to Jesus Christ.*

# What We Can Expect from God

Russian cosmonauts exploring outer space said that they did not see God—a foolish comment, for God is an invisible Spirit. Another man who knew about outer space, the astronomer Copernicus, came to a different conviction. His Christian faith is clearly confessed in the epitaph he chose for his grave. It reads in translation:

> I require not the grace that was given to Paul;
> I demand not the kindness which was given to Peter;
> But as Thou gavest to the thief on the cross,
> I pray, give also to me.

We can ask—and expect—of God what, on the basis of His Word, we know He has promised. He has not led us to believe that great riches will be ours, nor a life of ease and pleasure, nor worldly honor and recognition, not even escape from sickness and suffering. St. Paul had his thorn in the flesh, probably a sickness, to go with all the other deprivations he endured. But this God had promised him, "My grace is sufficient for you, for My power is made perfect in weakness" (2 Cor. 12:9).

To be at peace with God, to have His forgiveness thanks to the atoning merit of Jesus Christ, to enjoy, even in this life, a foretaste of eternal life, to be made strong by God's power working in us—this God has promised. All the blessings God wants to give us "with Christ"—these we may expect from God in answer to prayer.

*Prayer Suggestion: Ask God to grant you what He has promised: love, joy, peace, and all the other blessings in Christ.*

# The Art of Living with Others

Of Edith, a character in a novel, it was said, "Edith was a little country bounded on the north, south, east, and west by Edith." She was locked into herself.

The prophet Isaiah speaks of selfish, greedy persons who want to deny others the right of existence. He says, "Woe to you who add house to house and join field to field till no space is left and you live alone in the land" (Is. 5:8).

It is good for us to have other people live with us here on earth. How lonesome we would be without neighbors, friends, and family members! God knows this too, and therefore He created Eve to be Adam's helpmate, saying, "It is not good for the man to be alone" (Gen. 2:18). As Psalm 68:6 declares, God "sets the lonely in families." Psalm 128:3 says: "Your wife will be like a fruitful vine within your house; your sons will be like olive shoots around your table." Spouses and children are blessings of God who bring blessings.

Life in home, school, at work, and in the community is to be shared with others. It will not do anyone any good to be like the aforementioned Edith, surrounded by only her own concerns, thinking that she is a country in which the sun rises and sets. Such a life is barren and counterproductive. Life is fruitful when these words of the apostle Paul are followed: "Be kind and compassionate to one another, forgiving each other, just as in Christ God forgave you" (Eph. 4:32). Having come to live the life in Christ, we acquire the fine art of living with others in love.

*Prayer Suggestion: Ask God to open your heart to Christ and to His brothers and sisters who are in need of your love.*

# Every Christian, a "Book" Christ Is Writing

If you were to go to the library and look up Jesus of Nazareth as an author, you would find no entries. Thousands and thousands of books have been written about Jesus, but He Himself wrote no books, not even pamphlets or tracts. He was able to write, of course. When a woman accused of adultery was brought to Him, Jesus "bent down and started to write on the ground with His finger" (John 8:6).

Our Lord wrote His words of truth on material more permanent than parchment or paper; He wrote His message on human hearts. As a Roman mother once pointed to her children as her jewels, so Jesus could point to His disciples—to Mary, Martha, and Lazarus, to Nicodemus and Joseph of Arimathea, to all people who took His words to heart—as His "books." These are the people who, thanks to Jesus' words of spirit and life, became spiritually alive.

What is more, Jesus was Himself the Word—the one through whom the Father declared His love for all people, sending His own dear Son to die for their salvation.

If Jesus thought of His followers as His "books," St. Paul thought of Christians as Christ's letters. Paul wrote, "You show that you are a letter from Christ, the result of our ministry, written not with ink but with the Spirit of the living God, not on tablets of stone but on tablets of human hearts" (2 Cor. 3:3).

Because Jesus is the author and finisher of our faith, our lives are open books to be read by those around us.

*Prayer Suggestion: Ask that each day you live may write another chapter of Christ's saving love in your life.*

# How Precious Is the Book Divine!

One wealthy man, whose hobby is collecting valuable antique books, especially Bibles, was reported to have paid $150,000 for an original Bay Psalm Book. Rare, historic copies of the Bible, or parts of it, have commanded prices running into the millions.

The true value of the Bible, however, cannot be calculated in terms of dollars and cents. While some people value a given copy of the Bible because it is old or because of its history or because they love its poetry and prose or the noble language, the true value of the Holy Scripture lies in its message. The Bible is the Word of God—His ordinances and His promises of salvation. Of them the psalmist declares, "They are more precious than gold, than much pure gold; they are sweeter than honey, than honey from the comb" (Ps. 19:10).

The teachings of the Bible meet human needs, especially the greatest needs of all: to be at peace with God and to have His promise of forgiveness and of life eternal. The Scripture is very plain in this respect, always bearing witness to Jesus Christ. He is the one who, by His obedient life, death, and resurrection, procured life, here and hereafter, for all people and conveys it to all who believe in Him. The Bible, having shown us the way to heaven, also shows us the right way to live.

This precious Book, telling us about the precious Savior and Lover of our souls, is meant for all. It is truly the "Jesus Book," offering us His love. Thus our children sing, "Jesus loves me, this I know, for the Bible tells me so."

***Prayer Suggestion:*** *Pray that Christ may increase your love for the Bible, for it is His Book.*

# Words and Deeds That Come Back to Bless

During World War I an army would release poison gas against its enemy when the wind blew in that direction. Sometimes the wind would reverse itself during an attack, with the result that the lethal fumes were blown back upon the sender. Similarly, evil words directed at someone else can come back to hurt the one who originally spoke them.

As with evil words, so it is with evil works. Contrary winds can blow them back with a vengeance. A case in point is wicked Haman, who according to the book of Esther (chapters 3–7) plotted especially against Mordecai, Queen Esther's relative, for whose death Haman had erected a gallows. Hearing of this evil plot, the king of Persia ordered Haman to be executed on his own gallows.

By way of contrast, God's blessing rests on those who speak well of the neighbor and befriend him with deeds of love, as it is written in the book of Ecclesiastes (11:1), "Cast your bread upon the waters, for after many days you will find it again"—find it increased and multiplied to your own good by the grace of God. There is a divine principle that works both ways, as St. Paul declares, "A man reaps what he sows. The one who sows to please his sinful nature, from that nature will reap destruction; the one who sows to please the Spirit, from the Spirit will reap eternal life" (Gal. 6:7–8).

Eternal life—what a great blessing of God! It is His gift to all who believe in His Son, Jesus Christ, and in that faith do His will.

**Prayer Suggestion:** *Ask God to help you say and do what is to His glory and the good of all.*

# The Rebuilding of Persons

In his book *Peace of Mind,* Joshua Liebman stated the obvious: "No reconstructed society can be built on unreconstructed individuals." By the same token, you cannot have a strong chain that has weak links, a good forest without good trees, a productive farm with unproductive fields.

Society is people, not impersonal institutions, welfare agencies, libraries, schools, churches, parks, playgrounds, job-producing firms and factories. As desirable and necessary as these are—and readily granting that they can contribute to the good of society—what we need the most is upright, honest, virtuous, reconstructed persons. Sometimes this is forgotten, and vast sums of money are spent on things that leave people morally and spiritually unimproved.

What are "reconstructed individuals"? At the level of civil righteousness, they are the ones who set good examples in home, school, community, at work, being prompted by the love of righteousness, by the understanding that democracy can work only if all do their part.

But "rebuilt persons" in God's sight are those who are born anew by water and the Spirit in Baptism, by the Gospel that has brought the Savior Jesus Christ into their newborn hearts and that keeps Him there. What we have is a structure of the Christian life that is cleansed and renewed by the shed blood of Christ, a place where the Holy Spirit has found a home, a living temple to the honor of the living God.

*Prayer Suggestion: Pray that the Holy Spirit may implant you into the newness of life in Christ.*

# The Abiding Monuments of Love

In a cemetery in Genoa, Italy, stands the pretentious statue of a poor woman. The tour guide says, "She worked hard all her life selling flowers, saved every penny, had not even enough to eat, so that she could have a big monument built in her honor when she wouldn't be here to see it."

People sometimes set foolish, unworthy, and selfish goals. For many the goal is to enjoy the pleasures of life, to acquire riches, to establish personal security. Then there are those who, like the woman of Genoa, hope to establish a name for themselves in death. In contrast, a woman mentioned in the Bible expressed her love for Jesus by anointing Him, and He said, "Wherever the Gospel is preached throughout the world, what she has done will also be told, in memory of her" (Mark 14:9).

There is something lasting that we, too, can do as we build, not for time but for eternity, not for ourselves but for others. Parents live on through their well-instructed children. The same goes for teachers, as the writer of the book of Hebrews (13:7) declares, "Remember your leaders, who spoke the Word of God to you. Consider the outcome of their way of life and imitate their faith."

What a monument to the grace and glory of God is a life devoted to doing God's will! People who come after us may not know our names, but God knows. The blessings of such life—a life redeemed for service by the blood of Jesus Christ—go on and on. They abide, for the love that prompted such a consecrated life abides.

*Prayer Suggestion: Pray that God may increase your love for doing His will in word and deed.*

# There Is Hope for Humanity

Many people consider the biblical doctrine of original sin outrageous. They can't accept Jesus' words in Matthew 15:19, "out of the heart come evil thoughts, murder, adultery, sexual immorality, theft, false testimony, slander." Many used to say that such words applied to criminals but not to good people—good being used more or less of people whose lives were outwardly respectable.

But now the news media are very frank in telling us what also some good, outwardly respectable people are like. Recently a psychiatrist, discussing child molestation, issued this broadside in the public press: "Psychoanalysts will tell you there is nothing on the front page of newspapers that any of us is incapable of doing."

While this may border a bit on the extreme, it does tend to support what the Bible has been saying about original sin: (1) It keeps every one of us from self-righteousness, from being too judgmental about others, and (2) it shows the great need for the new life in Jesus Christ.

Our Lord, who knew what was in man and knew human nature, said to Nicodemus (in the well-known night conversation) that human beings need to be born anew by the Holy Spirit's power. And the new self has to be motivated by the same kind of love that prompted the Savior to suffer and die on the cross in behalf of us all.

This is God's program for reconstructing individuals in their total lives.

*Prayer Suggestion: Pray that Christ's sin-conquering power may become a stronger force in your life.*

# Giant Footsteps for Us

On July 20, 1969, astronaut Neil A. Armstrong stepped from his landing craft on to the moon's surface and said, "One small step for a man; one giant leap for mankind."

Everywhere human beings go, they reach places where the Creator of the universe has been long before. The biblical writers are aware of God's presence and performance in nature. The psalmist exclaims, "The heavens declare the glory of God" (Ps. 19:1). What the psalmist sees as he looks up raises a question for him, "When I consider Your heavens, the work of Your fingers … what is man that You are mindful of him?" (Ps. 8:3–4).

Stated another way, why should God, who made the vast universe, be at all concerned about the sinful human world? Why should He so love this community of human beings as to give His only Son for its salvation?

Here we confront a great mystery, immeasurable love that is "higher than the heavens" (Ps. 108:4). All we can say is that no goodness in us moved God to provide for our salvation. All is due to His pure grace, His unspeakable love.

This love took form in the person of Jesus Christ, who after three years of teaching and healing went to Jerusalem to suffer and die.

St. Peter tells us in his first letter (2:21), "Christ suffered for you, leaving you an example, that you should follow in His steps." We follow His steps when we carry our crosses after Him.

***Prayer Suggestion:*** *Pray for a better grasp of the love of God, which gave you a Savior in Jesus Christ, and ask for strength to follow in His footsteps.*

# What to Do about Our Wishes

It is an old custom to throw two coins into the Trevi Fountain in Rome: one, to assure a happy return to Rome, the other to fulfill a wish.

We all have wishes for others and for ourselves. We wish someone a safe journey, a happy birthday, an enjoyable vacation or holiday. We wish many things in behalf of ourselves—good health and happiness among them. Some people, though, wish for things of doubtful value—winning the lottery, for example. Some wishes, of course, are downright evil, as we learn from examples in the Bible. Adam and Eve wished to be as wise as God; King Saul wished to destroy David, his rival; Judas Iscariot betrayed Jesus out of a wish for money.

Needless to say, Christians wish for what is good and God-pleasing, for others and for themselves. St. Paul writes to the Philippians about Christian virtues to seek: whatever is true, noble, right, pure, lovely, admirable, excellent, praiseworthy. The desire to have peace in one's marriage, home, school, business, church, and community is a good wish. Young people desiring an education to enhance their God-given talents for service have a good wish. What remains is that we work for the fulfillment of such a wish, asking God to bless our efforts. St. Paul tells the Philippians (4:6), "In everything, by prayer and petition, with thanksgiving, present your requests to God."

God-pleasing wishes are a fruit of faith in Jesus Christ.

*Prayer Suggestion: Ask God to grant you the desires of your heart in keeping with His good and gracious will.*

# The Hand You Hold

The mental and physical powers God has given you can be compared to four kinds of cards you hold in your hand.

The first power may be symbolized by clubs. Just as a club can be used to strike others, so can words and deeds. However, the club can also represent our effort to strike down evil that arises in our hearts. For this we need God's Word.

In your hand you also hold spades. God has given you the ability to dig, to investigate, to search for treasures in many fields of endeavor. The most promising and productive field in which to dig is the Holy Scripture. There we find the truths of our salvation.

The hand you hold contains also diamonds, precious stones. Of infinite value are spiritual diamonds, the most precious of which is faith—for it gets you into heaven. St. Peter speaks of them as adornments far superior to "gold jewelry and fine clothes." The life of a Christian sparkles with the diamonds of truthfulness, sincerity, honesty, honor.

Then there are hearts. Among God's gifts to you is not only the heart pulsating in your breast, but also the inner self that abounds with love, compassion, courage. You have a heart for the poor, a heart enabling you to go on amid life's difficulties, a heart given to God in response to His great love to you.

In your hand you hold clubs, spades, diamonds, and hearts. Use them to God's glory.

***Prayer Suggestion:*** *Pray that God may help you to make greater use for good of the personal gifts and powers He has given you.*

# God's People: Oaks of Righteousness

During the days of paganism in northern Europe, oak trees were revered, even worshiped as homes of benign spirits. The same may have been true of pagans in the Old Testament.

However, oak trees are mentioned in the Bible also as symbols of strength. When the prophet Amos wanted to underscore the power of God over the enemies of His people, he quoted God as saying, "I destroyed the Amorite before them, though he was tall as the cedars and strong as the oaks" (Amos 2:9).

What is more, the comparison of people to oak trees bespeaks the strength and stateliness of the believers of God. The prophet Isaiah envisions the coming of the Messiah as imparting, beauty, strength, and righteousness to all the people of God. Isaiah says that God would grant to all mourners in Zion "a crown of beauty instead of ashes. … They will be called oaks of righteousness, a planting of the LORD for the display of His splendor" (Is. 61:3).

"Oaks of righteousness"—that is what Christians have become through faith in Jesus Christ. There is beauty and holiness in the robe of Christ's righteousness in which they are clothed, for they have washed their garments and made them white in the blood of the Lamb. And there is also strength—strength like that of an oak tree—for people who live their life in Christ. All who rely on the Savior are strong indeed, for Christ's strength is fulfilled in their weakness.

***Prayer Suggestion:*** *Pray that the power of Christ may be made perfect in you so your weakness may be turned into strength.*

# God Is Satisfied

Joaquin Andujar, a native of the Dominican Republic, pitched for the St. Louis Cardinals. Even when he lost he said that God was his "Amigo," his friend. When he lost a game, he kept up his faith. At one time he struggled through this sentence to ward off criticism, "Do you know why Jesus Christ died? He tried to satisfy everybody."

Well, not quite! Jesus made no attempt to satisfy His opponents within the scribes and Pharisees. Yet already in His youth, He had found favor with God and man. He did satisfy those who came to Him in repentance, promising them the forgiveness of sins and acceptance by the heavenly Father. But His enemies He could not please. He antagonized them to the point that they brought about His death.

What counted most of all was that Jesus satisfied His heavenly Father, who on several occasions declared, "This is My Son, whom I love; with Him I am well pleased" (Matt. 3:17; 17:5). Jesus gave up His life so He might satisfy the demands for righteousness that God's Law made on all people. He endured the penalty that the Law assessed for our disobedience. Now God is pleased with what He did, and He is pleased with us who believe in Jesus.

We cannot satisfy everybody. Some will be displeased when we stand up for what is right. Our main concern is that we satisfy and please God.

***Prayer Suggestion:*** *Add to this prayer: "For Jesus' sake keep me this day, this night, from sin and every evil, that all my doings and life may please You."*

# Borne on Eagles' Wings

The eagle, with its sharp eyesight, can be considered the original "eye in the sky."

Eagles are known for other qualities, especially for their great strength that surpasses that of other birds. The psalmist declares, "[The Lord] satisfies your desires with good things so that your youth is renewed like the eagle's" (Ps. 103:5). Isaiah writes much the same: "Those who hope in the LORD will renew their strength. They will soar on wings like eagles" (40:31).

As the parent eagle carefully attends the young as they learn to fly and "spreads its wings to catch them and carries them on its pinions" (Deut. 32:11), so God delivered His people from bondage in Egypt, saying, "I carried you on eagles' wings and brought you to Myself " (Ex. 19:4).

God brings salvation to His people today as on eagles' wings. Through Jesus Christ He has redeemed them, granting them faith to lift them up and sustain them. We read in St. John's gospel, "No one has ever gone into heaven except the one who came from heaven—the Son of Man … For God so loved the world that He gave His one and only Son, that whoever believes in Him shall not perish but have eternal life" (John 3:13, 16). How uplifting and sustaining are these words! Little wonder that John's gospel is symbolized by the eagle. Through His Word and Spirit, God wants to strengthen you and bear you up to Himself.

*Prayer Suggestion: Pray that God may give you a lift, as on eagles' wings, by strengthening your faith in Jesus Christ.*

# The Owl: Symbol of Wisdom

In the Bible, the owl is mentioned usually in connection with desolation foretold for nations and their proud cities. Zephaniah prophesied that Nineveh would be left "utterly desolate and dry as the desert" (2:13) and that the call of the desert owl and the screech owl "will echo through the windows" (2:14). Because owls lived in the ruins and caves of desolate, forsaken places, the psalmist said when he was feeling alone and distressed, "I am … like an owl among the ruins" (Ps. 102:6). In the Bible (for example, Micah 1:3–8) the owl is associated with God's judgment on unbelief because its haunting sound in the night can scare us.

We today picture the owl as solemnly wise, and human beings are told to take its wisdom to heart. A much better source of wisdom is the Bible. It has a body of sacred literature known as the "wisdom" books—Proverbs, Ecclesiastes, the Song of Solomon. Such "wisdom" is more than learning; it includes understanding, spiritual insight, and discretion, which stem from one's right relation to God and result in right relation to others.

The highest wisdom is found in the Holy Scriptures, for, as St. Paul declares, they "are able to make you wise for salvation through faith in Christ Jesus" (2 Tim. 3:15).

So we need to increase our wisdom of God's grace. Jesus Christ became "for us wisdom from God—that is, our righteousness, holiness and redemption" (1 Cor. 1:30). In Him we have all we need.

*Prayer Suggestion: Ask the Holy Spirit to increase your wisdom, particularly the wisdom of putting full faith in Jesus Christ.*

# Striving for the Prize

Awards and prizes abound in our society—Pulitzer Prizes in literature and journalism, Emmy Awards for television programs, Oscars for the movies, a variety of achievement awards. A prize may have a financial reward to go with it; but mostly it proclaims work well done.

In St. Paul's day prizes were awarded for athletic excellence. He writes that many run in a race but only one receives the prize, and he applies this truth to people running the race of their Christian faith. Let them not be drop-outs, lest they forego the prize: the crown of everlasting life.

The apostle considered himself as being in a race that allowed for no letups, saying, "Not that I have already obtained all this [eternal life], or have already been made perfect, but I press on to take hold of that for which Christ Jesus took hold of me. Brothers, I do not consider myself to have taken hold of it. But one thing I do: Forgetting what is behind and straining toward what is ahead, I press on toward the goal to win the prize for which God has called me heavenward in Christ Jesus" (Phil. 3:12–14).

The prize—life with Christ here and hereafter—of course, is not earned. It is not a wage but an outright gift of God. In receiving this gift, we cannot boast, but must give all thanks and glory to God, who sustains us in the faith until the end.

We also thank Jesus Christ, who in our behalf ran His race to the death and received His prize.

What's in it for you if you stay close to Jesus to the end? Far more than a Nobel prize. For you it's the gift of eternal life.

**Prayer Suggestion:** *Pray for strength to keep on following Jesus, even when the going is rough.*

# Ravens: Bad News, Good News

For the poet Edgar Allen Poe, the raven was bad news. Having lost his beloved Lenore, Poe lets the raven be, as he says, "emblematical of mournful and never-ending remembrance."

But ravens stand also for good news. During a great famine, God sent the ravens to feed the prophet Elijah. This was good news then, and it is good news now, for us. We know that God cares for us.

Through the ravens, God fed Elijah; but who feeds the ravens? The psalmist answers, "[God] provides food for the cattle and for the young ravens when they call" (Ps. 147:9). Jesus said, "Consider the ravens: They do not sow or reap, they have no storeroom or barn; yet God feeds them" (Luke 12:24). Doesn't God do the same for us?

The Son of God became man—a poor, homeless man who had less than the birds with their nests. We know the reasons why He became poor: "For you know the grace of our Lord Jesus Christ, that though He was rich, yet for your sakes He became poor, so that you through His poverty might become rich" (2 Cor. 8:9). In Christ we are rich in forgiveness and eternal life.

*Prayer Suggestion:* Ask God for a faith that will enable you to rely on Him for the help you need, leaving the method to Him.

# The Voice of the Dove

In the Old Testament doves were sacrificed as sin offerings and burnt offerings. Ordinarily when a child was born, the mother was to bring to the priest "a year-old lamb for a burnt offering and a young pigeon or a dove for a sin offering" (Lev. 12:6). If she were poor, she could substitute a turtledove or a young pigeon for the lamb.

When Jesus ousted the sellers of sacrificial animals from the temple, He dealt leniently with those who sold doves. He didn't let the doves loose but said to the owners, "Get these out of here!" (John 2:16).

These sacrifices pointed ahead to the perfect sacrifice for sin that Jesus would bring when He would offer up Himself on the cross. As symbols of this sacrifice to come, the doves in their innocence and gentleness gave up their lives.

Doves enter the story of our salvation in another way. As Jesus began His ministry after His baptism by John the Baptist, the Holy Spirit descended on Him "like a dove." Thus was Jesus visibly anointed "with the Holy Spirit and power" (Acts 2:38) so He might fulfill His mission as the Messiah. And when it was time for the upbuilding of Jesus' church to be continued by His followers, the Holy Spirit again descended visibly—as tongues of fire on the disciples on Pentecost Day.

The Holy Spirit continues to descend upon God's people in Christ. Although we may not see it happen visibly today, we are assured that it is happening. As St. Peter wrote, "The Spirit of glory and of God rests on you" (1 Peter 4:14).

*Prayer Suggestion: Ask that the same Holy Spirit who descended on Jesus at His baptism may enter your heart and bring peace.*

# Jesus Christ Is Lord of All

Scientists have told us about things on the earth and around the earth in outer space. They also tell us what is in the earth or under its surface. There is, first, the 15-mile deep outer crust; second, a mantel of hot rock, some 1,800 miles deep; and third, the earth's core, perhaps like a liquid-center golf ball.

It's mind-boggling! How could all this exist? The letter to the Hebrews explains, "By faith we understand that the universe was formed at God's command" (11:3). Our creed is this: "I believe in God the Father, Maker of heaven and earth."

Not only God the Father but also God the Son is the Creator. "Through Him all things were made," writes St. John in his gospel (1:3).

Jesus Christ is Lord of all, not only because He is the co-Creator but also because, by His resurrection from the dead and His elevation to God's right hand in heaven, He is established as the Redeemer of the human race. He is Regent of the universe, Conqueror of Satan, the King of the angels, Judge of the living and the dead.

St. Paul writes: "God exalted Him [exalted Christ after His death on the cross as our Servant] to the highest place and gave Him the name that is above every name, that at the name of Jesus every knee should bow, in heaven and on earth and under the earth, and every tongue confess that Jesus Christ is Lord, to the glory of God the Father" (Phil. 2:9–11).

Even at a time when He is not universally acknowledged as such, Jesus Christ is Lord of all.

*Prayer Suggestion: Pray that you may come to know Jesus Christ better as your Savior and friend who bears all your sins and griefs.*

# Learn to Love Them

It is not hard to love our friends and to return their favors. But things get more difficult when we must reach people on the other side—people who are different, people whom we may consider a nuisance.

When applied to undesirable people, this is a hard lesson to learn and to translate into practice. But that is what our Lord wants us to do—learn to love them! As Jesus said, "Love your enemies and pray for those who persecute you" (Matt. 5:44).

What about your relation to people who, at work, in community life, in school, even in church and home, get on your nerves? Learn to love them—and to favor them with words and deeds that proceed from love. Love does wonders for them and for you.

Learning to love the unloved and unlovable would be difficult—in fact, impossible—without help from God. Jesus realized this, saying that when we love our enemies we are the sons and daughters of our heavenly Father. The Father makes His sun rise on the evil and on the good and sends rain on the just and unjust. What is infinitely more, He sent the Sun of Righteousness, His own Son, to die for the sins of all. He gives us also the Holy Spirit to work faith, thus engendering both the willingness and power to love others.

What about you and the people in the garden of your life who are more like dandelions than daises, more like rogues than roses? For Jesus' sake—and yours—learn to love them.

*Prayer Suggestion: Ask God to help you to love others, even your enemies.*

# Building the King's Highway

The Christian faith was at first called the Way (Acts 9:2; 24:14)—the way leading to salvation. The only road to peace with the Father and to a place in His heavenly mansions is faith in Jesus Christ as God's Son and our Savior. When Thomas asked about the way to God, Jesus replied, "I am the Way. … No one comes to the Father except through Me" (John 14:6).

By themselves, people do not know the way of salvation in Christ. St. Paul asks, "How can they believe in the one of whom they have not heard?" (Rom. 10:14). So God sends preachers to tell people about Jesus Christ. Such a herald was John the Baptist. God had said through Malachi (3:1), "See, I send My messenger, who will prepare the way before Me." This prophecy was fulfilled with the coming of John the Baptist.

John had to be more than a pathfinder or explorer. He had to be a road builder, had to prepare the way before Christ. This John did, not with road graders but with spiritual tools—with the Word of God and with baptism. The essence of his message was "Repent, for the kingdom of heaven is near" (Matt. 3:2) and "Look, the Lamb of God, who takes away the sin of the world!" (John 1:29).

That is how we today prepare the way for Jesus Christ, our King. The means of grace—Word and sacraments—are the King's highway into our hearts. Let there be diligent use of these means!

**Prayer Suggestion:** *Pray that the Lord Jesus may come into your heart through His Word and abide with you.*

# The Pomegranate: An All-Purpose Tree

The pomegranate tree (along with the fig tree, the olive tree, and the vine) is mentioned in the Bible as an appreciated fruit tree. Its pulpy fruit was very tasty. Because of its eye appeal, pomegranates also were worked into the architectural design of Solomon's temple. Embroidered pomegranates, alternating with golden bells, adorned the fringe of the high priest's robes. With taste and eye appeal, the pomegranate was an all-purpose tree.

There are also all-purpose people, people of many facets, people of appealing character and pleasing personality. Wherever God puts them in the orchard of His church, they bear fruit. Undoubtedly Timothy was such a man. He was not as talented as St. Paul, but certainly he was an excellent number two man. Wherever St. Paul sent him—to Corinth, Philippi, or Thessalonica—he performed well. He was flexible enough to adapt himself to many situations.

Dorcas, in Joppa, was another all-purpose Christian. As a friend and helper of the poor, an artist with her seamstress needle, she "was always doing good and helping the poor" (Acts 9:36). There is no church or community anywhere in the world that wouldn't like to have a Dorcas in its midst.

As "trees," we may not be able to grow apples made of real gold, but we can be pomegranate trees, whose productivity and diversity of talents makes us welcome wherever we go. We can be Christians who can serve wherever God puts us. It is for this that Jesus Christ has redeemed us.

*Prayer Suggestion: Pray that God may find a place for you where you can serve with the gifts you have.*

# The Cedars of Lebanon: Good Timber

The cedars of Lebanon around Tyre and Sidon were highly prized. The seafaring Phoenicians used the timber to make masts for their tall ships. Solomon's temple in Jerusalem was built of these aromatic cedars.

Notable visitors coming to ancient Tyre and Sidon must have admired these stately trees. Elijah found refuge there (in nearby Zeraphath) during the famine in Israel, and St. Paul spent a week with Christians in Tyre while the ship in which he was sailing was being unloaded.

But the greatest guest ever in that area was Jesus. We are told that He, under great pressure from the crowds, "withdrew to the region of Tyre and Sidon" (Matt. 15:21). But He didn't have much of a vacation. While He was there, perhaps just beginning to admire the scenery—mountains, valleys, cedar forests—there came a Canaanite mother who sought His help for her demon-possessed daughter.

At another time Jesus came close to the north country when in the presence of three disciples He was transfigured—gloriously changed—on a mountaintop, perhaps Mount Hermon. From that height He could have seen the cedars of Lebanon.

Individuals of quality and character are said to be persons of good timber. That is what our Lord wants everyone to be. He went to the tree of the cross to redeem all people from sin, and by His Spirit, He makes them the spiritual cedars of Lebanon from which to build His temple, the holy Christian church.

**Prayer Suggestion:** *You want to be a growing Christian? Ask the Holy Spirit to dwell in you and make you His temple.*

# The Fig Tree: Foliage and Fruit

The fig tree is mentioned early in the Bible. After Adam and Eve had sinned, they became aware of their nudity and tried to cover themselves with fig leaves.

Jesus, the second Adam, came into the world to undo the power and guilt of sin. At the beginning of His ministry, He was introduced to one Nathanael, whom Philip was recruiting as a disciple. But the Lord already knew him. He said, "I saw you while you were still under the fig tree before Philip called you" (John 1:48).

Using fig trees as illustrations, Jesus taught His disciples many things about the kingdom of God. He said, "Now learn this lesson from the fig tree: As soon as its twigs get tender and its leaves come out, you know that summer is near" (Matt. 24:32).

A fig tree, however, is not fulfilling its purpose when it bears leaves but no fruit. On a fig tree the fruit appears before the leaves. Consequently, if a tree is full of foliage but has no figs, it is a pretty good sign that it will never have any figs.

This presents us with an important truth about salvation: People cannot cover their sinfulness—their lack of the fruitfulness God desires—by wearing a patched-together, makeshift, fig-leaf apron of their own making. They can stand before a holy God only when by faith they are dressed in the robe of Christ's righteousness.

Having the saving faith, people will not be like fig trees with leaves only but will bring forth the fruit of faith.

***Prayer Suggestion:*** *Pray that God may make you to be like a tree that brings forth its fruit in its season.*

# The Olive Tree: A Source of Goodness

Olive trees are the source of many good products. For example, olive oil was used medicinally by the Good Samaritan, who poured oil and wine on the wounds of the injured man. Olive oil was a lamp fuel, as used by the wise virgins in Jesus' parable. In ceremonial rites, kings were anointed with it. In general, fruitful olive groves were the picture of prosperity. Such plenty was to be shared with the poor, as Moses said, "When you beat the olives from your trees, do not go over the branches a second time. Leave what remains for the alien, the fatherless and the widow" (Deut. 24:20).

God's people are like olive trees—alive, fruitful, productive. Far from being dead timber, they are, in the psalmist's words, "like an olive tree flourishing in the house of God" (Ps. 52:8). They are that also in the home. God promises them bliss and happiness in the family: "Your sons will be like olive shoots around your table" (Ps. 128:3).

In another word picture, St. Paul tells the Gentiles that they were once "separate from Christ, excluded from citizenship in Israel and foreigners to the covenant of the promise" (Eph. 2:12). They were like wild olive shoots, useless and unfruitful, which God grafted into His church and were made fruitful. God blessed them and made them a blessing to others.

It wasn't easy. To bring about this change, the Lord Jesus Christ had to suffer—had to go to Gethsemane to agonize. (Significantly, "Gethsemane" means "oil press.") There and on Calvary's cross, life was pressed out of Him so we might have life and the energy we need to serve Him.

*Prayer Suggestion:* Ask God, for Jesus' sake and by the power of His Spirit, to bless you and make you a blessing to many.

# The Palm Tree: An Emblem of Victory

In Bible times, palm branches were symbols of joy and peace, of victory and triumph. As such, they were used for festivals, for making booths during the Feast of Tabernacles.

There was a special time when God's people used palm branches to express joy. You know the story—how Jesus' friends welcomed Him to Jerusalem as the Messiah by singing and spreading palm branches along the road. The occasion was Palm Sunday, a day still observed by Christians.

Palm branches symbolize the victory of Christians through their faith in Jesus Christ, the risen one. St. John writes, "Everyone born of God overcomes the world. This is the victory that has overcome the world, even our faith" (1 John 5:4). The same apostle describes this triumph of Christians in a heavenly tableau scene in which he shows us "a great multitude that no one could count, from every nation, tribe, people and language, standing before the throne and in front of the Lamb. They were wearing white robes and were holding palm branches in their hands" (Rev. 7:9).

Palm trees, with their fruit (dates) and foliage, typify what Christians can do to give honor to Christ and to serve Him— serve Him by serving His brothers and sisters with the fruits of their faith. They can rejoice and sing. They can hold up palm branches as tokens of their victory in Jesus Christ, who by His self-sacrifice on a cross and His rising from the tomb fulfilled all things necessary for their salvation.

Every time we see a palm, we remember the victory that Christ has won for us.

*Prayer Suggestion: Thank God for all the help He has given you in Christ to win life's battles, especially the battle over sin.*

# From under the Juniper Tree

The juniper tree, also known as a broom tree, has berrylike cones that yield an oil for medicinal use. The ancients burned its wood to protect against plagues.

The prophet Elijah, sitting under a juniper tree, had need for a healing that no tree could impart. He had completed a day's journey into the wilderness as he fled from King Ahab and Queen Jezebel because he had opposed Baal worship. Fatigued and deeply depressed, he said, "I have had enough, LORD. Take my life; I am no better than my ancestors" (1 Kings 19:4).

Undoubtedly we all know such feelings—the blues, the blahs. Instead of verbalizing them while lying on a psychiatrist's couch, we may experience them while sitting under the proverbial juniper tree. Life seems so out of focus. We are on the run, trying to get away from our problems.

What about this juniper-tree experience? We need to face our feelings and address ourselves to them, and we need to remember that depression is not unique; many others experience it. As others before us, we can get out from under the juniper tree. In Elijah's case, an angel provided food and drink so in the strength of this nourishment he could continue his 40-day and 40-night journey to Horeb, the mount of God.

God likewise strengthens us with His Word, the bread of life. That Word leads us to another tree, the tree of the cross on which Jesus Christ gave His life so God might enfold us in His fellowship. Under the shelter of that tree we can rest.

*Prayer Suggestion: Ask God to give you a faith-lift, working in you the Holy Spirit's fruit of love, joy, and peace.*

# Laurels for Your Life

When the British under Wellington had defeated Napoleon at Waterloo in 1815, the mail coaches bearing the news of victory were adorned with laurel branches.

Laurels denote victory, fame, and honor, not only for a Greek athlete or a Roman general but also for an outstanding scholar. We still speak of a poet laureate.

However, what tokens of victory can go to a person who seems to be a born loser? Before looking at the answer to that question, we need to evaluate our use of the unenviable title of "born loser." One who by outward appearance is a loser actually may be a winner, (if not now, then eventually). Nor does the lack of fame and fortune make people losers, for if they are serving others, they are winners, and they deserve recognition (although that is not for what they strive). Their crown is not a laurel wreath but something more meaningful and lasting: a thankful son or daughter, gratitude from someone who was given a second chance, and, above all, God's seal of approval.

No victory is won without great effort, patience, and persistence. St. Paul compares himself to an athlete who goes into intensive training in preparation for the race. The athlete does it to receive a perishable wreath, but we an imperishable one: the crown of eternal life (1 Cor. 9:24–27).

Hard as we may try to overcome the problems and temptations of sin, we cannot succeed by ourselves. Someone else has to do it. As we run the race of life, Jesus is running with us and grants us the laurels of victory.

**Prayer Suggestion:** *Pray that God may supply you with courage and strength to continue the race and in His own time give you the victory.*

# The View from a Mountain

When we find ourselves in the valleys of mental depression, God wants to lead us to mountaintops so we can see our life in a clearer perspective. Our worship in God's house is such an experience, for the church is a spiritual Mount Zion set in the midst of our world. Outside of church, we often experience such vantage points when special occasions occur—a promotion in our work, recognition of services performed, the celebration of a birthday.

High points in life, however, are not the only times when we can have a good perspective. Unpleasant experiences—sickness, loss, a deep disappointment—also can give us a better view of life, if we rise from the "dumps" and let God show us His love. These are pauses that refresh, moments when we can say, "I will lift up mine eyes unto the hills, from whence cometh my help" (Ps. 121:1 KJV).

When God's people were about to enter the land of promise, He said to Moses, "Go up into the Abarim Range to Mount Nebo in Moab, across from Jericho, and view Canaan, the land I am giving the Israelites as their own possession" (Deut. 32:49). What a thrill for Moses to see the land!

Inspiration Point in Yosemite Park offers a spectacular view of the 7,500-foot-high granite monolith called El Capitan and the Bridalveil Falls. There is an inspiration point in your life too. It is the upward look, the look to Jesus, the Lamb of God, to Jesus the pioneer and perfecter of our salvation. He who gave His life for us and rose again is the high point of our lives.

*Prayer Suggestion: Pray for God's guidance to gain a better perspective of your life as you turn to Jesus.*

# A Rich Bread Supply

After St. Louis, Missouri, was founded in 1763, some French families from earlier settlements in Illinois began to move in. Their neighbors back home didn't think much of the move. They nicknamed the new town Pain Court (pan coor), which in English means "short of bread."

Many cities and communities today, especially in the Third World, are literally short of bread. In fact, some sections in our modern, thriving North American cities are populated by people who are actually starving.

Their situation isn't much different from that of the multitude that came to Jesus in the wilderness. However, when they did, Jesus affirmed that people do not live by bread alone. He doesn't deny the need for bodily food; He asserts instead that human beings need more than that. They need the bread of life, the Word of God, which nourishes minds, hearts, and souls. Jesus is Himself the Word and the Bread of Life.

Interestingly enough, our Lord was born in Bethlehem, a city whose name means "house of bread." But as a native of this city He did not aspire to be a "bread king," that is, a supplier of goods that please the appetites and desires of human nature. He came to make His spiritual kingdom, His church, a true "house of bread," where all that He has gained for our salvation—forgiveness, peace with God, eternal life—is conveyed to us through Word and Sacrament.

Christ well supplies His church so it is never short of bread but well provided with the Bread of Life.

*Prayer Suggestion: Consider what all is included when you pray, "Give us this day our daily bread," and then ask God for these blessings.*

# Life's Experiences: As Ballast and for Building

The old Brick House, now a restaurant in historic St. Genevieve, Missouri, is said to be the oldest brick building west of the Mississippi River. It was erected in 1785 with bricks brought from France. The bricks served a double purpose: as ballast in the ship and as building material.

Life's experiences—the lessons we learn, the input of education, the successes we enjoy, and the reverses we suffer—can be regarded as being the ballast, the stability we need in life, and the materials we need to build a life.

Imagine how troubled Job would have fared if he had not had ballast when he endured all his losses! But he remained upright because he had God's truth in his heart: "I know that my Redeemer lives" (Job 19:25). Job's experiences were not dead weight, but they provided him with the material—the bricks, if you will—to rebuild his life. After it was all over, Job prayed, "My ears had heard of You but now my eyes have seen You" (Job 42:5). The account goes on: "The LORD blessed the latter part of Job's life more than the first" (Job 42:12).

So it can be with all of us. Life's truths, including our burdens and afflictions, serve a double purpose: as ballast in our ship and as pieces we can put together to build a worthwhile life, to rebuild life after a setback. We can do this when we take to heart that He, the Son of God, came among us as a human being to give His life as a ransom for all—to redeem us from sin and the fear of death so we can live to His glory, in this world and in the world to come.

*Prayer Suggestion: Ask God for steadfastness and strength to carry life's load.*

# Serving with Our Talents

The former Helen Traubel, an operatic and concert soprano, also wrote two mystery novels. Thomas Jefferson was a lawyer, political philosopher, and scientific farmer, as well as a statesman. Martin Luther was a theologian, linguist, and hymn writer. The comic Red Skelton painted clowns.

Some people have multiple talents; others have fewer. When you count up your talents, don't limit yourself to the musical or literary, to the scientific or the popular. God's talents given to us include many kinds, like group-leadership ability, creative housekeeping, friendliness, being good in a repair shop, being a healer of hurts by words and deeds.

God gives us talents for a reason: to equip us for service. Just as eyes and ears, hands and feet, mind and muscles are differently equipped so they can serve the whole human being, so God equips us for the good of all—be that in church, community, society, state, or the business world.

Talents vary also in degree. We may not be able to sing arias or write novels, but we can nevertheless sing to the glory of God in worship and at home, and we can write encouraging letters and notes to people who need uplifting. This, too, is using our talents as good stewards. St. Paul says, "It is required that those who have been given a trust must prove faithful" (1 Cor. 4:2).

The motivation for that, like the talents themselves, comes from God, who made us and who, through Christ Jesus, redeemed us. In love to Him who first loved us we serve Him and one another with our talents.

***Prayer Suggestion:*** *Ask that God help you discover your talents and to give you the willingness to use them for Him and for others.*

# How to Have a Happy Life

Sally Benson, 1900–72, an interesting storyteller, shaped much of her material into plays. In her "Meet Me in St. Louis," which was published in 1942 and made into a movie in 1944, she tells about her childhood in the city named.

Many people have happy memories of their childhood. Their parents loved them, cared for them, and imparted moral and spiritual guidance. Parents who fail to give character training are, as someone has said, "fashioning sparrows and then sending them out to fight hawks."

In the Bible, Timothy had enjoyed a good upbringing. St. Paul writes to him, "I have been reminded of your sincere faith, which first lived in your grandmother Lois and in your mother Eunice and, I am persuaded, now lives in you also" (2 Tim. 1:5).

Teaching little children how to pray; telling them Bible stories, especially telling them about Jesus; explaining to them their Baptism; setting a good example—these add greatly to the joys of childhood. How blessed are people who can say, "My parents cared enough about me to provide the very best—not always earthly riches, but something much finer than gold and silver: a Christian education." This is putting first things first, seeking first God's kingdom.

Parents and their grown children may not meet again in St. Louis or in whatever other community they were once together as a family, but they will certainly meet again in the heavenly Father's home of many mansions.

*Prayer Suggestion: Thank God for all your happy childhood experiences and for your present nearness to Jesus Christ.*

# A Clear Title to Your Home

Robert M. Snyder, a wealthy Kansas City industrialist, in 1904 bought 2,500 acres of scenic land in the Ozark country. There, from his native Scotland he brought stone masons to build a castle-size mansion of 60 rooms, together with a greenhouse, water tower, and stables. Snyder never got to live in it; in 1906 he lost his life in a street accident. The mansion stands unfinished to this day.

There can be other reasons why people never get to live in their dream house: high interest rates, loss of money in a bad business deal, fires, and floods. Others move into their home only to find that they cannot keep up the payments.

Jesus told His disciples before He was parted from them, "In My Father's house are many rooms [mansions] ... I am going there to prepare a place for you" (John 14:2). The clear and unencumbered title to that eternal dwelling place is not one we earned by the labor of our hands. It is an outright gift from Christ, who earned eternal life for us.

While Jesus was here on earth, He had no home, no place where to lay His head. He had come to be the Servant, suffering deprivation and death itself so He might provide a place for us in the Father's house—complete with title.

> He lives and grants me daily breath;
> He lives, and I shall conquer death;
> He lives my mansion to prepare;
> He lives to bring me safely there.

*Prayer Suggestion: Ask God for His help to make your earthly home a picture of the heavenly one to come.*

# Knowing Oneself

A generation ago, Augustus Thomas was esteemed "one of America's most highly regarded dramatists." Earlier in life he had trouble finding himself. He had been a page boy in Congress, studied law, tried railroading, and edited a newspaper. Then he started writing plays and had 60 of them published, including one titled "As a Man Thinks."

It is important how people think of themselves and that they know their talents and capabilities, for only then can they find themselves.

What is there for us to know about ourselves, and how can we find it out? Aptitude tests are helpful, although it is recognized that some personal qualities and potentialities escape them. For a total-person evaluation, with emphasis on the spiritual, we need the Word of God—both Law and Gospel.

The Law shows us our sins, not only outward misdeeds and wrongful words, but also the sinful thoughts of the mind and the evil desires of the heart.

The Word of the Gospel, however, reveals that we are loved by the heavenly Father, redeemed by His Son, Jesus Christ, and made into clean, sacred temples by the Holy Spirit. All our gifts are then heightened—our natural talents and the special gifts of the Spirit. New confidence comes, for we can do all things through Christ, who strengthens us.

With the Word, then, we evaluate ourselves by new standards, no longer asking what serves my selfish ends, but how can I glorify God and help my neighbor.

*Prayer Suggestion: Pray that God may help you to know yourself as one whom He loves in Jesus Christ.*

# The Resurrection Body

In 1981, Adele Starbird, a gracious lady who had been dean of women at Washington University and a columnist for the *St. Louis Post-Dispatch,* celebrated her 90th birthday. In chatting with friends she referred to her aging body as "an old jalopy" and added, "I'm looking forward to the day when I get to turn it in on a brand-new, shining model."

In the Bible we find aging human bodies compared to houses or dwelling places, tents. St. Paul referred to his body as an "earthly tent," and added that we are looking forward to a glorified, permanent body: "We have a building from God, an eternal house in heaven, not built by human hands" (2 Cor. 5:1).

The basis for the belief in the resurrection of the body is the bodily resurrection of Jesus Christ, to whom we are tied by faith and in whose victory over sin and death we share by faith in Him. Our Lord returned from the grave in the same body, easily identifiable by the nail marks and the wounded side. But the body in which He returned was glorified.

What does this mean to us? St. Paul declares, "The Lord Jesus Christ ... will transform our lowly bodies so that they will be like His glorious body" (Phil. 3:20–21). The differences between the buried body and the raised body are pointed out in 1 Corinthians 15:43: "It is sown in dishonor, it is raised in glory." Therefore, on the basis of Holy Scripture we confess, "I believe in the resurrection of the body."

***Prayer Suggestion:*** *Pray for a stronger faith in Jesus that you may enjoy and share the fruits of His resurrection.*

# Winning Life's Skirmishes

Visitors looking for Fort Davidson in the Ozark country at Pilot Knob, Missouri, find only the remaining earthworks. A Civil War battle was fought there September 27, 1864. Although some 1,000 men were lost in the 20-minute engagement, it was not considered a major battle. The outcome did, however, save St. Louis, a key city on the Mississippi, and that had a great bearing on the Civil War outcome.

In everyday life, ever so many situations can be easily dismissed as minor. But when unattended to, a minor problem can develop into a major tragedy. A concession to Satan by cheating a little, lying a little, or hating a little can easily prepare the way for a major surrender. An initial argument not ending in reconciliation or a solution can become a festering wound, bringing serious trouble into the family and home.

Life's troubles go back to an event in the Garden of Eden, where an encounter took place between Satan and two people. A minor event? Not so. By the fall of Adam and Eve, sin entered the world, and death by sin. What many consider a minor skirmish was a major defeat for the human race, and it set the stage for the great duel involving Satan and the woman's Seed, Jesus. It was fought not only at our Lord's temptation in the wilderness but ultimately in the battle He won on Calvary's cross, as celebrated by His resurrection.

Thanks to Christ's victory, we can win life's little, everyday battles, and in that way stay the course leading to peace with God and with one another.

***Prayer Suggestion:*** *Pray for God's help in solving also life's problems, great and small.*

# Love One Another

The Lord Jesus described the true mark of His followers when He said, "By this all men will know that you are My disciples, if you love one another" (John 13:35).

The love of Christ sets a very high standard. No one can love as He does, yet He desires that we love on that basis. He says, "As I have loved you, so you must love one another" (John 13:34).

Loving as Christ loves is not the same as loving the neighbor as oneself. Some love themselves very little—even hate themselves—and to love the brother or sister like that is not enough. Neither is it enough to love only those who love us. Such love falls far short of what Jesus has in mind.

We cannot conceive of Christ's kind of love unless we first become His disciples. Disciples are persons reborn in the water and Word of Baptism, persons whose heart the Holy Spirit has changed through the Gospel. They receive new powers, for they are renewed in the life of Christ.

Such people cannot keep their commitment to Christ locked up in the inside. Their mutual love becomes a noticeable mark by which everyone knows whose people they are. What a confession of faith such love is!

St. Paul speaks of "Christ in you, the hope of glory" (Col. 1:27). Christ needs to be the new tenant in our hearts. With Him in us, we can begin to love others as He loved us and daily grow in this grace.

*Prayer Suggestion: Pray that God would make you a mirror reflecting His love to you in Christ.*

# God's Name—More than an Ornament

This week, you undoubtedly may have heard profanity—the vain use of God's name in cursing or swearing—either in person or on TV. Although you may have heard this often, it is still shocking because it offends against the God you love.

There are other ways in which God's name is profaned—lying, for example, or deceiving by God's name for selfish ends. Some people try to adorn false religion by adding God's name to it, thus misleading people into accepting it as God-given. This was known in Shakespeare's time, for in his play *The Merchant of Venice* he has one of the actors say, "The world is still deceived with ornament. In law, what plea so tainted and corrupt, but, being season'd with a gracious voice, obscures the show of evil? In religion, what gross error, but some sober brow will bless it, and approve it with a text, hiding the grossness with fair ornament."

We need to probe our lives and lips to see how we have used God's name. We are always tempted to hide behind the name of God, as though to be named after Him were a guarantee of the genuineness of our faith. It takes more than calling oneself a Christian to really be one.

What does it take? Believe on the Lord Jesus Christ as Savior. It means to call on God's name in every trouble—even when there is no special trouble—and to pray, praise, and give thanks. Then God's name, more than an ornament, is a badge of honor that tells people who we are and whose we are.

*Prayer Suggestion: Ask for the help of the Holy Spirit for the right use of God's name in prayer and in all of life.*

# The Eternal Drama of Life

In many respects life differs for each of us. For example, the life of a computer operator's daughter obviously differs from that of the daughter of the company's CEO.

Yet there is a sameness in life for all of us in many of the events between birth and death. As Jesus said about life before the flood (and it's still true today), "People were eating and drinking, marrying and giving in marriage" (Matt. 24:38). St. James points to the universal brevity of life when he says, "You are a mist that appears for a little while and then vanishes" (James 4:14).

What is your life like? In *The Merchant of Venice*, Shakespeare has an actor say, "I hold the world but as a stage, where every man must play a part, and mine is a sad one."

However, if life is a drama, it is not one in which we are puppets. God gives us freedom—freedom to choose marriage partners; the whereabouts of our home, work, vacation; the type of government we want; the kind of candidates we want for public office. Yes, God even lets us choose sin and its inevitable consequences. At the same time, God wants all people to be saved and to come to faith in Jesus Christ. He appeals to us with His love, with the promise of reconstructed life, with the assurance that life is the scene of His merciful acts all the days of our sojourn on earth.

Life is more than a stage play on which the final curtain comes down with the words, "The End." In Christ, God gives us eternal life.

*Prayer Suggestion: Ask God to help you play your part in life joyfully and to the best of your ability.*

# Jesus Loves Little Children

Many communities throughout the United States have a public school named after Eugene Field, the poet-laureate of children. Such a name for a school is fitting because, as one teacher noted, "The world of little people was left unrepresented in the realm of poetry until Eugene Field came along."

The world of little people was of great spiritual concern to Jesus. Remember His words: "Let the little children come to Me and do not hinder them, for the kingdom of God belongs to such as these" (Matt. 19:14). St. Mark continues the account: "He took the children in His arms, put His hands on them and blessed them" (Mark 10:16).

The love of Jesus for children needs to be revived in an age that can produce technological wonders but that is darkened by child neglect and abuse, most of it by parents who themselves may have been mistreated as children.

To say the least, our Lord takes a dim view of adult attitudes and actions that harm children, which includes child pornography, televised violence, or any failure to show love and consideration for children. On the other hand, we hear the Savior's words of approval when child care makes use of the love He Himself has revealed. He declares, "Whoever welcomes a little child [a humble child] like this in My name welcomes Me" (Matt. 18:5). Always we bear in mind that God, the Giver of children, loved also the little ones so much that He gave His Son into death for their salvation.

Jesus gives us the love that blesses little children.

*Prayer Suggestion: Ask the Lord Jesus to fill your heart with love toward children and the power to apply that love.*

# Let Your Light Shine

Jesus' exhortation to let our light shine has gone over into everyday language. However dark the corner where we live and work, we can brighten it and be a light. Better to light a candle than curse the darkness.

In Shakespeare's *The Merchant of Venice,* Portia sees the light in her house and exclaims, "How far that little candle throws his beams! So shines a good deed in a naughty world." Because of the contrast with the darkness of evil, good deeds and their doers stand out as lights. St. Paul praised the Philippians because they "shine like stars in the universe as [they] hold out the Word of life" (Phil. 2:15–16).

A greater light, however, will always eclipse a lesser one. As the aforementioned Portia goes along in the night and sees the candle burning in her house, her companion, Nerissa, observes, "When the moon shone, we did not see the candle." That is as it should be. When Christ lets His full light shine— and He will do this in heaven—our light is no longer needed. But until that time, His words to us are, "Let your light shine"—to the glory of God.

This light of ours comes not from within but from the Word of God. The psalmist declares, "Your Word is a lamp to my feet and a light for my path" (Ps. 119:105).

This Word shines from the pages of the Holy Scriptures. The Bible is God's light because it instructs us for salvation through faith in Christ Jesus. It teaches that while we were yet sinners, Christ died for us and rose again.

***Prayer Suggestion:*** *Pray that the Holy Spirit may enlighten your heart and mind so you can be one of God's candles.*

# Be What You Are

Sometimes people don't want to be themselves but pretend to be somebody else. F. Scott Fitzgerald's novel *The Great Gatsby* deals with such a man. A native of North Dakota, this man changes his name from James Gatz to Jay Gatsby. While in military training for World War I, he falls in love with a Southern belle far his superior in wealth and culture. When he works for a rich man who has a yacht, he learns what it means to be rich. Gatsby wants to be like that, so he becomes a prominent bootlegger and soon has enough money to buy a big mansion on Long Island. People attend his parties, not because they are his friends but because the drinks are free. Even in death he plays the role of another, for he is shot by someone who mistakes him for another.

Be what you are! Those who blindly copy the lifestyles of others easily become phonies, and it doesn't take long before people recognize this. God made each one a unique person, giving distinctive talents to each. Our Creator wants us to be the way He made us—true to ourselves.

Those who want to carbon copy other people may not like themselves. But, God loves them, each one as an individual. St. Paul declares, "God demonstrates His own love for us in this: While we were still sinners, Christ died for us" (Rom. 5:8).

Having by faith become a new creation in Christ, you have the right to be what you are—an honest, upright person using the distinctive talents and gifts God has given you.

*Prayer Suggestion: Pray that God may remove all pretense from your heart and give you the desire to be yourself: a redeemed child of God.*

# Names in the Book of Life

In Elephant Rock State Park in Missouri's Ozark region one can see huge granite boulders into which master stone cutters chiseled their names over a hundred years ago. The names are as legible now as they were then.

Rock is very durable writing material. Large-size stone inscriptions are not only lasting but also very legible. That's why pious Job of the Bible, about to confess his faith in the living Redeemer, exclaims, "Oh, that my words were recorded, … that they were inscribed with an iron tool on lead, or engraved in rock forever!" (Job 19:23–24).

For the inscription of names, one medium is even more durable than granite: the Book of Life, mentioned several times in the Bible. All who by faith in Jesus Christ have become God's children and heirs of salvation have their names entered into the Book of Life. This is the heart and memory of God, which is far more reliable than man's records, computers, memory banks. God remembers all His people, no matter how long ago they died, for their names are written in His book.

What if your name is not in histories, blue books, social registers? Let that be of no concern to you, but do care whether your name is written in the Lamb's book. All who trust in Jesus as Redeemer and Peacemaker with God have their names in it.

The tombstone of the English poet John Keats reads, "Here lies one whose name was writ in water." Of a Christian it can be said, "Here lies one whose name is written in the Book of Life.

*Prayer Suggestion:* *Pray that God may keep you in His favor through your faith in Jesus and thus write your name in His book.*

# What Time Is It?

For the people of Tuscumbia, Missouri, it is always eight o'clock—at least so says the Miller County courthouse. When it was built there years ago, no clock was put into the cupola. Instead, someone painted a dial on the outside with the hands pointing to eight o'clock.

When we ask "What time is it?" we should be inviting deep, very significant answers—answers that say that time has wings, that your life is fleeting, that it is later than you think. As St. Paul says, "The hour has come for you to wake up from your slumber, because our salvation is nearer now than when we first believed. The night is nearly over; the day is almost here. So let us put aside the deeds of darkness and put on the armor of light" (Rom. 13:11–12). This is an appropriate reminder, regardless of whether this devotion is read morning, noon, or evening.

Jesus, our Lord and Savior, was aware of the time while He was here on earth. That is why He worked so hard while it was day; He knew the night was coming when no one could work. What did He do? He labored—all the way to Calvary's cross to save us. Now, regardless of whether it is morning or night, regardless what the clock in the courthouse dome says or doesn't say, we have rest and peace through faith in Him. Young or old, we can say with the psalmist, "My times are in Your hand" (Ps. 31:15). With the Emmaus disciples we can say: "Stay with us, for it is nearly evening; the day is almost over" (Luke 24:29). Jesus will accept that invitation.

**Prayer Suggestion:** *Pray that God may keep you aware of times and seasons and always draw you closer to Him.*

# Jesus, the Bread of Life

Maize, or Indian corn, was supposedly named after Mahiz, a good spirit who gave the grain to an Indian boy.

The Indians of old did not know the true God but worshiped the Great Spirit and lesser spirits. Consequently, they gave to them the credit and glory that belong to God. It is indeed true that all good gifts, grain included, come from God. St. Paul said in Lystra of Asia Minor, where the people worshiped the sun as the source of all good: "[God] did good, and gave us rain from heaven, and fruitful seasons, filling our hearts with food and gladness" (Acts 14:17 KJV).

God avails Himself of the laws and forces of nature, also of human resourcefulness and diligence, to provide daily bread for the people. A case in point is hybrid corn, which scientists developed to greatly increase the quantity and quality of corn. In the end the glory belongs to God, for He created the basic materials with which scientists work, and He gives people the health, strength, and brain power to do their work.

God does more than give us corn or grain from which we bake bread for the body. For our souls He provides the bread of life. Jesus says: "I am the bread of life. He who comes to Me will never go hungry" (John 6:35).

When our Savior was crucified, dead, and buried, He became as grain sown into the ground. But that was not the end. He rose again, thus verifying that the salvation He came to effect was valid, and that His Word would now produce much fruit. His Word is bread that satisfies.

*Prayer Suggestion: As you pray "Give us this day our daily bread," count the gifts God gives you along with it.*

# Bypassing Boredom

Much of what people do or don't do is related to boredom. It may go by other names—tedium, ennui, dullness, the blahs—but its nature is the same: a physical, mental, and emotional weariness because of life's drab routines and its recurring sameness. Boredom drives some people to drink and to use drugs.

We can devise no single, sure-fire formula for bypassing boredom to fit everyone, for our lives differ. We can, however, pick up hints from others. That's why the study of biographies can be so helpful. Look at some lives pictured in the Bible. St. Paul, so often in prison, overcame the boredom of those behind bars by writing letters, conversing with his jailers, speaking to God in prayer, singing God's praises, and making plans for his next mission trips. Can you imagine Dorcas of Joppa (Tel-Aviv) being bored while she sewed coats and garments for the poor? Timothy could not have been bored if he did only half the things St. Paul suggested to him: use the gifts that were in him, give attendance to reading, teaching, visiting people, and witnessing to the faith.

These examples from the Bible are significant for us because these people believed and lived the Christian faith. They stood close to Jesus, wanting their lives to count for Him because He had given His life for them. With that as their motivation, they chased away the blues. This power is available also to us.

**Prayer Suggestion:** *Pray God that you may find meaning in life by serving.*

# What Is Christ Worth?

The man who commissioned Leonardo da Vinci to paint a portrait of his wife was so displeased with the work—the "Mona Lisa"—that he refused to pay for it. In later years it came to be recognized as a masterpiece. When in 1962 it was sent from the Louvre for exhibition in the United States, it was insured for $100,000,000.

Quite often in life, better judgment comes with the passage of time. Although the prodigal son once despised his home and father's love, he appreciated them greatly when things went wrong.

That is what repentance does—repentance, which in Greek means a change of mind, and in Christian usage, a change of heart.

At about the time Jesus of Nazareth was proclaiming the kingdom of God, a contemporary, Saul of Tarsus, was in Jerusalem studying under the great teacher Gamaliel. Jesus did many wonderful works. His teachings, illustrated by His incomparable parables, were mind-gripping. Then on a cross outside the Jerusalem city limits He performed His greatest masterwork: redemption.

But where was Saul of Tarsus all this time? Undoubtedly preoccupied with his studies; undoubtedly also very hostile to Jesus' teaching. But when he was converted, a most fundamental change came about. St. Paul declared, "For to me, to live is Christ" (Phil. 1:21).

What if someone had asked St. Paul, "What is Christ worth to you?" He would have answered, "Christ is everything to me."

***Prayer Suggestion:*** *Pray that you may come to know the love of Christ that passes knowledge.*

# The Power of Intercession

Are your prayers always answered? All proper prayers have the promise of God's answer, as declared by the prophet Isaiah, "Before they call I will answer; while they are still speaking I will hear" (Is. 65:24).

Although it may not seem so to our human hearts, God gives special attention to prayers of intercession, request, appeal, and pleading for our fellow human beings, whether friends or foes. We see this from many instances in the Bible: Abraham praying for the inhabitants of Sodom (Gen. 18:22–33), Moses interceding for the people of Israel (Ex. 32:31–32), the Canaanite mother pleading for her demon-possessed daughter (Matt. 15:21–28), the apostle Paul making his requests in behalf of converts (Phil. 1:7–11). These great intercessions were pleasing to God; they were "powerful and effective" (James 5:16) because they conformed so closely to the intercessory prayers of Jesus, particularly to His High Priestly Prayer in John 17. What is more, not only the example of Jesus but, above all, His reconciling work in giving up His life for the world both prompts and enables us to pray for others.

Our intercessions have the promise of God's audience and answer because they are an expression of the divine will that we love our neighbor. Such prayers, spoken in love, put selfish interests aside and instead focus on the needs of people around us. Knowing God will answer encourages us to follow our intercessions with thanksgiving for God's blessings.

Answered prayers are a tribute to the love of God that prompts the caring and sharing love of Christians.

**Prayer Suggestion:** *Include others in your prayer today.*

# Christ's Peace in Everyday Life

More than 2,000 years ago in Rome, it is said that mothers quieted their crying children by saying, "Hush, Hannibal is at the gates!" Hannibal, of Carthage in northern Africa, was Rome's enemy. With his elephants he crossed the Alps into Italy and defeated the Roman army. Eventually, in 146 B.C., the Romans destroyed Carthage and salted the site so nothing would grow. That is how things stood until February 1985, when the mayor of modern Rome and someone representing ancient Carthage (near Tunis) signed a peace treaty as a symbolic act of friendship.

Some 150 years after Rome's final victory, Jesus, the Prince of Peace, was born in the Roman Empire. He was not a man of war. He had nothing against the people of North Africa. In fact, it was a man from there, Simon of Cyrene, who carried His cross to Calvary. Jesus did more than advocate peace. As St. Paul tells the Ephesians, " [Christ] Himself is our peace" (Eph. 2:14). Christ offered up Himself for our sins, and through Him God reconciled the world to Himself.

Although there are still wars and rumors of wars in our world, we can well imagine how much worse things would be if Christ had never come. Christ's peace reaches down into our personal lives, affecting our person-to-person relationship in our everyday lives: peaceful relations in homes, schools, the workplace, the community. We settle our differences in open discussion; in love we give a little; we bear one another's burdens. This is the fruit of Christ's work in our hearts.

*Prayer Suggestion: Pray that Christ may bring His peace into your heart and enable you to share it with people around you.*

# Be a Friend—to Yourself and Others

We are often our own worst enemies. A character in the Pogo comic strip declared, "We have met the enemy, and he is us." To refuse to learn in school (and throughout life), to neglect one's health, to waste opportunities, to be abrasive, to alienate friends—is to be one's own enemy.

The other side of the coin says: Be a true friend to yourself, do yourself favors. Some will say that such encouragement is unnecessary, since people by nature love themselves and seek their own interests first. True, but self-seeking is not the same as being one's own best friend. In fact, it is self-love, the "me first" attitude, that underscores the saying of the comic strip that "the enemy is us."

Some feel that friendship to oneself is ego-centered and has too narrow a base; friendship is a relationship with other people. True. But it is also true that many people hate others because they hate themselves. So, it would seem, if you feel right about yourself and know how to be a true friend to yourself, you are in a better position to be a friend to other people.

You do yourself a favor when you are truthful about yourself. Honest introspection, difficult as it is, is needed. It reveals many unpleasant facts, and these must be known before they can be dealt with. To confess honestly "I am a sinner" is a prerequisite, immediately to be followed by reliance on Jesus Christ as the Redeemer, forgiver, friend, reconciler, healer. Now spiritual growth can begin. Now you can be a friend to yourself and to others.

**Prayer Suggestion:** *Pray that all you think, say, and do may glorify God and reveal His love.*

# The Way of True Wisdom

When the noted painter and muralist Thomas Hart Benton left his native Neosho, Missouri, to study art in Chicago, he didn't think there was much more to learn. Years later he wrote, "I held the idea that I was a genius. As time passed, however, I realized that very few people around me shared that notion."

Some exaggerated notions of self can be attributed to the enthusiasm of youth, but the give-and-take of life corrects these opinions. There is, however, a conceit that is utterly vain and is a roadblock to personal growth, particularly to spiritual progress: the conceit of false pride, arrogance, and of a bloated egotism. As persons whom God has made and redeemed, we do need to think highly of ourselves, but not more highly than we ought. As St. Paul says, "Think of yourself with sober judgment, in accordance with the measure of faith God has given you" (Rom. 12:3).

To be wise is one thing, a thing God wants, but it is quite another to be wise in one's own conceits, as the same apostle puts it.

The way to true wisdom begins with one's relationship to Jesus Christ. The witness of Holy Scripture concerning Jesus as the Savior makes us wise unto salvation through faith that is in Christ Jesus. Where there is this faith, there Christian life can flourish. The adversities of life cannot destroy such a house.

The way to true wisdom is acceptance of the words of Jesus and applying them in everyday situations.

***Prayer Suggestion:*** *Pray that God may impart to you the wisdom of the life in Christ.*

# Knowing and Doing

On a construction site, sidewalk superintendents—spectators—commonly think they know what needs to be done, but few are capable of doing it. There is a vast difference between knowing and doing, between the theoretical and the practical.

In *The Merchant of Venice*, Shakespeare has Portia say, "If to do were as easy as to know what were good to do, chapels had been churches, and poor men's cottages princes' palaces."

To know, to do—both are important. Without knowing and planning, we are apt to rush into all kinds of projects but accomplish little. Conversely, to know but not to do is to let the best-laid plans of mice and men go to waste.

Jesus emphasized knowing and doing. For three years He taught His disciples so they might know the truth. This, so that in subsequent years they might do the truth, that is, proclaim and apply the Gospel for the salvation of people. Doing the truth serves as a test, to see if it works out as claimed. Jesus said, "If anyone chooses to do God's will, he will find out whether My teaching comes from God" (John 7:17).

Jesus was a knower and a doer. He knew the Holy Scriptures—knew the Father's will, knew His mission in life. Then He did what He knew He had to do. He offered Himself up on the cross as a sacrifice for sin. Thus He built not a little wayside chapel but a worldwide holy Christian church, a communion of saints. Thus He opened not a poor man's cottage in heaven but the Father's house of many mansions.

*Prayer Suggestion: Ask that the Holy Spirit may open your mind to God's truth, and then give you the strength to do it.*

# Christian Growth: Program and Process

St. Paul prayed for the Christians in Colossae, "Asking God to fill you with the knowledge of His will through all spiritual wisdom and understanding … that you may live a life worthy of the Lord and may please Him in every way: bearing fruit in every good work, growing in the knowledge of God" (Col. 1:9–10).

Having come to faith in Jesus Christ as the Savior, Christians begin their spiritual development through the seed of God's Word implanted in them. Their growth in Christian knowledge, wisdom, and understanding progresses as, over the span of a lifetime, they take to heart and apply the Word proclaimed in sermons, studied in Bible classes, and read individually in the Holy Scripture. Christians need to keep in close contact with the Word, for from it they learn God's "good, pleasing and perfect will" (Rom. 12:2).

Through the power of God's Word and Spirit, the Christian's knowledge of the divine will turn to the performance of it. The result is not only a life consistent with the faith professed, but also "a life worthy of the Lord." When the will of God is carried out, God's purpose in strewing out the seed of the Word comes to fruition: The Christian will be "bearing fruit in every good work."

In his statement to the Colossians, the apostle has briefly outlined a program of knowledge leading to fruitfulness. What remains is that it becomes a process of Christian growth.

*Prayer Suggestion: Ask the Holy Spirit to nurture you through the Word so you may grow in grace and in the knowledge of Christ, your Savior.*

# Growing into Christian Maturity

When Prince Charles of England was four years old, it was reported that Queen Elizabeth tried to bring him up as a normal child. At that time he thought that all children were like him, and that every child's mother was a queen. In the ensuing years the world of Prince Charles opened up. He had to confront the reality of royalty to be ready to assume the responsibilities of a king some day. Unfortunately, that reality has been a rocky road for Charles.

Life doesn't always work out as we expect it to. Jacob's son Joseph probably envisioned himself as a prosperous, nomadic shepherd when he would grow up. Jeremiah certainly didn't want to be a prophet of doom and gloom.

The same can be said of countless people since Bible times. Joan of Arc likely expected to be a peasant wife. Martin Luther was encouraged to be a lawyer. We are told today that the best trained people are those who are capable and willing to be retrained for a new profession, a necessity because society is changing so quickly.

God has another approach to training, to the unending preparation for life: "The LORD gives wisdom, and from His mouth comes knowledge and understanding" (Prov. 2:6). That wisdom is the knowledge of who and what we are—and why—knowledge gained only through God-given faith in Jesus. The true wisdom that trains us is understanding how to live the faith that the Holy Spirit of God puts into our hearts.

*Prayer Suggestion: Ask God to bless your study of the Bible so you may prepare daily for a life of wisdom under God's direction.*

# Honest Work Is Honorable

In the play *The Solid Gold Cadillac,* all kinds of action develop when a small stockholder asks why the board chairman gets so much money for doing so little.

This question can be asked on all levels of life. Many are inclined to be critical of people on public welfare who do little work. But why should anybody, including a wealthy, prominent person, get paid much for doing little?

The Bible is not a textbook on economics, but it does lay down basic principles that apply across the board. One principle is that "the worker deserves his wages" (Luke 10:7). The Bible reminds all employers and bosses not to threaten or abuse anyone, knowing that they have a Master in heaven. Employees are encouraged to render faithful services. And to all, whether white collar or blue collar, whether board chairman or broom pusher, whether owners of solid gold Cadillacs or a compact car, God says, "If a man will not work, he shall not eat" (2 Thess. 3:10). (Obviously these words don't apply to persons unable to work because of old age or physical disability or because of the inability to find work.)

Honest, constructive work on all levels is honorable. Jesus of Nazareth worked with His hands as a carpenter until age 30. After that, He did the work of His heavenly Father: preaching the Word, healing the sick. Then these same hands were extended on Calvary's cross for the salvation of us all. God raised His Son from the dead, and He invites and enlists us all to work together with Christ in His kingdom.

*Prayer Suggestion: Pray that God may enable you to find pleasure in your work and prepare you for even greater services.*

# Well-Balanced Growth

For a cover of the *Saturday Evening Post,* Norman Rockwell painted the picture of a girl who was in a transitional stage. In one hand she held a doll, and in the other a picture of a motion picture actress whom she apparently admired.

As we pass from childhood to adulthood, our interests change. It is not healthy for a person to be a perpetual Peter Pan who never grows up. St. Paul writes, "When I was a child, I talked like a child, I thought like a child, I reasoned like a child. When I became a man, I put childish ways behind me" (1 Cor. 13:11). His point was that, amid all the changes in and about us, love does not change; it abides.

Along with physical and mental growth should go spiritual maturation. This the holy apostles stress. Peter urges us, especially those of us who are beginners in the Christian faith, to nourish ourselves with the milk of God's Word so we may grow up in our salvation (1 Peter 2:2).

Likewise, St. Paul tells us we are no longer infants, for we know the truth and speak the truth in love, as adults should. In so doing, "we will in all things grow up into Him who is the Head, that is, Christ" (Eph. 4:15). Christ is the Head, and all Christians are the growing members of His body.

Jesus Himself, while He was here on earth, "grew in wisdom and stature, and in favor with God and men" (Luke 2:52). He Himself searched the Scriptures, and He bids us do likewise, for they testify of Him as our Lord and Savior who gave His life that we may have eternal life.

***Prayer Suggestion:*** *Pray that the Holy Spirit may enable you to make progress in your Christian faith and love as you daily read the Bible.*

# Why a Guru When We Have Jesus?

Many North Americans, especially young people who have dropped out of the church, profess to benefit from the instruction of a guru. A guru is a religious teacher and spiritual guide in Hinduism.

One is prompted to ask, What can a guru teach us that we cannot learn better from Jesus? In His time Jesus was considered a teacher, a rabbi, and, if you will, a "guru." He taught the people on many occasions.

Is it inner peace that troubled people desire? Jesus not only talks about peace but also imparts it: "Peace I leave with you: My peace I give to you. I do not give to you as the world gives" (John 14:27).

Is it harmony with God that people desire? Jesus not only discusses such harmony but also conveys it: "I am the way and the truth and the life. No one comes to the Father except through Me" (John 14:6).

Is it freedom from the prison of oneself that people desire? Jesus not only extols freedom verbally but also outlines a simple program for achieving it: "If you hold to My teaching, you are really My disciples. Then you will know the truth, and the truth will set you free" (John 8:31–32).

Are people troubled because they know they did what was wrong, left undone what was right, and can do nothing to make restitution? Jesus not only has words of wisdom but also imparts salvation: "The Son of Man did not come to be served, but to serve, and to give His life as a ransom for many" (Mark 10:45).

*Prayer Suggestion:* Tell Jesus you come to Him as your teacher and Savior.

# Integrated Education

The yellow school bus is as much a symbol of public education today as was the little red schoolhouse in its day. In some areas of our country, the bus is used to effect racial integration in education. However much that may be needed, our children need even more a spiritual integration.

If children learn all the secular subjects but remain uninstructed as to the way of salvation through faith in Christ Jesus, their education is unbalanced and incomplete. Their growth is certainly not as symmetrical as was that of the boy Jesus, who "grew in wisdom and stature, and in favor with God and men" (Luke 2:52). This was coordinated mental, physical, spiritual, and social growth.

Further, if our children's total education is not integrated in the Christian sense, if all secular knowledge is in one drawer and spiritual knowledge in another, then we teach our children to live in two worlds and to become "split personalities." Then faith in the Savior and love for Him does not motivate learning and everyday living. Then we are bringing up a generation that believes that Christianity pertains only to church for one hour on Sunday morning, while the rest of the week is lived by worldly standards.

The admonition in today's Bible reading is to fathers, but it applies to parents in general, as well as to Christian parents collectively: the church. It too has the responsibility and privilege of bringing children to the Lord Jesus and keeping them with Him through Christian education, "teaching them to obey everything" (Matt. 28:20) He has commanded us.

*Prayer Suggestion: Thank Christ for teaching you His Gospel, and ask His help in teaching it to the next generation.*

# The Lispings of a Lily

In a well-known hymn line, William Cowper refers to his speech organ as "this poor lisping, stammering tongue." A flower, along with other members of the plant kingdom, has no tongue at all. Yet the lily manages to testify to us not only of the Creator's wisdom but also of our heavenly Father's tender love.

In a Civil War song, Julia Ward Howe has us sing, "In the beauty of the lilies Christ was born across the sea, With a glory in His bosom that transfigures you and me." It is doubtful that there were lilies in the stable where Jesus was born, and it is just as doubtful whether lilies adorned the tomb from which He rose on Easter morning. Yet lilies did play a part in His life and ministry. As a teacher He used them as visual aids. Who can forget the words of His outdoor sermon: "Consider how the lilies grow. They do not labor or spin. Yet I tell you, not even Solomon in all his splendor was dressed like one of these" (Luke 12:27).

As the lilies instruct us to rely on God, so they teach us also the beauty of innocence and holiness. Lilies often are an expression of purity. Of course, human beings are sinners all and are never totally pure. Only Jesus Christ was altogether without sin. As the heavenly High Priest who offered up Himself for our sins, Jesus was "holy, blameless, pure, set apart from sinners, exalted above the heavens" (Heb. 7:26).

Through faith in Him, we are now made pure, clean, and like lilies in God's sight, our robes have been made clean in the blood of Jesus Christ.

***Prayer Suggestion:*** *Pray that God strengthen your faith, for it covers you with the robe of Christ's righteousness.*

# Do You Remember?

Rosemary, a shrub of the mint family, is used for cooking and as perfume. The ancients thought that it strengthened memory, so in folklore, rosemary was the emblem of remembrance, fidelity, and constancy. As the name implies, the plant honors Mary, the mother of Jesus, of whom it is said, "Mary treasured up all these things and pondered them in her heart" (Luke 2:19).

But there was another Mary who remembered and is remembered. It was Mary, the sister of Martha and Lazarus in Bethany, who toward the end of Jesus' life anointed His head with an expensive ointment. When some quibbled, Jesus defended this act of devotion and said, "Wherever this Gospel is preached throughout the world, what she has done will also be told, in memory of her" (Matt. 26:13).

How good it is for all of us to remember. The Bible is full of exhortations to remember. The writer of Ecclesiastes stated, "Remember your Creator in the days of your youth" (12:1). The psalmist said, "Praise the LORD, O my soul, and forget not all His benefits—who forgives all your sins and heals all your diseases" (103:2–3). Jesus said, as He instituted the Holy Supper, "Do this in remembrance of Me" (Luke 22:19).

Do we remember? Yes, though we need not tie a string on our finger or grow rosemary plants in our gardens as memory helps. The goodness of God surrounding us every day won't let us forget. Now—this very day—remember someone with a gift, a token of love, a letter, a phone call.

*Prayer Suggestion: Ask God to help you recall His many blessings to you and thank Him for them.*

# More Free Time—For What?

The scarlet pimpernel, a plant in the primrose family, has interesting habits. At the approach of cloudy or rainy weather it closes up, making it the "poor man's weather glass." Further, it seems to observe hours on the clock, opening its flowers at seven and closing them at two.

The plant has counterparts in human society. Some people close up at the approach of adversity. The hours the scarlet pimpernel keeps are reminiscent of the shorter hours we have to work these days, thanks largely to our technology. Compared to the former six-day work week with its 14-hour days, we seem to observe "banker's hours," to say nothing of our long holiday weekends and generous vacations.

Freed from the drudgery and slavery of long work days, we enjoy more leisure. We can use it for R and R—rest and recreation. Leisure hours can be put to constructive use: spending more time with our families, carrying out do-it-yourself projects at home, reading and continuing one's education, doing community work. Especially can we do volunteer work for Christ and His church.

By both our labor and our leisure, we show our thankfulness to Jesus Christ, who, unlike the scarlet pimpernel, did not close shop at the approach of adversity, did not observe a schedule of set hours. He had work which the heavenly Father had given Him to do, namely, proclaim the Good News of the kingdom, heal the sick, cast out demons, and especially do the work of our salvation. That He did—all the way to Calvary.

***Prayer Suggestion:*** *Pray that God may direct you to the profitable use of your free time.*

# Rich in God's Love

When all goes well with people, they are said to be "in clover." Clover, the state flower of Vermont, is a symbol of prosperity, of good fortune. According to popular superstition, a four-leaf clover brings good luck.

Clover also has an association with religion. Early missionaries used the trefoil, the clover's triple leaf, as a symbol of the Holy Trinity. Not sheer luck, but He who is Father, Son, and Holy Spirit—three persons in one divine being—is the source of all blessings. Therefore, let all creatures here below join the heavenly host in praising God.

Yes, God is good. It is noteworthy that people who seem to have so few earthly goods consider themselves to be in the clover of God's rich grace. St. Peter, who never had much gold or silver, reminds the persecuted, impoverished readers of his first epistle that God's abundant mercy had given them "new birth into a living hope through the resurrection of Jesus Christ from the dead" (1 Peter 1:3).

Change the scene to a Roman prison where Paul sits, awaiting his execution. Yet he writes to Timothy, "The grace of our Lord was poured out on me abundantly, along with the faith and love that are in Christ Jesus" (1 Tim. 1:14). Grateful for this wonderful gift, the apostle was willing to give up his life for the sake of Him who died for him and rose again.

Your life may not seem to be a field of luscious red clover, but make no mistake about it: If the love of God in Christ has entered your life so you are both beloved and loving, you are immeasurably rich—you are in the clover.

*Prayer Suggestion: Pray that God may not only enrich you with His love but also enlist you to bring His love to others.*

# Follow Up the Clues!

How did Thomas James of Chillicothe, Ohio, early in the 1800s, find out there was iron ore at St. James, Missouri? He saw that Shawnee Indians, camping on his farm while en route to see the president in Washington, D. C., had smeared themselves with the red color of ore called hematite. That indicated the presence of iron. He followed up the clue and ran a successful smelter at St. James for 50 years.

God has not promised that Bible study will lead to material wealth, but He has promised spiritual riches. Bible study enriches the heart and mind, and quite often these bonanzas are found when we follow clues—clues that lead us to Jesus Christ, in whom are hid all wisdom and knowledge.

On the road from Jerusalem to Gaza, an Ethiopian official was reading the Bible as he rode in his vehicle. The section he read was from Isaiah 53:7, which reads, "He was led like a lamb to the slaughter, and as a sheep before her shearers is silent, so He did not open His mouth."

The Ethiopian had come upon a clue—a prophecy of the coming Christ—but he needed clarification of the clue. So he asked the evangelist Philip, who had come to ride with him, "Who is the prophet talking about, himself or someone else?" (Acts 8:34). Philip seized the opportunity to bear witness of Jesus Christ as the Lamb of God offered up for the sin of the world. Now the Ethiopian had found the key to the Scriptures. He had found the great treasure of forgiveness of sins in Christ the Savior.

*Prayer Suggestion: Pray that you may accept the Scripture's testimonies that always lead you to Christ to enrich you spiritually.*

# Three Great Truths

Bo Giertz, the Lutheran bishop of Gothenburg, Sweden, once wrote that these were the three big lies: (1) There is no God; (2) There is no devil; and (3) Everyone can be saved in his own way.

We can balance this out with three big truths. First, there is the true God, the Creator of us all and the Father of all believers. He is a God of justice, mercy, righteousness, and love.

The second great truth is this: Not only is there a devil, but there is also the one who destroyed Satan's kingdom and power: Jesus Christ, the Son of God—He who gave His life on the cross as an offering for the sins of the world.

The third great truth involves the Holy Spirit. He brings us to faith in Jesus Christ as the Savior. If it were true that everyone could be saved in his own way—by serving idols, by doing works, by bringing great sacrifices such as bestowing all his goods on the poor or even giving his body to be burned—then there would be no need for faith in Christ and no need for the Holy Spirit to implant the saving faith in us through the Gospel.

God said through St. Paul that faith comes through hearing the Word of God, the Gospel, which alone is the power of God unto salvation. Salvation is not humanly achieved; it is God's outright gift of grace.

We can put the three great truths like this: The Father thought (planned) it; the Son wrought it; and the Holy Spirit has brought it to us in the Gospel.

*Prayer Suggestion: Pray that your faith may be more firmly rooted in God the Father, the Son, and the Holy Spirit.*

# The Honor of Serving Our King

During the time when the emperor of Japan was considered divine (before the end of World War II), it was a traditional and coveted honor for some Japanese women to spend three or four days sweeping and cleaning the emperor's palace. It was a volunteer service cheerfully rendered.

In the New Testament we read of women who followed Jesus, ministering to Him from their substance. Having accepted Jesus as the promised Messiah and Son of God, they considered it a privilege to serve Him. Similarly, all Christians who have come to know the love of Jesus gladly honor Him by following Him and doing the works that please Him.

So it has always been. Believers in the Old Testament deemed it an honor and a delight to serve God—serve Him in His house and elsewhere, however lowly the service. Said the psalmist, "I would rather be a doorkeeper in the house of my God than dwell in the tents of the wicked" (Ps. 84:10). God's people, as Psalm 100:2 encourages them, serve the Lord with gladness, spontaneously, joyfully, and with pleasure. They do not regard it a chore or irksome duty or a reluctant performance to be held to a minimum.

We honor Jesus, our King, by serving Him, being prompted by the knowledge that He served and honored us. As St. John the Divine writes in Revelation, "To Him who loves us and has freed us from our sins by His blood, and made us to be a kingdom and priests to serve His God and Father—to Him be glory and power for ever and ever! Amen" (Rev. 1:5–6).

*Prayer Suggestion: Pray that you may find life's greatest delight in serving Christ Jesus, your King.*

# The Right Door

Jesus makes two points—one pertaining to spiritual leaders, the other to their followers—in His reference to the door or gate of a sheepfold.

First, He speaks of the gate as the shepherd-owner's proper means of entering the sheep enclosure, while thieves and robbers get in by climbing over the back fence. Such a shepherd stands for the properly called and ordained servant of the Word who comes to serve the church. This is in contrast to spiritual charlatans whose only desire is to exploit Christians. The true pastor comes, enters, and does his work in the name of the Good Shepherd. He preaches the Gospel of salvation.

In the second gate or door reference, Jesus shifts the meaning toward Himself as the Good Shepherd. He is to be recognized as the door to the sheepfold, the only proper entrance to God's kingdom. He is the only way to peace with God and to eternal life; there is no other way, no other door. He declares, "I am the gate; whoever enters through Me will be saved. He will come in and go out, and find pasture" (John 10:9).

The Good Shepherd came to give His life for the sheep. (Interestingly, the first people to be told this were the shepherds at Bethlehem.) Jesus died on Calvary's accursed cross so we might be blessed with life in Him.

There is no other entrance or exit in the Father's house of many mansions. Jesus is the only door. All who believe in Him as Lord and Savior are saved.

*Prayer Suggestion: Tell Christ that you are grateful that He came as the true shepherd and that He speaks to you through His under-shepherds.*

# The Extent of Jesus' Love

The Hessian soldiers whom King George III engaged to fight in the Revolutionary War knew nothing of love for England. They were mercenaries, hirelings. For every man killed, they received a sum of cash. Three men wounded counted as one dead man.

A hireling does only what he is paid to do. In that respect he differs from the owner, as Jesus said: "The hired hand is not the shepherd who owns the sheep. So when he sees the wolf coming, he abandons the sheep and runs away" (John 10:12).

In contrast, Jesus is the Good Shepherd. He is truly and lovingly concerned about His sheep. He cared so much that He laid down His life for our salvation. Had He been a hireling, that is, had He hoped for personal gain in playing the role of Savior, He would have fled when He saw Judas coming with a band of soldiers to arrest Him. Had He come to seek fame and fortune for Himself, He might have enacted the role of a mercenary, collecting cash or credits for every follower He gained.

But Jesus did the opposite. He emphatically declared that He had not come into the world to deprive people of their life, liberty, or happiness, but to give them life. To that end He, the Good Shepherd, met the ultimate test of love: He gave up His life for us on the cross, and this at a time when we were still His enemies. Then, on the third day, that great Shepherd of the sheep rose again from the dead, taking up again the life He had voluntarily laid down. Because He lives, we too live, now and forever.

*Prayer Suggestion: Pray that Jesus' great love to you may prompt you to thank Him and to share it with others.*

# Redeeming the Time

What can you do if you are confined or are taken away from your regular activities? Held in protective custody at a castle known as the Wartburg, Martin Luther began his translation of the New Testament Bible. The bird man at Alcatraz studied bird life and used this knowledge to good advantage. While in a Philadelphia prison for his failure to pay his debts, Charles Goodyear began making experiments in rubber.

The apostle Paul was also active in prison. There he carried on his work for Christ by writing epistles to mission congregations and evangelizing the prison guards. He set us a good example of redeeming the time, of making the most of every opportunity.

People say, "Here we are, confined in hospitals or other institutions—some of us sick, some weakened by advancing age, some in situations where there is no access to resources."

Whatever our circumstances, we can all pray, for ourselves and for others. We can do some upbeat, creative, positive thinking—like the psalmist who meditated on God's Word and wonderful works. We can write letters—if not long epistles, then shorter notes that express our appreciation for the good others have done. We can have friendly chats with people who feel down and out. We can do someone a favor or lend a helping hand. We can develop our skills and talents.

The best example of redeeming the time is our Savior Jesus Christ, who did the heavenly Father's work in our behalf. Christ's love to us prompts us to make the most of our time.

*Prayer Suggestion: Ask God to help you discover opportunities to serve Him with your time.*

# Who Is Your God?

Visitors in Rome are shown the Pantheon, a temple built about 2,000 years ago by Agrippa, the son-in-law of Caesar Augustus. As the name implies, it was a temple dedicated to all the gods.

The God who has revealed Himself in Holy Scripture and who is the Father of our Lord Jesus Christ is the one true God. When we worship Him, we need not be concerned as to whether we have overlooked any other deity. This seems to have worried the heathen from time to time. As said, Agrippa built a temple to all the gods; and in Athens, St. Paul saw an altar dedicated to the unknown god. People then tried to make sure that no supposed god or goddess was slighted.

The problem of people today is not serving too many gods but serving none at all—neglecting the one true God who made them, redeemed them, and gave them everything they have.

There is another aspect to the problem. Although most people do not formally worship the gods once honored in the Pantheon, they in effect do have idols. These little gods are things like money and ideas or purposes such as self-love or self-fulfillment.

Who is your God? Whom do you really love and serve? Surely it can be none other than the heavenly Father who has revealed His love in Jesus Christ. To believe in Him is to bring life and happiness, as our Lord prayed the night before His death, "This is eternal life: that they may know You, the only true God, and Jesus Christ, whom You have sent" (John 17:3).

*Prayer Suggestion:* Ask God to draw you closer to Him with His everlasting arms of love in Jesus, His Son.

# Suffering with Christ

Living in this vale of tears, Christ's modern followers must suffer, along with other people. Sickness and death, disappointments and heartache invade their homes too. Reverend Winemiller, in Tennessee Williams' play *The Eccentricities of a Nightingale,* didn't have an easy life ministering to his flock in a Mississippi town. He was aging, his wife's mental health was failing, and his daughter, Alma, was a misfit.

Sometimes Christ's disciples today must suffer in another way. They are persecuted for His sake. Jerusalem killed the prophets, and the apostles were to fare no better, as Jesus foretold, "A time is coming when anyone who kills you will think he is offering a service to God" (John 16:2). But to all His followers who must suffer, Jesus gives this promise: "Blessed are you when people insult you, persecute you and falsely say all kinds of evil against you because of Me" (Matt. 5:11).

Our Lord suffered a lot. St. Peter tells us why Jesus endured the ultimate persecution: "Christ suffered for you, leaving you an example … He Himself bore our sins in His body on the tree, so that we might die to sins and live for righteousness; by His wounds you have been healed" (1 Peter 2:21, 24).

Jesus did indeed leave us an example, that we should follow in His steps. When we do this, we shall be blessed, even as our Lord Himself was blessed. Having endured the cross, He knew only the joy of victory in our behalf and in token of it was seated at the right hand of the throne of God.

*Prayer Suggestion: Thank God for having blessed you amid all your sufferings and for giving you joy.*

# The Greater Baptism of Jesus

The man who preached in the wilderness as Christ's forerunner was called John the Baptizer. He was called that because baptizing people was an important part of his ministry. Shortly before His ascension our Lord referred to this baptism when He said, "John baptized with water, but in a few days you will be baptized with the Holy Spirit" (Acts 1:5). John's baptism was in its time a means through which the Holy Spirit was given to kindle and strengthen faith.

John's baptism, however, was temporary. It was superseded by the Baptism instituted by Jesus, the one greater than John, when He said: "Therefore go and make disciples of all nations, baptizing them in the name of the Father and of the Son and of the Holy Spirit" (Matt. 28:19).

Before the disciples went into all the world to preach, teach, and baptize, they received the Holy Spirit, who was poured out on them in extraordinary measure on Pentecost.

The greater Baptism instituted by Jesus is still in effect. It bears the unabridged power to work forgiveness of sins, to deliver from death and the devil, and to give eternal salvation. A man high in his 70s recently said that the Baptism certificates of him and his wife hang over their beds so every day they are reminded of the great blessings still coming to them through their Baptism. This because, as St. Paul has written, "[God] saved us through the washing of rebirth and renewal by the Holy Spirit, whom He poured out on us generously through Jesus Christ our Savior" (Titus 3:5–6).

***Prayer Suggestion:*** *Pray that God may bring your Baptism to mind when you are weak in faith.*

# Following the Christ Road

Sometimes finding and following the right road is made easy. In L. Frank Baum's *The Wonderful Wizard of Oz*, all that Dorothy has to do to get to the Emerald City is to follow the yellow brick road.

In everyday life, the choice of roads is often difficult—to move or to stay, to go or to wait, to buy or to sell. Sometimes the decisions are crucial, a matter of life and death—when surgery is involved or when a personal risk has to be taken.

Consider how much more bewildering life would be if we couldn't find the road to heaven—if we didn't know the true God, what His will is, how we can be at peace with Him. Those who don't know the right road may stay bewildered and lost.

But God has spared us this agony of choice by revealing to us the way of salvation by faith in the saving work of Jesus Christ, His Son. Jesus proclaimed Himself as the Way, the Truth, and the Life, as the only road to the heavenly Father. He became that road when by His atoning death and glorious resurrection He effected our reconciliation with God.

Having redeemed us, our Savior now invites us, "Follow Me!" We follow Him when we fulfill His will, do the works He desires, and in all things show love to our fellow human beings, friend or foe. This not to be saved, but because we are saved.

Following Jesus involves self-denial, taking up our crosses, and serving Him.

***Prayer Suggestion:*** *Express your gratitude to God for revealing to you the way of salvation in Jesus Christ.*

# Getting on the Right Boat

The expression "missing the boat" can have true-to-life meaning. In 1836 the Sisters of St. Joseph, a French order, began work in the St. Louis, Missouri, area. They awaited the arrival of two more members to open a school for deaf children. When they didn't come, the others feared that they were lost at sea. When the two finally showed up, the reason for their long delay was revealed: They had taken the wrong ship—one that took them to the West Indies instead of the United States.

"Missing the boat" had real meaning for the prophet Jonah, except that he intentionally took the wrong boat—one that took him far away from Nineveh where he was to preach God's Word. But God found the runaway missionary and sent him on his mission.

Ships heading for calm, untroubled seas are not necessarily the right ones for us to take. Jonah thought he would have smooth sailing in his escape from God, but he really got into a storm; he was on the wrong boat.

We need not hesitate to board the right ship, even if the voyage ahead seems stormy. The disciples on the storm-tossed boat on the Sea of Galilee were safe, for Jesus was with them. When we have Him with us—He who gave His life that we might live with Him forever—we are always on the right ship, for it is heading for the right port, for heaven.

So let the winds of life blow and the waves rise high; we are in the right boat.

*Prayer Suggestion: Pray for God's guidance in choosing the right way to go.*

# Peace and Order in the Church

Clarence Cannon, born in 1879 at Elsberry, Missouri, did more than put in his time as a United States representative; he was the author of "Rules of Procedure in Congress"—rules still followed there and elsewhere in the world.

To some, politics is a dirty word, and they avoid involvement in it. But they are wrong. When it is based on good order, politics benefits the citizens in state and nation.

God wants good order to prevail in all things. St. Paul tells the Corinthians, "Everything should be done in a fitting and orderly way" (1 Cor. 14:40). Again, he writes, "God is not a God of disorder but of peace" (1 Cor. 14:33). God has shown His orderliness in the universe He created. The heavenly bodies move precisely in their spheres. On earth, always in proper order, we have seedtime and harvest, cold and heat, summer and winter, day and night.

God created order in the church too, when He established His Son, Jesus Christ, as the head. Jesus became the head of the church when He gave His life for its redemption. Further, God gave the church apostles, prophets, evangelists, pastors, and teachers. To all members of Christ's body, the church, the Holy Spirit gives gifts and talents to be used for the good of all: wisdom and knowledge, administration, practical know-how in finances, and the like.

All is well in the church and in the local congregation when we take God's endowments and directives into consideration and do in the church what Clarence Cannon did in Congress: establish wise rules of procedure.

***Prayer Suggestion:*** *Pray that God grant you peace and an ordered life.*

# Loving and Giving

Americans give a reported 65 billion dollars annually for charities. Sometimes donors contribute to ease their conscience, to get rid of the solicitors, or to claim deductions on their income tax returns. This leaves out love.

The present-day word "charity" has wandered away from its original meaning. Charity, from the Latin *caritas*, meant dearness, affection, love. In early Christianity it designated the love of God for us and, in response, our love to God and to others. Writing in Greek, St. Paul used the word *agape*, which the King James Version of the Bible translates with "charity." In 1 Corinthians 13, for example, we read of the excellence of charity. The modern versions return to the original meaning: love.

Charity nowadays means giving for, or engaging in, works in behalf of the poor—works quite often performed impersonally, with no love involved.

The ideal is to put charity back into love and love back into charity. That would restore a person-to-person relationship and would cause our giving to flow from love. That would put the Gospel back into giving and helping, if not in community relationships, then certainly in the church or among Christians. The Gospel declares that God loved all people, then gave—gave His only Son to lay down His life for all.

Among Christian people, giving proceeds from love. Organized charities are necessary, but they do not—should not—replace personal giving prompted by personal love.

*Prayer Suggestion: Pray that your love to Christ may increase, to be expressed in words and deeds that show love in action.*

# The Rugged Road of Discipleship

The way of Christianity is both easy and hard. It depends on what aspect of it one is examining. Jesus expressed both views: "My yoke is easy and My burden is light" (Matt. 11:30), and "If anyone would come after Me, he must deny himself and take up his cross and follow Me" (Matt. 16:24).

On the one hand, the way to peace with God is like wearing an easy yoke and bearing a light burden because Jesus Christ carried the load—the whole load of our sins and their just deserts. We contribute nothing to forgiveness of our sins or to the inheritance of eternal life. Salvation is God's outright gift, which we receive by Spirit-created faith. This is not to say that grace is cheap or that we are going to heaven on a free ride, for our reconciliation with God cost Jesus Christ His life.

The way of Christianity is also hard, for our discipleship has to be fulfilled in the face of opposition. The world hates Christ and His followers as much today as it did then. The Christian's other two enemies, Satan and one's own sinful flesh, likewise make following Jesus a difficult journey. To live under Christ in His kingdom and to serve Him faithfully is like entering through a narrow gate and walking a hard road.

There are awards of grace for walking in Jesus' footsteps and for scaling the steep, rugged mountain with Him. You have a glorious view. You cannot help but admire the grandeur of the way on which Christ is leading you. To follow Jesus is to take the high road.

***Prayer Suggestion:*** *Thank Christ for opening the way of salvation, and ask Him for strength to follow Him.*

# A Few Can Destroy—and Quickly

One of the evils of war is that relatively few men can in a short time destroy what it took many people decades to build up. Only some 1,300 soldiers were involved in the minor Civil War battle at Pilot Knob, Missouri, on September 27, 1864. Yet as many as a thousand officers and men were casualties—all this in a battle that lasted only 20 minutes.

In civilian life, it doesn't take long for a few culprits to do much harm—terrorists with their bombs, arsonists, children with guns, the proverbial "black sheep" who with a few misdeeds can bring evil on generations of families.

The Bible speaks of a confrontation in the Garden of Eden, where the tempter and two persons, Adam and Eve, in very short order brought sin and death on the whole human race.

Thank God, the reverse is also true: a few people working together can do a tremendous amount of good. A good example of that are the 12 apostles, who in a few years turned the world upside down for Christ. Consider how St. Paul, assisted by Timothy, Titus, and others, spread the Gospel, bringing thousands to the saving faith in Jesus, the Savior.

Perhaps today you had—or will have—the opportunity to join others to do something good. You don't have to wait for the majority; you may not have to spend hours and hours in talking about it. So with a few friends and neighbors, you do it: clean up the trash in your neighborhood, prepare a playground for youngsters, visit the sick and the elderly.

***Prayer Suggestion:*** *Pray that God may show you the right thing to do and give you the strength to do it, to improve life for yourself and for others.*

# A Childish or a Childlike Faith?

At the burial service of the well-known musician Meredith Willson, a fellow composer paid him this tribute: "He had … the genuine humility and childlike lack of guile that Christ wanted all of us to have."

Great talents, a lifetime of accomplishments, but a humble attitude is what our Lord desired His followers to have. When the disciples argued as to who of them was the greatest in His kingdom, He said, "I tell you the truth, unless you change and become like little children, you will never enter the kingdom of heaven. … whoever humbles himself like this child is the greatest in the kingdom of heaven" (Matt. 18:3–4).

Christ did not advocate a childish but a childlike faith, that is, unquestioning trust and confidence in His love. Such a faith not only survives, it grows. It adds Christian knowledge and understanding and spiritual maturity through the diligent study of God's Word. The apostle Peter urges, "Grow in the grace and knowledge of our Lord and Savior Jesus Christ" (2 Peter 3:18).

No matter how long we live or how much wisdom we acquire, this remains our faith, namely, that God so loved us all that He gave His beloved Son, Jesus Christ, to gain salvation by His obedient life, atoning death, and triumphant resurrection. On this foundation we build our Christianity, striving every day to grasp more and more of "how wide and long and high and deep is the love of Christ" (Eph. 3:18).

*Prayer Suggestion: Pray for a faith that takes God at His Word, also when He calls for humility.*

# Keeping Our Spiritual Health

Health books, those dealing with diets and physical exercise, sell well these days.

The Bible can be called a book concerned with one's spiritual health—with one's total well-being, for spiritual health has a wholesome effect on the body also. The Bible speaks on spiritual diets. St. Peter tells beginners in Christianity, "Like newborn babies, crave pure spiritual milk, so that by it you may grow up in your salvation" (1 Peter 2:2). This "pure spiritual milk" is the Word of God. Its basics are the Law that convicts us of sin and the Gospel to declare Jesus Christ to us as the Savior, crucified for our sins and risen from the dead.

God desires that we grow in the grace and knowledge of our Lord and Savior Jesus Christ. For this we need solid foods, the meat and potatoes of God's Word. This points to continuing, lifelong Bible study.

The Bible is also God's book for spiritual exercises. Such exercises help us get rid of the flab of sin and build up the muscles of faith.

Here is a resolution in which all Christians join: "Let us throw off everything that hinders and the sin that so easily entangles, and let us run with perseverance the race marked out for us. Let us fix our eyes on Jesus, the Author and Perfecter of our faith, who for the joy set before Him endured the cross, scorning its shame, and sat down at the right hand of the throne of God" (Heb. 12:1–2).

*Prayer Suggestion:* Ask the Holy Spirit to lead you deeper into God's Word and draw you closer to Jesus, who is the core of God's Word.

# Christ's Cleansing Water

A "signature in stone" that the ancient Romans left in every land where they ruled were buildings for bathing and for immersing themselves in healing waters. Tourists in England can visit such a place in Bath, a city near Bristol, established in A.D. 75. To give this health resort a religious touch, the Romans also built a temple to Minerva near the baths.

A "signature" of Christians is the objects we build for Holy Baptism, the washing of water by the Word, for taking a spiritual bath. By means of water and the Word, our Lord makes people His own. All that Christ procured for their salvation when He died and rose again—forgiveness of sins, reconciliation and peace with God, power to lead a life worthy of their Christian calling—all this is offered, transmitted, and sealed in Holy Baptism.

St. Paul says, "Don't you know that all of us who were baptized into Christ Jesus were baptized into His death? We were therefore buried with Him through baptism into death in order that, just as Christ was raised from the dead by the glory of the Father, we too may live a new life" (Rom. 6:3–4).

Christians gather around the sin-cleansing, healing water of Baptism to become Christ's own and to be brothers and sisters to one another. St. Paul does indeed say, "The body is a unit, though it is made up of many parts. ... So it is with Christ. For we were all baptized by one Spirit into one body—whether Jews or Greeks, slave or free" (1 Cor. 12:12–13). What a unifying power is Baptism!

*Prayer Suggestion: Ask God that the power of Holy Baptism may continue to work in you to give you strength for Christian living.*

# Weeds and Wheat Together: For How Long?

God's rejection of the wicked and His intervention for the righteous is not a question of "whether" but of "when."

Sometimes it seems to us that the mills of divine justice are grinding too slowly, if at all. We wonder why doesn't God intervene in behalf of justice in this world. Why doesn't He stop the hand that destroys, put an end to wars and conflicts, stop Satan in his tracks, separate the evil from the good in the outward fellowship of the church?

Because God's time schedule often differs from human calendars and clocks, some people assume that God has completely withdrawn from human affairs.

This is a false conclusion to draw. God is deeply involved in the affairs of world and church because He is concerned about them. In His hand, all that people call destiny is not blind fate but the enactment of events in which God has the final say. It is not a question of whether God will intervene and cause His good and gracious will to triumph; it is a question of when.

Jesus makes this plain in His parable of the tares among the wheat. Believers and unbelievers, genuine Christians and hypocrites, are in mutual company when and where the Word of God is proclaimed. In this life, given our inability to use a truth serum or a lie-detector test to determine whether every confessing church member is a true Christian, we have no choice but to "let both grow together until the harvest." That is the end-time, Judgment Day, when God Himself will effect the separation. In the meantime we pray, "Lord of the harvest, grant that we wholesome grain and pure may be."

***Prayer Suggestion:*** *Ask God to make you fruitful in every good work by increasing your faith in Jesus.*

# Christ's Finished Symphony

In October of 1822 Franz Schubert began writing his "Eighth Symphony in B Minor." After he had completed the first two movements, he delivered the manuscript to the sponsoring music society—and it was hailed a masterpiece. But for unknown reasons, Schubert did not complete the total work. Hence it is known as the "Unfinished Symphony."

Jesus Christ is the great composer of the symphony of salvation. When He, the Son of God, was obedient to God's Law in our behalf, and when He, as the great Prophet, proclaimed God's kingdom by word and deed, He completed, we might say, the first two movements of His symphony.

He came to do the heavenly Father's will and to finish His work. On the eve of His death, knowing that His work of redemption was certain of accomplishment, He said to the Father, "I have brought You glory on earth by completing the work You gave Me to do" (John 17:4). The next day, before bowing His head in death, He declared, "It is finished" (John 19:30).

Because our Savior's great symphony was finished, as attested by His resurrection, we can join in the chorus of praise to the enthroned Lamb: "You were slain, and with Your blood You purchased men for God from every tribe and language and people and nation. You have made them be a kingdom and priests" (Rev. 5:9–10).

Christ's completion of His symphony is not academic; it is essential and most vital to our Christian faith.

*Prayer Suggestion:* Give thanks to Jesus that He finished His symphony of your salvation, and ask Him to continue His work in you.

# The Reopened Channel

The Suez Canal in Egypt was opened in 1869 to connect the worlds of Europe and Asia. The ruler of Egypt commissioned Verdi to compose the opera "Aida," a love story set in Egypt, to commemorate the event.

The connecting link between the worlds of heaven and earth is none other than Jesus, the Mediator between God and sinful humankind. In Him God reconciled the world to Himself. Christ's coming for this purpose represents the greatest love story ever told.

The coming of Christ as Savior was made necessary because the communication between God and the human race was broken off because of sin. A great gap had developed. The channel had to be reopened, and only Jesus could do this.

During the Arab-Israeli War in 1967, the Suez Canal was closed to shipping. Before long the waterway was unnavigable because of silting, sunken ships, and other obstructions. In the 1970s the canal was reopened and cleaned up.

That is what Christ did when He became, as the epistle to the Hebrews states, "the Mediator of the new covenant." This covenant was far superior to the one established at Mount Sinai, and His priesthood far greater than Aaron's. This validity is because of "the sprinkled blood that speaks a better word than the blood of Abel" (Heb. 12:24). Truly, "the blood of Jesus, His Son, purifies us from all sin," as St. John testified (1 John 1:7). The channel is open again.

*Prayer Suggestion: Thank God for making it possible for you to approach Him in prayer, asking Him, for Jesus' sake, to keep you reconciled to Him as His child.*

# It All Comes Down to Love

Hillel, the great Old Testament religion teacher, once took up a dare. He claimed he could recite all of the wisdom of the law of Moses while standing on one leg. When challenged, he recited, "All the wisdom of the Torah consists in this: 'Thou shalt love the Lord with all thy heart, and all thy soul, and all thy strength, and thy neighbor as thyself.'"

A similar challenge had been given to Jesus long before Hillel. When asked to name the great commandment in the law, Jesus, too, used these quotes from Deuteronomy 6:5 and Leviticus 19:18. As Jesus said, on these two statements—love to God and love to the neighbor—depend the law and the prophets, all of God's revelation.

People today will have no problem with the Word of God—whether the Law (the Ten Commandments) or the Gospel promises God spoke through the prophets and apostles—when they love God and their fellow human beings. The entire religion God has revealed to us in Holy Scripture can be summed up in the one word "love."

Our love to God and to neighbor, however, is not spontaneous, not something that comes naturally. It is God's gift. It is a derivative of God's great love to us, as demonstrated in the giving of His Son, Jesus Christ, for our salvation. In response to that love, as created in us by the Holy Spirit in bringing us to the saving faith, we love God and all those whom He loves. Then everything falls into place. When we love God, we will gladly do the next thing: Keep His commandments.

*Prayer Suggestion: Pray for the help of the Holy Spirit to increase in love to God and the practice of it among people.*

# Love and Loyalty in Marriage

Love in marriage becomes all the more effective when it expresses itself in terms of mutual regard, helpfulness, and loyalty. Much good material has been written on the subject, but nothing surpasses the words of St. Paul in Ephesians 5. He tells husbands and wives to love each other. Such love looks away from selfishness, from self-fulfillment at the cost of love to the other spouse. In marriage, the partners nourish and cherish their mutual relationship, sacrificing personal advantage for its sake. The apostle declares as he introduces this section, "Submit to one another out of reverence for Christ" (v. 21).

In a good marriage relationship husbands and wives add loyalty to love. They come to each other's defense. A good example of that is found in United States history. On June 25, 1875, at Little Big Horn in Montana, General George A. Custer and his 264–member Seventh Cavalry Regiment were defeated and died in battle. When Custer was blamed for this loss, his wife, Elizabeth, spent the next 55 years in writing and lecturing to defend him.

It is good to note how love and loyalty speak even when husbands or wives are long dead. Love is enduring.

Love in marriage becomes enduring when it is connected with reverence for Christ, when it comes as a response to Christ's self-sacrificing love. Christ loves us and gave Himself for us all, that He might redeem us with His blood, and sanctify and cleanse us through His Word and Spirit.

Christ's love endures; so can ours, with His help.

***Prayer Suggestion:*** *Pray for a greater measure of love toward Christ and those who share your life.*

# Stand Firm

"Stand firm then," St. Paul tells us (Eph. 6:14), with the whole armor of God when the forces of evil attack us. Don't surrender; don't run away. Stand!

The verb "stand" is used in many combinations. There is the call: "Stand up, stand up, for Jesus, you soldiers of the cross." We do this when we bear witness of Him as the one crucified for the sins of all. We do this when in matters of faith we stand up to be counted.

A bit different is the emphasis in the charge to stand for—to stand for the truth of God's Word. It has been said that, unless we stand for something, we are apt to fall for anything.

An old spiritual declares that we Christians stand on the promises of God. We take our stand on the promise that God loves us in Christ, that He made us His children, that He cares, that He hears our prayers.

From the movie industry comes the expression stand in. When the scene is being prepared, someone takes the place of the actor on the set. In Christian life, many needs and opportunities arise for us to stand in and fill someone's place—in church, at home, at work.

Finally, when a courtroom witness has completed his or her testimony, the judge tells that person to stand down. Everywhere in Christendom and the world, God has His witnesses and workers. He is pleased when they speak and work for Him. But the time comes when He says, "It is enough; it is time for you to stand down, to come home."

***Prayer Suggestion:*** *Ask God to give you the strength to stand firmly in the faith in every situation of life.*

# Bad News, Good News

Job knew what bad news was. One after another came the messengers of doom: not only his cattle and sheep but also his children had perished. But note Job's reaction to his losses: "The LORD gave and the LORD has taken away; may the name of the LORD be praised" (Job 1:21).

Psalm 112:7 says of the righteous man, "He will have no fear of bad news." True, no one can be entirely unmoved or indifferent to bad news, but the righteous person—the one who is right with God—will not be bowled over by adverse tidings. Because his or her trust is in God, that person is able to cope with the situation.

This is possible because for God's children there is always Good News. The Good News not only outweighs the bad, but it draws them closer to the heavenly Father, who supports and sustains them. The assurance of God's love in Jesus Christ is a constant factor in the lives of Christians, be the days evil or good. Parents who don't love their children let them grow up wild. Parents who care about them prove their love by correcting and guiding their children.

Bad news is bearable because of the Good News of God's love. This Good News in the highest sense is the Gospel of salvation in Jesus Christ. At Christ's birth the angel proclaimed this Gospel, "I bring you good news of great joy ... a Savior has been born for you" (Luke 2:10–11).

Whatever is bothering you, you can live with it, for God so loved you that He gave you the best He had: His own Son.

*Prayer Suggestion: Pray that in times of trial the Holy Spirit may bring the Good News of Christ to your remembrance and sustain you.*

# The Joyful Outlook on Life

For some people, even for those perfectly healthy and in possession of needful things, life is dreary, like a cloudy day.

On the other hand, it is often the heavily burdened person who is thankful, hopeful, joyful. Much suffering has not deprived such a person of the treasure of happiness. A man who spent a great deal of time in prison and faced death on many occasions was St. Paul. He could live with seeming contradictions; he could be, in his own words, "sorrowful, yet always rejoicing" (2 Cor. 6:10).

Pessimism looks at the dark side of things. Instead of saying that a glass is half full, it is to the pessimist half empty. Nothing is ever half won; it is always half lost. Pessimism cannot find delight in wildflowers, for it sees them as weeds.

The Christian's joyful outlook on life is not fantasy or blue-sky optimism, but realism. It has a real foundation. It can exist when dark clouds blot out the sun, for it does not depend on changeable weather, nor on fickle human emotions, nor on here-today-gone-tomorrow success. It rests not on human beings but on Jesus Christ, who for us and for our salvation passed through the dark night of suffering and death only to rise again on Easter morning. The Holy Spirit He sends us is the author of our faith in the Savior and of all its fruits, as St. Paul has written, "The fruit of the Spirit is love, joy, peace ..." (Gal. 5:22–23).

Look out your window. What do you see? A glass half empty or half full? A field of weeds or of wheat?

***Prayer Suggestion:*** *Ask God to help you find the joy Jesus has promised you.*

# Being Honest with Ourselves and with Others

When Catherine the Great made a trip through southern Russia, she was impressed by the villages along the way. Unknown to her, these were fake villages, built by General Gregory Potemkin, to make the queen think that the peasants lived well.

Our hearts build such "Potemkin villages" all the time. The master deceiver, Satan, paints beautiful pictures for us. When tempting Jesus, he "showed Him all the kingdoms of the world and their splendor," adding, "All this I will give You … if You will bow down and worship me" (Matt. 4:8–9). It was a false world that Satan showed.

The boasting worshiper in Jesus' parable of the Pharisee and the publican built his own "Potemkin village" of pretended personal virtues. On display, for his own satisfaction and the admiration of others, were his would-be piety, generosity, self-righteousness. He painted everything, even his pride, in bright, attention-gaining colors.

It is time to look at our own lives. What is the setting of my life that I want others to see? Am I bearing genuine fruit, or am I a Christmas tree with all kinds of ornaments—glittering tinsel, gilded nuts, make-believe fruits?

The Bible declares, "He who conceals his sins does not prosper" (Prov. 28:13). However, "If we confess our sins, He is faithful and just and will forgive our sins and purify us from all unrighteousness" (1 John 1:9). We can be honest with ourselves, coming to God just as we are, for "the blood of Jesus, His Son, purifies us from all sin" (1 John 1:7).

*Prayer Suggestion: Pray for God's help to seek whatever is true and honest as a fruit of faith in Jesus.*

# The Good That Fire Can Do

Fire can be a fearsome force—a forest fire, flames destroying a home, a fire storm raging out of control in a city.

Fire can also be beneficial—not only in that it warms our homes, creates heat for smelters and foundries, and consumes trash. Thanks to fire, much of what is dead and destructive can be burned up. The world needs this kind of controlled cleansing.

When Jesus speaks of setting the world on fire, He is not referring to the destroying fire of the Last Day. Christ refers to the fire of affliction attending those who commit themselves to Him. Both He and His followers must submit to a "baptism of fire." This fire separates and divides people, even in the home. It kindles the anger of Christ's enemies. It brings pain and can touch off persecution.

The fire that Christ touched off and in which He would be engulfed, painful as it might be, was beneficial. As judgment, this fire consumes evil. As grace, it warms our hearts and enlightens our minds. The Holy Spirit, whom we address in a Pentecost hymn as "holy Fire," brings us to faith in Jesus Christ, who by passing through suffering and death became our Savior.

Is there fire in your life? Consider that it may be necessary to burn away the dross of sin and to purify your heart for a more dedicated life in Christ.

*Prayer Suggestion: Ask your Lord for patience and strength to survive all the fires of affliction to the glory of His name.*

# Be Ready!

Breaking and entering, burglarizing homes and stores, robbing and stealing are ancient crimes. Jesus Himself said, "If the owner of the house had known at what hour the thief was coming, he would not have let his house be broken into" (Luke 12:39). Through the centuries, human nature hasn't changed.

The lack of alertness is another old human failing. Here, too, people have not changed. Jesus Himself stresses the need for readiness. And well He might! Many people today are preoccupied with buying and selling, "eating and drinking, marrying and giving in marriage" (Matt. 24:38). They give little thought to being ready for Christ's impending return to judgment at an unannounced date.

The reminder is in place: "Be ready, because the Son of Man will come at an hour when you do not expect Him" (Matt. 24:44). The hour is late. The sun is setting on our world and on "life's little day." As Alfred Tennyson has well said, "Sunset and evening star, And one last call for me."

Christians are ready to receive their Lord when they continue in fellowship with Him, confident that He who suffered, died, and rose again for their salvation is always ready to receive them.

*Prayer Suggestion: Pray for readiness to receive the Lord Jesus when He comes. Thank Him for giving you so much to look forward to.*

# The Right Cover-Up

The effort of government and business to cover up wrong-doing is not new. Ever since the fall, people have tried to cover up sin or to misdirect attention by transferring the blame elsewhere. In the Garden of Eden Adam blamed Eve for his disobedience, and Eve blamed the serpent.

Judas Iscariot covered up not only his thefts from the disciples' treasury, but he also disguised his intent of betrayal by asking in the Upper Room, "Surely not I, Rabbi?" (Matt. 26:25). In the Garden of Gethsemane he tried to conceal his bitter enmity against Jesus by kissing Him.

The cover-up of sin doesn't work. The writer of Proverbs (28:13) declares, "He who conceals his sins does not prosper, but whoever confesses and renounces them finds mercy." The right way to deal with sin is to repent of it and confess it to God. In faith, we lay that sin on Jesus Christ, the Lamb of God, who made atonement for the sins of the whole world. Oh, what a friend we have in Jesus, for He bears all our sins and griefs! Because He has taken away our sin, we forsake it, leave it behind, and no longer worry about it. Not the cover-up of sin but the open acknowledgement of it in repentance and faith opens us to God's forgiving grace.

The psalmist exclaims, "Blessed is he whose transgressions are forgiven, whose sins are covered" (Ps. 32:1)—indeed not covered up by deceit but fully covered by the forgiveness Jesus has earned. If you are haunted by past sins, confess them and know that God has dealt with them by covering them with the forgiving blood of Jesus Christ.

*Prayer Suggestion: Give thanks to Jesus Christ for having atoned for all your sins on Calvary's cross.*

# God's Word Can Change Things

Some people regard words as useless. They may refer to something said as "mere words," adding that "words are cheap" or that "deeds are what we need, not words."

Yet words can be powerful and effective. A word or two, like "I do" or "I will," make for a marriage and then a family. A word or two of kindly advice can turn a discouraged person around. A few words from a person of authority can send another on an urgent mission, like the centurion of Capernaum said, "I tell this one, 'Go,' and he goes; and that one, 'Come,' and he comes" (Luke 7:8).

How much greater is the power of the words God speaks, for with Him, words are deeds! Whatever God says, you can consider it done.

Jesus Christ, the Son of God, declares, "The words I have spoken to you are spirit and they are life" (John 6:63). This bespeaks divine power. The Gospel that He proclaimed—that God loved the world so much that the Son came to give His life a ransom for all, that He would die but rise again to draw all people to Him—is the Word of God, bringing salvation to all who believe it.

The Holy Spirit, who was active with the Father and the Son at the creation of the world, is the Lord and giver of life. He is imparted into our hearts by the Word of Christ, and He creates life in us.

What power is in the Word of God, the Word of the Father, the Son, and the Holy Spirit! Let it come into your heart.

*Prayer Suggestion: Ask God to make His Word a force in your life, and thank Him for every blessing of the Word.*

# What Christ's Recruitment Poster Says

A man who lived the rather comfortable life of a scribe said to Jesus, "I will follow You wherever You go" (Luke 9:57). He apparently was not aware of the rigors of discipleship. So our Lord tells him, "Foxes have holes and birds of the air have nests, but the Son of Man has no place to lay His head" (Luke 9:58).

Christ is fair with people who have some interest in His ministry and mission. He does not recruit them by falsely promising: "Become a Christian and you will be free of problems; you will enjoy peace and happiness, honor and distinction. Join up with Me and see the world—see exotic and exciting places!" Nothing like that! Instead, His recruitment poster says, "If anyone would come after Me, he must deny himself and take up his cross and follow Me" (Matt. 16:24).

But our Lord also says, "Come to Me, all you who are weary and burdened, and I will give you rest. ... My yoke is easy and My burden is light" (Matt. 11:28, 30). Discipleship is most satisfying and pleasant to those who know that Christ for their sake became poor so by His poverty they might become rich. Their love to Him takes the edge off self-denial for His sake.

All who are following Jesus, especially if their loyalty previously lay elsewhere, can join the hymn writer in saying:

> Alas! that I so late have known Thee,
> who art the Fairest and the Best;
> nor sooner for my Lord could own Thee,
> our highest Good, our only Rest.

**Prayer Suggestion:** *In your prayer renew your allegiance to your blessed Lord and pledge Him your complete loyalty.*

# Up from Small Beginnings

Jesus spoke in a parable about the mustard seed, the smallest of all seeds. When it is planted, however, it grows and grows, from a large garden plant to a tree large enough for the birds to find shelter in its branches.

The kingdom of heaven is like that. After Christ's ascension, Christianity had a small beginning; only a dozen men went out to preach the Gospel. They didn't use force, high-pressure methods, or trickery. They simply told people that Jesus, having died on the cross for the forgiveness of sins, had risen from the dead, overcoming death for all sinners. God blessed their preaching, and the church grew.

The life of an individual Christian usually has small beginnings too. Faith is like a mustard seed. But it grows, bringing forth the fruits of faith. Faith becomes like a tree laden with the fruit of the Holy Spirit: love, joy, peace, patience, kindness, goodness, faithfulness, gentleness, and self-control.

Likewise, small beginnings often mark our Christian vocation. We need not hesitate to start at the bottom. In 1921 the world-famous actor Sir John Gielgud began his career in London's Old Vic Theater. He was not an instant star. He had only a one-line part in Shakespeare's play *Henry V.* From that he went on to more important roles.

So, too, in our Christian life. Our Lord gives His "Well done!" to faithful servants, saying, "You have been faithful with a few things; I will put you in charge of many things. Come and share your master's happiness!" (Matt. 25:23).

*Prayer Suggestion: Pray for God's help to grow daily in your faith and in the faithful performance of your work.*

# Does Your Word Carry Weight?

Some people complain that their words are not heeded. When there is no obedience, compliance, and cooperation, the words of parents, of teachers, of law-enforcing officers do indeed carry no weight.

In Shakespeare's play *Henry IV* someone boasts, "I can call spirits from the vast deep." Another replies, "Why so can I, or so can any man, but will they come when you call them?" There is a vast difference between calling someone and having that someone respond.

It was different with the centurion of Capernaum. He said, "I tell this one, 'Go' and he goes; and that one, 'Come,' and he comes. I say to my servant, 'Do this' and he does it" (Luke 7:8).

Whether our words carry weight depends largely on ourselves. People will honor you for standing behind your words. If you are a parent or a teacher, you must mean what you say and say what you mean.

Whether or not our words carry weight, they will never carry the power of God's Word. He is almighty, always capable of fulfilling His promises. He promised to send His Son for our salvation, and He kept that promise. So, too, His promise to hear our prayers: "[God] who did not spare His own Son, but gave Him up for us all—how will He not also, along with Him, graciously give us all things?" (Rom. 8:32).

God's Word carries weight; His words enable our word to do likewise.

***Prayer Suggestion:*** *Pray that the words you speak may always be truthful and be spoken in Christian love.*

# A Friend Always with Us

Along the rugged Italian coast not far from Genoa, an unusual statue of Christ stands 56 feet under water. His hands are lifted up to bless all who perish at sea.

Statues of Christ, whether in churches or out in the open like the impressive Christ of the Andes, remind us that Christ is Lord. He is everywhere, even in the sea. Christ demonstrated that power when He stilled the storm on the Sea of Galilee and brought the disciples safely to shore.

A power so great—and especially a power motivated by so great a love and compassion—certainly extends also to our lives. It finds and befriends us in hospitals, in our homes, at work, or in our travels on land, sea, and in the air. He has promised, "I am with you always" (Matt. 28:20).

Sometimes we have to make a trip. It may be to attend to a sick friend or relative far away (or even to accompany them to their last resting place). Our work may require travel, and this takes us away from our loved ones. Young people must leave home to enter college or take a job. The elderly may have to move into a nursing home. Our trips may not be easy, but this is sure: Jesus is with us wherever we go.

What a friend, then, we have in Jesus! He bore all our sins and griefs, taking them with Him to the cross and the tomb and leaving them there. He exchanges our guilt and grievances for peace with God, peace with our fellow human beings, peace with ourselves, and even peace in ourselves. Surely, such a friend will not abandon us in life's dark hours.

*Prayer Suggestion: Thank the Lord Jesus for His presence with you at all times and in all places. He has promised this.*

# Worshiping God Only

Some people trust in things made rather than in the Maker of things. St. Paul writes in the opening chapter of his letter to the Romans (1:25) that the heathen have "worshiped and served created things rather than the Creator."

A very open and obvious form of idolatry is to worship things God made: the sun, moon, and stars; animals; even human beings. Another form is to bow down and worship things people themselves have made: statues of wood and stone; images; any representation of God. God forbids this, telling His people not to make for themselves graven images. A more recent translation reads, "You shall not make for yourself an idol in the form of anything in heaven above or on the earth beneath or in the waters below" (Ex. 20:4).

Another less obvious form of idolatry is trusting in and loving earthly things, although not worshiping them. The Bible gives many examples of this, and they can be duplicated from our modern society: loving money more than God, considering pleasure to be one's highest good, trusting in medical technology more than in God.

God has placed many things at our disposal for rightful use, but these are not substitutes for God. "Fear the LORD your God, serve Him only" (Deut. 6:13). As the Mediator between God and humankind, Jesus has atoned for our sins and reconciled us to God as His children. He has made it possible for us to worship God and serve Him only. What a privilege!

*Prayer Suggestion: Ask God to help you turn your heart more and more from earthly things to Him, the source of all blessings.*

# Christ Died for One and All

After the Civil War, a man very diligently and devotedly attended to the grave of a man who fell in the battle of Chickamauga. He was asked whether this man had been a brother or other close relative. "No," he said, "this man is special to me since he died in my place. I was drafted to go into the army, but since I had a family, he volunteered to take my place. He died for me."

Many people today are alive because of the heroic deeds of others: parents, law-enforcement officers, firefighters, lifeguards, and the like.

Does not all this remind us of the great love of Jesus Christ, who died so we might live? You and I, being sinners, ought to have gone to the cross to die, for the wages of sin is death. But here comes Jesus Christ, volunteering to take our place. He, the sinless one, was treated as the consummate sinner, as the most lowly criminal, so you and I, believing in Him as our Savior, might go free.

True, other people also have laid down their lives for loved ones. The love of Jesus, however, exceeds all human deeds of devotion, for He was willing and able to die not only for one person but for the whole human race. As Paul declares, "He died for all," for He loved all, the whole human race—"that those who live should no longer live for themselves but for Him who died for them and was raised again" (2 Cor. 5:15).

Because Christ was the one for all, we all, in gratitude, are now for the one.

*Prayer Suggestion: Ask for the help of the Holy Spirit to dedicate your life to Jesus Christ, the best friend you ever had.*

# Truth with Love

A man in the barber chair was liberally sprinkling his conversation with profanity, using God's name in vain. But when the barber thanked him for the money he paid for the haircut, the man said, "Don't thank me; thank the Lord who gave it to me." Though we might wonder about a faith that takes God's name in vain, what the man said was true: Every gift we have comes from God. Truth is truth regardless of who speaks it—a nonbeliever, a robot, or the devil himself.

Didn't the devil say through a demon-possessed man that Jesus is "the Son of the Most High God" (Mark 5:7)?

Truth is truth, no matter who speaks it. How much better, though, when people who speak the truth believe it, for then they speak with conviction. Yet how much more effective when the truth is spoken in love! When St. Paul said to the jailer of Philippi "Believe in the Lord Jesus, and you will be saved" (Acts 16:31), you can be sure that he said it with kindness to the man who had earlier beaten him. The apostle spoke the truth in love—what a difference that made!

What a difference it makes today, when in our association with other people in the home, at work, in school, at church, or while traveling, we speak the truth in love! Then what we say comes from a source deeper than the mouth; it comes from the heart. The apostle bids us, "Be kind and compassionate to one another, forgiving each other, just as in Christ God forgave you" (Eph. 4:32). Out of love to Jesus Christ, who died to save you, we can speak the truth with kindness.

***Prayer Suggestion:*** *Pray that the Holy Spirit's twin fruits of truthfulness and love may abound in your life.*

# Why We Love Baptism

Does the devil hate water? He does when it's the water of Holy Baptism, which, joined to the Word of God, brings forgiveness of sins, delivers from death and the devil, and gives eternal salvation to all who continue in their baptismal grace. Holy Baptism unites us with Christ and makes us the beneficiaries of the forgiveness and freedom Christ has gained for us. St. Paul writes, "All of you who were baptized into Christ have clothed yourselves with Christ" (Gal. 3:27). Those baptized are living their lives in close fellowship with Christ, rising daily from sin and walking in the newness of life.

It is not hard to see how the devil makes his hatred known. He does this by trying to dissuade people from being baptized. He gives them wrong ideas. At the time of St. Augustine in the fourth century, Satan had people believing that they should postpone their Baptism until shortly before they died, lest by their sinning they render the sacrament ineffective.

That the devil hates Baptism is evident also from the fact that he tempts baptized people to forget all about the covenant the triune God made with them at their Baptism. They had promised to renounce the devil and all his ways; faith engendered in Baptism gave them the power to do so. But many play into the devil's hand by living contrary to their promise.

God's people, joined by the angels of heaven, who rejoice over the conversion of every sinner, love the water of Baptism, not because the water itself has magical power but because it is connected with the power and promises of God's Word.

*Prayer Suggestion: Pray to Father, Son, and Holy Spirit to keep you mindful of your baptismal covenant.*

# Once Deformed, Now Transformed

The movie "The Elephant Man" is the story of a deformed man who achieves dignity. Human dignity includes a sense of personal worthiness, the belief that human beings were once created in the image of God, that they have a purpose for being here. People should not be deprived of human dignity simply because they are poor, deprived, or deformed.

People are still people, although in a spiritual sense sin has deformed them. Sin has caused them to lose the image of God, that is, the righteousness and holiness in which Adam and Eve were originally created. Sin has conformed them to evil—to the image of Satan.

God, however, has intervened to change the spiritual and moral deformity caused by sin. He has acted to change us back into His image and thus to restore us to the human dignity of being His children. To do this, more was required than to apply a bandage. Outward reform, that is, no more bad or anti-social habits, is not enough. The Bible calls for regeneration, a being born anew, a coming to faith in Jesus Christ as the Redeemer from sin and as our loving Lord.

Transformation describes this change and this attainment of true human dignity. We must not let this regeneration get away once we have it. Such backsliding is avoided when we grow daily in faith and the life in Christ. St. Paul says it plainly, "Do not conform any longer to the pattern of this world, but be transformed by the renewing of your mind" (Rom. 12:2). How? By the Holy Spirit, through the Gospel.

*Prayer Suggestion: Pray that the Holy Spirit may continue His upbuilding, uplifting work in you through the Gospel of Jesus Christ.*

# Amnesty or Amends?

After a war, the government and citizenry of a country confront the question of what to do about draft dodgers and deserters. Should they be pardoned by an amnesty declaration? Should they be required to make some amends before they can be reinstated as good citizens?

Spiritually speaking, Adam and Eve and all their descendants were and are deserters, fleeing from the presence of God and refusing to serve Him. Scripture says that all people have sinned, all have gone astray, all have taken refuge in places where they think God can't find them.

How has God dealt with the disobedient human race? He did not simply declare an amnesty or blanket forgiveness, for the God of grace and love is also just, holy, and righteous. He cannot go contrary to the holiness and righteousness of His nature by disregarding sin and pronounce a pardon.

God found a way out of this dilemma. He laid our sin on another, on Jesus Christ, who as our substitute was obedient unto death. We sinners had refused to render service to God, but here is the Servant who takes our place. Here is Jesus Christ, the one who knew no sin, who was made sin for us. Now God forgives all, not by virtue of an act of amnesty but because Christ has made full amends for all.

We all can now come out from our hiding places and return home to God, thanks to Jesus Christ. There are no charges against us; we are declared righteous before God.

*Prayer Suggestion: Say thanks to God for sending His Son to serve, suffer, die, and rise again so your forgiveness might be certain.*

# What Is Rightful Obedience?

Obedience is not popular in our time. Some think of it as conflicting with self-fulfillment. Some confuse authority with authoritarianism. The counterpart of rightful authority is rightful obedience.

Perhaps the present situation came about in part because, in the past, an obedience was demanded that was less than rightful—a blind obedience like that given by the spirit-servant Ariel to his master Prospero in Shakespeare's *The Tempest*, "I come to answer thy best pleasure, be it to fly, to swim, to dive into the fire, to ride on the curled clouds."

No one should be asked to render an obedience when the order given goes contrary to God's Law. That's why for such instances the apostle Peter said, "We must obey God rather than men" (Acts 5:29).

It is a different situation when those in rightful authority—parents in the home, teachers in school, officers of the law in our town, the boss at work—ask compliance and cooperation in matters that involve the good of both the individual as well as the larger community.

Christians know a higher motivation for obedience. They render it for the Lord's sake, that is to say, out of love to Him who in love gave Himself for them. They become the willing servants of Him who became the supreme Servant in their behalf. As St. Paul writes, "Being found in appearance as a man, [Christ] humbled Himself and became obedient to death—even death on a cross" (Phil. 2:8).

*Prayer Suggestion: Ask God to give you a better insight into His gracious and good will so the doing of it will be a pleasure for you.*

# How Big Are We?

According to one story, a dictator of a Communist country was visiting in the United States and saw a suit he admired. An American tailor took his measurements and sold him enough material for a suit. When the dictator got home to have the suit made, his own tailor told him there wasn't enough material. "How can that be?" the dictator said. "The U.S. tailor assured me there was enough for a three-piece suit." To this his private tailor replied, "Comrade, in America you aren't as big as you are here."

By human standards, someone can be considered very big, but not so in the eyes of God. Egypt's proud Pharaoh said to Moses, "Who is the LORD, that I should obey Him and let Israel go? I do not know the LORD and I will not let Israel go" (Ex. 5:2). From the New Testament, add Pontius Pilate. He said to Him who has all the power in heaven and on earth, the Lord Jesus, "Don't You realize I have power either to free You or to crucify You?" (John 19:10). What arrogance!

How big are we? When we see ourselves in the mirror of the love of God—the love that sent Christ into the world to make us the redeemed children of God—we see our true stature. "Because of His great love for us, God, who is rich in mercy, made us alive with Christ even when we were dead in transgressions … and … raised us up with Christ and seated us with Him in the heavenly realm in Christ Jesus" (Eph. 2:4–6).

We must not dishonor what God has honored, but seek to live worthy of the high position God has given us.

*Prayer Suggestion: Pray for God's help so you may always see yourself in the light of God's love for you, a love that exalts you.*

# When God Uses His Eraser

Years ago, one man made a rather large fortune by inventing erasers for pencils. Someone else made an even bigger fortune when he invented the delete key for computers. God, however, makes no mistakes, and consequently He needs no eraser. Yet, in a sense, He erases not His, but our mistakes.

The Bible does not use the word "erase" to describe God's forgiveness, but expressions like these are used: God removes our sins, puts them behind Him, buries them in the deep sea, cleanses and washes them away with the blood of Jesus, blots them out, cancels them, nails them to Christ's cross, covers them with Christ's mantle of righteousness. We could also say that God uses a delete key, and when He does, the screens on which our sins were recorded are thoroughly blank.

Of course, God is holy and righteous, and as such He is not indifferent to sins, nor does He just ignore them or gloss them over. Whatever is sinful and unholy cannot abide in His presence.

Because Jesus took all our sins upon Himself and atoned for them by His death, He paid all our debts. With faith in Jesus Christ as our Savior, His righteousness becomes our righteousness. For His sake, God declares us just and holy.

The prophet Isaiah stated it another way: "'Come now, let us reason together,' says the LORD. 'Though your sins are like scarlet, they shall be as white as snow; though they be as red as crimson, they shall be like wool'" (Is. 1:18).

*Prayer Suggestion:* *Thank God because He, by grace, for Jesus' sake, through faith, has removed all your sins.*

# Faith Religion, Not Rules Religion

Some people think Christianity is essentially living according to the golden rule and other rules. In their rule-mindedness, they are apt to do one of two things: either elevate human rules to the level of divine law or treat God's commandments as though they were given by a human being.

Many people at Christ's time, notably the Pharisees, tried to bind human mandates and "the tradition of the elders" on peoples' consciences, equating them with God's Law. The reverse of this is to take God's Ten Commandments and give them human standing, that is, regard them as social mores that may become outdated and can be ignored. One need look no farther than the TV screen to see where this belief has led.

Despite what many think, the Ten Commandments have a place in life. We cannot get along without them. Nor should we add to or take away from them.

The sure way of getting away from legalism or the rules-mentality in our religious life is to make the Gospel of Jesus Christ central in our lives. Salvation is a matter of faith in the Savior Jesus Christ, not of keeping rules. The Scripture teaches that "[God] saved us, not because of righteous things we had done, but because of His mercy. He saved us through the washing of rebirth and renewal by the Holy Spirit, whom He poured out on us generously through Jesus Christ our Savior, so that, having been justified by His grace, we might become heirs having the hope of eternal life" (Titus 3:5–7).

God grant you this faith.

*Prayer Suggestion: Pray that through the Word the Holy Spirit may be poured out upon you richly so you may grow more and more in grace and in the knowledge of our Lord and Savior Jesus Christ.*

# The Church's One Foundation

Jesus Christ Himself is really the Rock on which His church is built. Christ is the "chosen and precious cornerstone" (1 Peter 2:6) that God laid in Zion. The church is "built on the foundation of the apostles and prophets, with Christ Jesus Himself as the chief cornerstone" (Eph. 2:20).

Accordingly, Peter and the other apostles have a place in the foundation of the church. Our Lord, alluding to the name Peter (from the Greek *petros,* a stone), calls this discipline a "rock man." Jesus did not imply that He would build His church on the person of Peter, for He knew only too well Peter's impetuosity, instability, and rashness. Left to his own personal powers, Peter was more a reed than a rock.

The rock on which Jesus purposed to build His church— again in a play on words—was the *petra,* the rock of the truth Peter had confessed as his faith: "You are the Christ, the Son of the living God" (Matt. 16:16). Other people second-guessed Jesus to be a prophet, perhaps even Jeremiah, or John the Baptist come back to life. How firm a foundation is the truth Peter confessed! God's Word is always abiding, steadfast, firm, and sure. It gives great strength to those who believe and confess it.

When Peter's confession becomes our own, then we too become rock-like. The apostle bids us, "Come to Him, the living Stone ... [and] like living stones" be "built into a spiritual house to be a holy priesthood, offering spiritual sacrifices acceptable to God through Jesus Christ" (1 Peter 2:4–5).

***Prayer Suggestion:*** *Ask God to make your faith in Christ as firm as a rock.*

# God's Word Stirs Us Up

In her mystery book *The Theft of the Royal Ruby,* the English author Agatha Christie has one of her characters explain how to know when to start preparing Christmas pudding: "We'd start listening for the collect that begins, 'Stir up, O Lord, we beseech Thee,' because that collect was the signal, as it were, that the puddings should be made that week."

"Stir up"—that is what God does to our hearts when He speaks in His Word, also what the risen Christ did to two disciples on the way to Emmaus. They said, in retrospect, "Were not our hearts burning within us while He talked with us on the road and opened the Scriptures to us?" (Luke 24:32).

Everyday talk—about the weather, politics, professional sports—hardly stirs up fire in our hearts. But the Word of God does, especially when we hear it from the mouth of the Lord Jesus. As the great Prophet, His function was to preach, interpret, and apply the Holy Scriptures. He told us to search the Scriptures, for they "bear witness of Me."

By divine inspiration the prophets interpreted God's plan of salvation (1 Peter 1:10–12), and Jesus inerrantly interpreted the writings of the prophets. The result is that "we have the word of the prophets made more certain" (2 Peter 1:19), not only because the apostolic Word in the New Testament shows how the prophetic Word was fulfilled, but mostly because Jesus Christ Himself, who is the Prophet and the Word personified, put His stamp of certainty on it.

***Prayer Suggestion:*** *Pray that the prophetic and apostolic Word concerning Jesus may warm your heart.*

# We Have God's Word in Words

People use looks and hand motions—"body language"—to convey much. In writing, too, one can practice utmost word economy. After Victor Hugo had written his novel *Les Miserables*, he was anxious to know how it was selling. He wrote his publisher, "?" and the publisher replied, "!"

How does God communicate with us? In the realm of nature, He does it without words. In what we see before our eyes—mountains, seas, vegetation, living beings, the heavenly bodies—He reveals His wisdom and power.

Nature, however, tells us nothing about God's love and compassion. For that we need God's words. In the Old Testament, God spoke through the prophets, in both their spoken and written words. St. Peter writes, "Men spoke from God as they were carried along [moved, inspired] by the Holy Spirit" (2 Peter 1:21).

God spoke to us through the person of His Son, and what a message it is! God so loved the world that He gave His only Son as its Savior. What is more, God speaks to us through the words that Jesus spoke. These are the words of the Holy Scriptures, of which Jesus said that they testified of Him. In the Bible, which includes also the writings of the evangelists and apostles, we have God's Word given to us in words. Precious words indeed, for they include us in God's every promise of salvation!

***Prayer Suggestion:*** *Tell your Savior to open to you the Scriptures as He did to the Emmaus disciples so you may come to know Him better.*

# God's Word, Our Gibraltar

In Memorial Estates Cemetery near Chicago, one can see a massive stone Bible weighing 37 tons—thought to be the largest in the world. While such a monument is impressive, it cannot begin to represent the true strength of the Word of God, which prompted England's prime minister William E. Gladstone to speak of "the impregnable rock of Holy Scripture."

The Word of God, written by the inspired prophets and apostles, is central to the Reformation. Martin Luther has us sing, "A mighty Fortress is our God" because He has given us His might in which we take refuge. In defiance of all enemies of the pure Gospel, this Word "they still shall let remain" for the simple reason that they cannot destroy it.

The Word of God proclaims the Valiant one, Jesus Christ, the Sabaoth Lord and sole Savior. *Sola Scriptura*—"Scripture Alone"—is written in large letters on Reformation banners, for it testifies to Christ alone as the Savior from sin. "Scripture Alone" strips away human philosophy and reason as co-sources of doctrine. Jesus stood firmly on the "It is written" of the Holy Scripture because it could not be broken.

As the sole source of Christian doctrine, Holy Scripture can and does teach authoritatively the other two great principles of the Reformation: "Grace Alone" and "Faith Alone." The apostle Paul teaches very clearly, "It is by grace you have been saved, through faith—and this not from yourselves, it is the gift of God—not by works, so that no one can boast" (Eph. 2:8–9). Now all glory belongs to God.

*Prayer Suggestion: With a thankful heart praise God for giving us His Word, which testifies of Jesus Christ as the only Savior.*

# Sanctified to Serve

On November 1, All Saints' Day is observed in some churches. The occasion raises the question of who a saint is. We restrict the meaning too much when we refer the term only to such dead Christians who once led exceptionally holy lives and performed miracles.

The Bible speaks of all Christians as sanctified people, as saints. St. Paul, for example, addresses the Corinthians as follows: "To the church of God which is at Corinth, to those sanctified in Christ Jesus, called to be saints" (1 Cor. 1:2 RSV). Christians are saints despite the fact that they are still sinners. They are saints—from the Latin word *sanctus*, which means holy, sanctified, consecrated—not because they are sinless but because by faith in Jesus Christ all their sins are forgiven and God declares them just and holy in His sight. They are sanctified, born again, regenerated, enlightened, and lead a new life in Christ. "If anyone is in Christ, he is a new creation," St. Paul teaches in 2 Corinthians 5:17.

St. Paul also urges those who are declared holy by faith to serve God with holy works in their everyday lives, not to be saved by them but to express their thanks to God. Where God's sanctified people serve and where the saints go marching in, there darkness turns to light. The apostle tells the Ephesians (5:8), "You were once darkness, but now you are light in the Lord. Live as children of light." Because God the Holy Spirit has called us by the Gospel, enlightened us with His gifts, and given us faith, we too are saints.

***Prayer Suggestion:*** *Pray that the Holy Spirit may make you a true saint by giving you a faith that works by love.*

# The All-Knowing God

Prayers offered at political conventions are sometimes verbose, pompous, and "God-informing," as when a churchman is supposed to have opened his prayer on the platform with these words: "Lord, as You have read in the morning paper ..." More acceptable is the prayer of Tevya in *The Fiddler on the Roof* who looked heavenward and said, "Lord, it says in the Scripture—well, You should know, for You wrote it ..."

Yes, God is all-knowing; there is no need to inform Him on what He has said or done. God knows everything people say and do, even the sins that people do in secret: the evil plotting, the practice of dishonesty under the guise of respectability, the unfaithfulness in marriage relationships.

God knows the little events in our lives, as the psalmist declares, "You know when I sit and when I rise ... Before a word is on my tongue You know it completely" (Ps. 139:2, 4).

"You are the God who sees me" said Sarah's maid, Hagar, to God when she was in distress (Gen. 16:13). The fact of God's ever-present eye, ear, and mind should keep us from sinning—as happened to a young man who, after he returned from the army, told his pastor, "I was kept from much sin by remembering that God always sees me."

God's all-knowing power, however, should give us comfort and assurance. Because of it, He knows our needs, our afflictions, our weaknesses, and these move Him to compassion. Above all, He knows our need for the salvation Jesus Christ procured for us. He knows that we love Him in return.

*Prayer Suggestion: Pray that you may come to know God's love in Christ more fully, and then to trust more completely in your all-knowing God.*

# Life in God's Commune

A commune is a group of people on a piece of land or in a city apartment house whose members have a common interest and are bound together by friendship (and often economic) ties. They eat together and hold property jointly.

We may say that the first Christians in Jerusalem, bunching together around faith in Jesus Christ, formed a commune. Perhaps several communes made up the larger community of faith, for we are told, "All the believers were one in heart and mind."

In one sense, the Christian church can be called a commune. It is the communion of saints, the fellowship of believers. Jesus Christ is the head of this body and is its Savior. He became that when He "loved the church and gave Himself up for her" (Eph. 5:25). All who believe in Him as Lord and Redeemer are members of His church. It would be hard to imagine a union more closely knit together than this one.

Life in God's commune—the church—brings the blessings of God's grace: forgiveness, favor as His children, the promise of eternal life, and life in the Holy Spirit now. This is a wonderful relationship—with God as our Father and with one another. We are brothers and sisters in Christ. We love and serve one another. We commune together at God's altar.

Are you getting tired of living alone in a cold world? As a member of His church where you can worship and work for Him, you are in a commune, the communion of saints.

*Prayer Suggestion: Pray that the Holy Spirit may, through the Gospel, bring many to Christ, making them members of His body.*

# Your Life Can Be Changed

In his play *The Star Wagon*, Maxwell Anderson portrays a man who goes back in time and tries to change the course of his life. In real life, past events cannot be relived or undone.

What about the present—can it be changed? Can something be done now to give shape to the future? Some determinists or fatalists affirm that we are locked into our situations, that the course of events cannot be altered by what we do or leave undone.

Jesus teaches that our lives can change. He tells us to pray, for prayer changes things. He believed that immoral lives could be changed. He kept company with publicans and sinners, the moral outcasts of society, not to condone their sins but to give them another chance.

How can lives be changed? Not by making a few outward improvements for cosmetic reasons. The change Jesus wants—and helps us to effect—penetrates to the heart. He speaks of a change so complete that it can be called a new birth.

The new life, as Jesus told Nicodemus (John 3:1–21), is effected by water and the Holy Spirit. This is the water of Holy Baptism, which together with Christ's Gospel promise brings about a new heart, a re-created life. It makes mind and body the temple or dwelling place of the Holy Spirit. The Spirit grants faith so the repentant sinner turns to Jesus Christ and calls Him Lord and Savior.

Jesus promises to give strength to cope, courage to continue, and hope for the future.

***Prayer Suggestion:*** *Ask Christ to so enter your heart that conditions in your life will be changed for the better.*

# The Well-Built Home

Before people buy a home, they want to assure themselves that it is well built. Jesus, a carpenter's son and Himself a carpenter, said that a house founded on a rock can withstand downpours, floods, and winds.

There is another kind of home that is much more durable: our heavenly home, whose builder and maker is God. Because God is eternal, also heaven, His dwelling place, will last forever. Here on earth, we are reminded, "We do not have an enduring city, but we are looking for the city that is to come"(Heb. 13:14). In this heavenly city, also called "New Jerusalem" and "My Father's house," there are many mansions, many rooms (John 14:2).

We do well not to become too fond of the world and the things in the world, even so precious a place as our earthly home, for they are material and temporal. Not the things we see but the things we do not see are eternal.

How does heaven become our home? Eternal life in an eternal home with an eternal Father is ours through faith in Jesus Christ. He, the Son of God, came into this world, suffered, died, and rose again so He might prepare for us a home in the heavenly Father's condominium. There we have a reservation waiting for us. There Jesus awaits us, He who said, "I will come back and take you to be with Me that you also may be where I am" (John 14:3).

People can lose their earthly homes through fires, floods, earthquakes, tornados, mud slides, or even poor construction. We can never lose our home above; it is well built; it is eternal.

***Prayer Suggestion:*** *Thank God for your eternal home, and pray that He may always keep you mindful of it.*

# How God Settles a Strike

Today most employee strikes are conducted peacefully. People have come to realize that gains are more apt to be made around a conference table than by violence in the streets.

It was different many years ago when St. Paul came to Ephesus. There a violent strike broke out among craftsmen who made silver shrines in honor of the goddess Artemis, or Diana. They sensed that St. Paul's preaching about the true God and his opposition to idolatry cut sharply into their business. The uproar was quieted when the city clerk (probably with the backing of the Roman army) told the unruly crowd to voice their grievance in an orderly, legal way.

In quite another sense—and perhaps without fully realizing it—many people go on a strike against God. They bear a grudge because of grief or losses they have experienced. They say, "God should not have let this happen to us, for we were always faithful to Him. Don't we deserve something better?" So they refuse to live and work for God anymore. In effect, they carry sandwich boards that say, "God is unfair; we are out on a strike!"

God invites all strikers to assemble with Him around a conference table. There He declares, "Come now, let us reason together." He says there is no need to be at odds, for Jesus Christ is the Mediator between God and humanity. He atoned for all our wrongdoing when He went to the cross. It is as St. Paul has said, "God was reconciling the world to Himself in Christ." (2 Cor. 5:19). When at the bargaining table God gives us so much, yes, everything in Christ, can we still go on a strike against Him? Must we not love Him instead?

***Prayer Suggestion:*** *Instead of complaining, be thankful to God.*

# Jesus: Precious Truth

With science uncovering so many facts and computers storing them, one might think that truth abounds in our age. But this is not necessarily so, for there is a difference between factual data and truth. One can have all kinds of facts at the fingertips and not know what they add up to.

Mark Twain said, "Truth is such a precious article that we should all economize its use." Truth is not to be handled loosely, carelessly, or recklessly.

In the realm of spiritual beliefs, truth is even more precious—yet not so scarce as to be economized. God has revealed His truth abundantly in the Word; in the Gospel of Jesus Christ, He broadcasts it. But people are all too often preoccupied with self-centered pursuits. They have not "tuned in"—or, if they have, they have quickly forgotten what was said.

Because this has always been so, God sent His Truth to earth in the form of flesh and blood, in the person of Jesus Christ, His incarnate Son. Our Lord testified before Pilate that He had come into the world to bear witness to the truth. He not only proclaims the truth, He is "full of grace and truth" (John 1:14).

This is the truth: Because Jesus fulfilled all righteousness for us and endured death for our unrighteousness, we have peace with God. What remains is that we listen and take His truth to heart. Then we are truly blessed.

***Prayer Suggestion:*** *Pray that the Spirit of truth, who comes through the Word, may lead you deeper into the truth that Jesus personified and proclaimed.*

# Asking for Too Little?

"Why are our prayers not answered?" many people ask.

There may be several reasons for God's seeming silence. St. James mentions two possible reasons in his epistle: "You do not have, because you do not ask God. When you ask, you do not receive, because you ask with wrong motives" (James 4:2–3).

Wrong prayers are those in which people ask for God's gifts so they may be spent on their own pleasures, as St. James goes on to say. God will not give petitioners what they want if they intend to use it to fulfill sinful pleasures and desires. Wrong prayers are also those in which demands are made on God regarding the time and manner of God's help.

But there is also that other reason Jesus gives for prayers going unanswered: "You do not have, because you do not ask God"—either asking not at all or asking for too little, as though little were all that God could grant.

St. Paul would have us trust in God, "who is able to do immeasurably more than all we ask or imagine, according to His power that is at work within us" (Eph. 3:20).

Jesus Christ made it possible for us to pray to God. He atoned for our sins on Golgotha's cross and thus reconciled us to the Father. We are now God's children, who in Jesus' name can bring "large petitions" before God's throne—can pray boldly, confidently, and adequately.

***Prayer Suggestion:*** *Ask Jesus not only to teach you to pray but also to pray confidently and in His name.*

# Delayed Recognition

"A prophet has no honor in his own country," Jesus pointed out (John 4:44). A prophet may be without honor also in his own time. The same can be true for people in other callings. Johann Sebastian Bach was not appreciated until some 80 years after his death when Felix Mendelssohn revived Bach's setting of "The Passion According to St. Matthew."

Of Jesus, John 1:10–11 declares, "The world did not recognize Him. He came to that which was His own, but His own did not receive Him." In fact, the people of Nazareth, where He grew up, ran Him out of town. But He did not quit. He continued to do the will of the heavenly Father.

Delayed recognition may result from various factors. The person in question may have been a generation or more ahead of his time. The mood of the time may have changed.

The work of parents is very much on this order. Children usually don't view it in the right perspective. Perhaps years later, when they themselves have become parents, they will recognize the value of their Christian upbringing.

Delayed recognition—or no recognition at all in one's lifetime—is a possibility for each one of us. St. Paul urges us not to be pleasers of people or to be diligent "only when [the employers'] eye is on you and to win their favor, but with sincerity of heart and reverence for the Lord" (Col. 3:22). The concern of Christians is to be faithful, realizing that it is God's approval that counts.

*Prayer Suggestion: Pray for courage and dedication to carry on with your work and thereby glorify God.*

# Where Have All Our Heroes Gone?

Our era is hard on heroes. We seem to want to cut public figures down to size. Boys used to admire baseball stars—Babe Ruth, Joe DiMaggio, Dizzy Dean. Today we are told that professional athletes not only have feet of clay but also shoes with mud on them. The players themselves write books to debunk what people used to believe about them.

We used to say that every mother wanted her son or daughter to grow up to be president of the United States. But presidents today are not the heroes they once were; they are caught in the middle of every national controversy. Former employees of the White House publish their private diaries that demythologize presidents and their spouses. Not even Christopher Columbus or George Washington is safe.

Still, children need heroes—Christian persons who impress them in the right way and whose example they can follow. All of us, for that matter, benefit from studying the lives of biblical heroes, particularly those mentioned in Hebrews 11.

Towering over all heroes of faith is our Lord. We do well to "fix our eyes on Jesus, the author and perfecter of our faith" (Heb. 12:2). For us, Jesus is truly—and in a reverent sense—our superstar. In the hymn "A Mighty Fortress," we refer to Him "the valiant One, Whom God Himself elected. ... Jesus Christ ... of Sabaoth Lord." Him we believe and adore.

***Prayer Suggestion:*** *In your prayer thank Christ, the Son of God, for all His great deeds for His people.*

# The Citizen's "Thank You!"

Ernest Hemingway gave a very low estimate of patriotism when he stated, "They wrote in the old days that it is sweet and fitting in your dying. You will die like a dog for no good reason."

While we may disagree with Hemingway's view of patriotic death, we still admit that war is a great evil. In his *Large Catechism*, Martin Luther wrote that it is the devil who "causes so much contention, murder, sedition, and war." Sometimes war is thrust upon a country, and then the government has no choice but to wage a defensive and just war. Then all the citizens—those in uniform and the civilians—have the duty to come to the support of their homeland.

To lay down one's life for loved ones, whether in peace or in war, is a noble deed by which the individual renders to Caesar what is Caesar's.

On Veterans Day we honor all, the living and the dead, who have served their country and have made it possible for us to live in peace and to enjoy our freedom. Jesus said, "Greater love has no one than this, that he lay down his life for his friends" (John 15:13). With regard to our veterans, they gave much of their life—if not all of it—for their beloved country. And even if a compulsive draft rather than love led to their induction, it is right that we convey our "thank you!" to them.

***Prayer Suggestion:*** *Pray to the God of peace that it may not be necessary in the future for our citizens to go into battle.*

# Why the Bible Was Written

In bringing his gospel to a close, St. John states that he did not include everything Jesus said and did, for that would have made his book too voluminous. With the Holy Spirit guiding him, John was selective in the data he presented. Yet his purpose was clear: "These are written that you may believe that Jesus is the Christ, the Son of God, and that by believing you may have life in His name" (John 20:31). Not only John's gospel but the entire Scripture was written for this purpose. Even Jesus said, "The Scriptures ... testify about Me" (John 5:39).

The Bible was not written primarily to be a textbook of ancient history, although its history is accurate, purposeful, and instructive. Nor is its poetry offered for its own sake, though it is edifying. Nor is its psychology written to teach us that skill, though it is most profitable to take its lessons to heart.

Again, the purpose of Holy Scriptures is to lead us to faith in Jesus Christ, God's Son and our Savior, and from Him receive life in its fullness, eternal life.

"Do you know what's in the Bible?" a teacher asked the class.

"Yes," said a youngster. "Our Bible at home has in it a picture of my grandfather, my grandmother's last letter, and some dried flowers."

As a book, the Bible may have its extra uses, but its main purpose is to lead us to Christ.

**Prayer Suggestion:** *Pray to the Holy Spirit to arouse in you zeal and love for God's written Word.*

# The Original "Jesus People"

Some years ago, groups of young people who acknowledged Jesus as Savior and changed their lifestyle accordingly were called "Jesus people" or, less elegantly, "Jesus freaks."

The real Jesus people have been here for nearly 2,000 years. The first converts were two sets of brothers: Andrew and Peter, James and John. Then came Philip and Nathanael and the rest of the original 12 disciples.

After Christ's ascension into heaven, the followers numbered 120 men and women. On Pentecost Day the number suddenly increased by 3,000 newly baptized Christians, and soon the figure jumped to 5,000. Much to the dismay of the authorities in Jerusalem, the Jesus people filled all the city with their doctrine. Then other cities were evangelized. "The disciples were called Christians first at Antioch" (Acts 11:26).

To be the people of Jesus is both a hard task and a pleasant privilege. It is often hard to confess Jesus' name boldly and articulately before the general public; it may bring ridicule. But it is also an honor to bear His name, for He honored and accepted us, sinful as we were, redeemed us with His blood, and made us God's children. It is a privilege to be associated with Jesus, to think His thoughts after Him, to speak His words, and to live His kind life.

As true Jesus people we continue His Word. Then we shall know the truth, and the truth will set us free—free from fears and anxieties, free for a life of joyful service to Him. Says the hymn writer, "And then for work to do for Thee, Which shall so sweet a service be, That angels well might envy me."

*Prayer Suggestion: Ask that the Holy Spirit strengthen your faith and so make you a better Jesus person.*

# Obsession with Obscenity

In our day the preoccupation with sex—mostly abnormal sex—is both amazing and disgusting. Stores featuring pornographic books and magazines proliferate. The movie that does not feature either violence or sex, or both, is a rarity. Obscenity is an obsession. It is also big business. The pornography industry, as one newspaper put it, "makes dirty dollars out of dirty books."

Obscene language is not for Christians. St. Paul keeps reminding his readers that immorality in thought, word, and deed belongs to their former lives as pagans; for Christians it is now out of place.

The apostle writes, "Put to death, therefore, whatever belongs to your earthly nature; sexual immorality, impurity, lust, evil desires. … You used to walk in these ways, in the life you once lived. But now you must rid yourselves of all such things as these: anger, rage, malice, slander, and filthy language from your lips" (Col. 3:5–8). Note how obscene language, oral or in print, is not treated as innocuous; it is a form of immorality.

For language to improve, it is necessary for the heart to be cleaned up first, for it is out of the abundance of the heart that the mouth speaks or the hand writes. The human heart is changed when through the Gospel the Holy Spirit brings a person to believe in Jesus Christ as Savior, to love Him as the best friend, and to serve Him as one's beloved Lord. Then all things become new with that person. St. Paul writes, "If anyone is in Christ, he is a new creation; the old has gone, the new has come" (2 Cor. 5:17).

*Prayer Suggestion: Ask the Holy Spirit to create in you a new heart and to renew a right spirit within you.*

# God Sees Us

In winter the bald eagles come down from the north and settle down at Clarksville, Missouri, on the Mississippi River, their second largest gathering place in the lower 48 states. People by the thousands go out to look at them with their binoculars. But the eagles have an easier time to see them, for their eyes are six times sharper than a human's.

People have said they wanted to see God, but God can see them much better. In fact, since God is an invisible spirit, no human eye can see Him.

But God readily sees human beings. The psalmist says, "From heaven the LORD looks down and sees all mankind; from His dwelling place He watches all who live on earth" (Ps. 33:13–14). What is more, God sees what is inside our hearts and minds, as He said to Samuel (1 Sam. 16:7), "Man looks at the outward appearance, but the LORD looks at the heart."

It is a comfort for us to know that God sees us. When Hagar, Sarah's maid, was in misery, she said: "You are the God who sees me" (Gen. 16:13). God sees you and me and is aware of our needs. Our relationship to Him as Christians is very close. St. Paul told the philosophers in Athens, "God is not far from each one of us. For in Him we live and move and have our being." This is so because of Christ. We are God-reconciled, recognized children. We cannot see God with our natural eyes, but He sees us and provides for us, protects us, and will someday bring us to heaven, where we shall see Him face to face.

*Prayer Suggestion: Tell God that you draw confidence from the fact that He sees you and will grant what you need.*

# Consumers of God's Gifts

Consumers get quite a bit of help from private and public agencies that report to the public on the quality of merchandise, the comparative value of products offered, how to get the most for one's money. With this information, the consumers can be more discriminating.

Since God is ultimately the giver of all gifts, we are not so much consumers of humanity's goods as we are of God's, for He richly furnishes us with everything to enjoy. In Deuteronomy, Moses writes of one's earnings in the city, of the blessings of the field, of the fruits of the ground and the increase of cattle, of the full basket and the well-supplied kneading trough. All are God's gifts.

In the city of Lystra, when St. Paul healed a crippled man and was about to be revered as a god, the apostle turned the thoughts of the people to "the living God who made heaven and earth and sea and everything in them. ... He has shown kindness by giving you rain from heaven and crops in their seasons; He provides you with plenty of food and fills your hearts with joy" (Acts 14:15, 17).

We are consumers also of spiritual blessings, of which St. Paul speaks eloquently in the opening verses of his letter to the Ephesians: "Praise be to the God and Father of our Lord Jesus Christ, who has blessed us in the heavenly realms with every spiritual blessing in Christ" (Eph. 1:3). To be saved through Christ and have full forgiveness—for this we cannot pay with silver and gold. But we can thank God for them.

*Prayer Suggestion: Thank the Lord for all His blessings to you.*

## Blessed in Heavenly Places

Rostropovich, the renowned Russian-born former conductor of the National Symphony Orchestra in Washington, D.C., has a warm spot in his heart for an Armenian woman in Moscow. When he was a boy, his family moved to that city so he could get a musical education. But there was no place to live. So this woman took them into her two-room flat and kept them there for nearly three years without charging rent.

No room for newcomers in a crowded city—that was the experience of the Holy Family. Mary and Joseph laid Jesus in a manger "because there was no room for them in the inn" (Luke 2:7). The very Son of God, by whom all things were made and who for our salvation came down from heaven, rested in a cattle shelter in Bethlehem. St. Paul declares that our Lord was rich, but "for your sakes He became poor." Why poor? The answer follows immediately: "… so that you through His poverty might become rich" (2 Cor. 8:9).

And how rich? "Praise be to the God and Father of our Lord Jesus Christ, who has blessed us in the heavenly realms with *every* spiritual blessing in Christ" (Eph. 1:3, emphasis added). The stable in Bethlehem, the humble home in Nazareth, the wilderness where Jesus was tempted in our behalf, the sites and situations where He found the sick and suffering, the accursed tree of the cross on Calvary's hill—these do not impress us as "the heavenly places." But they were, for there God enriched us with every spiritual blessing.

In Christ, God has indeed blessed us abundantly.

***Prayer Suggestion:*** *Thank God for the many blessings He has given you, chiefly for having revealed Christ to you as Savior and friend.*

# Is Marriage Outdated?

In our time, more and more people are living together as husband and wife without bothering to get married. This relationship is considerably less than a common-law marriage, for there is not even an implicit agreement to stay together. When the partners tire of each other, they simply call it quits.

God instituted marriage in the Garden of Eden when He brought Eve to Adam, gave them to each other, and blessed them with the words, "Be fruitful and increase in number; fill the earth and subdue it" (Gen. 1:28). Throughout the Bible, marriage is regarded as a divine institution.

Can marriage ever grow out of date? Not unless God Himself terminates it. And that He will hardly do as long as human beings remain as they are now—sinful and lustful. St. Paul teaches, "It is better to marry than burn with passion" (1 Cor. 7:9).

St. Paul foresaw the time when "some will abandon the faith and follow deceiving spirits and things taught by demons. Such teachings come through hypocritical liars, whose consciences have been seared … They forbid people to marry …" (1 Tim. 4:1–3). Forbidding marriage, despising it, rejecting it as outdated desecrates one of God's ordinances.

Christ honored marriage by attending the wedding at Cana, performing the first of His miracles. This is the same Christ who "loved the church and gave Himself up for her to make her holy, cleansing her by the washing with water through the word …" (Eph. 5:25–26). This highest kind of love can be followed only by husbands and wives in marriage.

***Prayer Suggestion:*** *Ask God to help you do what you can to honor marriage.*

# God's Liberation of Women

Much has been said and done in the name of the women's liberation movement. The leaders, among many other demands, have called for equal employment opportunities and equal compensation for women. They have protested every demeaning custom and practice, such as the use of women as sex symbols. Unfortunately, some have used this call for rightful liberty as a call for license.

Long before there were feminist movements, God led a pan-gender liberation movement of His own. Our first parents and all who came after them were, of course, incapable of liberating themselves from the servitude to sin and their subjection to all of sin's consequences. As the writer to the Hebrews (2:15) puts it, all "were held in slavery."

It was up to God to take the initiative to free us from sin—and He did. At the fullness of time He caused His Son to be "born of a woman, born under the law, to redeem those under the law." Jesus Christ redeemed us all from the guilt, penalty, and dominion of sin.

This liberation applies to women as well as to men, for the apostle Paul states that there is neither male nor female (Gal. 3:28). All are one in Christ Jesus. Women are equal with men as participants of God's forgiveness and saving grace in Christ. In this respect Christianity differs radically from such other religions in which women are held to be inferior and, at worst, are not considered to be recipients of whatever "salvation" such religions have to offer.

Liberation from sin and self-serving commitments? Yes. God Himself is the leader of this movement.

***Prayer Suggestion:*** *Thank God for His grace to all in Christ Jesus.*

# Avoiding an Oil Crisis

People used to depend on oil lamps to give them light. Jesus refers to such lamps in His parable of the five wise and the five foolish virgins. The five wise had a sufficient supply of oil on hand to keep their lamps burning when the bridegroom finally arrived. The foolish five, on the other hand, experienced a fuel crisis at the most crucial moment. They cried to the others, "Give us some of your oil; our lamps are going out" (Matt. 25:8).

Our Lord teaches us to keep ourselves well provided with spiritual oil, that is faith in Him, our heavenly bridegroom. He truly loved the church as His spouse and gave Himself for her. Having died on the cross to save us, He arose from the dead and ascended into heaven. Before leaving, He promised that He would return to receive us to Himself and to take us to heaven. For reasons known only to Him, He is delaying His return; but this delay takes nothing away from the certainty of the promise.

In the meantime, we Christians need to remain alert, having made all preparations to receive the Lord Jesus when He comes. As the wise virgins knew where to obtain oil for their lamps, so we know where we procure the oil of faith: from the Word of God. Through the Gospel Christ gives us all that we need to stay spiritually alive. The Scriptures, says St. Paul, instruct and equip us for salvation through faith in Christ Jesus.

***Prayer Suggestion:*** *Pray the Lord to supply you richly with the oil of faith so you can go forward when He comes to meet you.*

# Ready to Receive the Bridegroom

In Scripture, the covenant of God with His people is compared to a marriage union. Isaiah told the children of Israel, "As a bridegroom rejoices over his bride, so will your God rejoice over you" (Is. 62:5). Hosea stressed that God took the initiative in this relationship, promising to bless the church of Old Testament believers: "I will betroth you to Me in righteousness and justice, in love and compassion" (Hosea 2:19).

The figure is continued in the New Testament, with Christ cast in the role of bridegroom and husband. St. Paul wrote to the Ephesians, "Christ loved the church and gave Himself up for her" (5:25). The church redeemed by Christ is pictured as the bride. St. John says, "I saw the Holy City, the new Jerusalem, coming down out of heaven from God, prepared as a bride beautifully dressed for her husband" (Rev. 21:2).

In the parable of the ten virgins, Christ is the bridegroom, who at the end of time will come from heaven to claim His bride, the church, and unite Himself with her in a heavenly marriage. But, as the five foolish virgins show, not all are prepared to receive Him, even if they are members of the visible church.

The point of the parable directs us to the conduct of the five wise virgins, who were ready to welcome the bridegroom, for they had provided their lamps with oil. They represent Christians who are "wise unto salvation," ready to meet Christ no matter when He comes. The truth they exemplify is expressly stated: "Therefore keep watch because you do not know the day or the hour" (Matt. 25:13).

*Prayer Suggestion: Ask for God's help to remain awake and watchful for Jesus' coming.*

# How Safe Are You in Church?

"Five of my parishioners were killed during vespers," wrote the pastor of a Florissant, Missouri, church in 1812. They were massacred by Indians. Early settlers everywhere were in peril, and not even the church was a safe sanctuary.

Today a church is usually regarded as a very safe place. But there are dangers, and they are not so much physical as spiritual. We learn from the book of Job that when God's people came together for worship, Satan too was present. Whenever the seed of God's Word is sown, the devil comes along and wants to snatch it away, as Jesus tells us in His parable of the seed and soils. The evil one is pleased when people in church don't have their minds on God's Word but engage in daydreams or even fall asleep. He is happy when false doctrine is proclaimed, for it leads people astray.

A further danger is that church-going can be regarded as a good work that merits God's favor and brings salvation. Reciting the creed, praying the Lord's Prayer, or singing a hymn can become a mere performance; the heart is not in it.

Yes, the church can become unsafe if we are not aware of potential dangers and react to them. St. Paul speaks of the perils on land and sea he experienced as a traveling missionary. He was also in peril when he preached in synagogues, for his hearers were often enraged at the preaching of Christ.

Nevertheless the church is a very good place to be when worship is conducted. We hear the Gospel of our salvation there. Believe in Him and you are safe, also in church.

*Prayer Suggestion: Tell your Lord that you will listen when He speaks in His Word and that you will gladly do His will.*

# God Took Us into His Household

When the United States of America was still a young nation, it was resolved that the president be provided with a free residence. To this end, the first White House in Washington, D.C., was built in 1800. The busy chief executives of the country were thus relieved of the expense and time-consuming tasks of finding suitable living quarters for themselves and their families. President John Adams, occupying the as-yet-unfinished White House alone, wrote in a letter to his wife, "I pray heaven to bestow the best of blessings on this house and all who inhabit it. May none but wise men ever rule under this roof."

The above words, now carved in the marble mantel in the State Dining Room, give us a glimpse into the kind of gratitude that befits us all for the loving kindness of God who has provided us with all blessings.

Even more important, God has given us a free spiritual home with Him as well. He took us into His household. How thankful we are for being members of God's family and household! By nature we were outsiders, but Jesus Christ lived, died, and rose again so we might have a spiritual home as God's reconciled children.

As we look into the future, we see a home much more glorious than the White House or any palace here on earth. Jesus declared, "In My Father's house are many rooms; if it were not so, I would have told you. I am going there to prepare a place for you" (John 14:2). How blessed we are to have heaven as our home!

**Prayer Suggestion:** *Ask God's blessing on your home and on all who inhabit it.*

# Remember Your "Thank You"

During a stormy night in 1860, two vessels, one a freighter and the other a passenger ship, collided on Lake Michigan. The latter ship, called the *Lady Elgin,* carried several hundred passengers. When the ship sank, the people jumped into the water, clinging to whatever came their way—lifeboats, floating timbers, even the bass drum from the ship's orchestra.

As the survivors struggled toward the Illinois shore, people from the land waded out into the water to extend a helping hand. Participating in the rescue mission was a university student by the name of Edward Spencer, an expert swimmer. During the early morning hours and through the day young Spencer succeeded in rescuing 17 persons from a watery grave. But so great was the strain that he lost his health and spent the rest of his life in a wheelchair.

In later years, this hero-for-a-day was asked what he remembered most about that tragic day. He replied, "I recall the fact that not one of the 17 rescued persons thanked me for saving their lives."

Jesus Christ sacrificed His life to rescue us from sin and death. Have we thanked Him? Is our thanksgiving by words accompanied by thanksliving? And do we live our thanks by giving ourselves for others? The apostle Paul tells the Philippians, "Do not be anxious about anything, but in everything, by prayer and petition, with thanksgiving, present your requests to God. And the God of peace, which transcends all understanding will guard your hearts and your minds in Christ Jesus" (Phil. 4:6–7).

***Prayer Suggestion:*** *In your prayer, state not only your needs—needs of body and soul—but also give thanks to Christ for His redemption.*

# No Need for Occultism

Recent years have seen an upswing of interest in the occult arts. Satan worship, incantation and the casting of spells, magical rites and mystical rituals, sorcery and witchcraft, astrology and fortune-telling are manifestations of it.

The black arts have been practiced in pagan society for many centuries. Old Testament writings not only mention witchcraft and assorted practices but also condemn them in strongest terms.

The book of Acts reports various encounters between the apostles and the advocates of occultism. In Ephesus, thanks to the teaching of St. Paul, the converts to the Christian faith made a big bonfire of books dealing with the magical arts, consuming a collection worth 50,000 pieces of silver (Acts 19:19). The production and sale of such books was big business even then.

Why the rebirth of occultism in our times is hard to say. Yet when the Christian religion declines in a country, the religious and irreligious cults have a tendency to flourish. When people turn from the worship of the true God, it is not uncommon for them to try to satisfy their spiritual needs on some substitute for true religion.

When the people in Ephesus consigned expensive books to the flames, they indicated their conviction that they had now found something much more precious: the Gospel of Jesus Christ. The same is true for all who have been discovered by Jesus Christ and have received His salvation. They neither need nor want the occult.

**Prayer Suggestion:** *Thank Jesus Christ for the light of His Gospel.*

# Thinking and Thanking

The words "thinking" and "thanking" are related. Before a person can thank properly, he or she must think properly. Those who think on and count their blessings are moved to thank Him who graciously gives all.

With the close of another harvest season, we have much to think about. In Psalm 100 the holy singer exhorts, "Know that the LORD is God!" Let the unwise think that they can be their own gods. Christians, however, think on God as the living source from whom all blessings flow.

The Lord who is God is the one who revealed Himself to Moses as Yahweh: "I AM WHO I AM" (Ex. 3:14). He entered into a covenant relationship with His people. He is our Father too, and we have become His children, thanks to Jesus' "blood of the covenant, which is poured out for many for the forgiveness of sins" (Matt. 26:28). Thus God is the believer's greatest good, for "His love endures forever; His faithfulness continues through all generations" (Ps. 100:5).

We belong to God also because He is our maker and provider. "It is He who made us, and we are His" (Ps. 100:3). He furnishes us with health, family, farmland, forest, town, city, police force, work opportunities, cars to take us to work, paychecks, and many more blessings.

The more you think on these great themes of God's gracious gifts, the more you are prompted to thank, to "enter His gates with thanksgiving and His courts with praise," to "come before Him with joyful songs" (Ps. 100:4). Thanksgiving is the result of right Christian thinking.

***Prayer Suggestion:*** *Think about God's gifts to you and your family. Then thank Him for His goodness, especially His grace in Christ Jesus.*

# What Shopping Centers Say

Very much a part of urban and suburban sprawls are the shopping centers with their street-level shops and stores, their landscaped malls, their acres of parking space. Shopping centers are the modern counterparts of the bazaars and marketplaces of other times and places. They are also social centers—especially for children and teens. So it was also in Jesus' day. He said His generation was "like children sitting in the marketplace and calling out to each other" (Luke 7:32).

Because of marketing techniques and advertising, shopping centers seem to say—to shout—"Buy! Buy!" If, however, we listen closely, we can hear another message. "Man shall not live by bread alone. You do not live by power mowers alone, by TV sets alone, by sports gear alone, by campers and minivans alone." To be truly alive, 21st-century people need Jesus Christ, the living Bread—He whose body was broken on a cross so, as at the breaking of bread, people might receive Him by faith, be nourished inwardly, and live eternally.

***Prayer Suggestion:*** *Pray for God's blessings, thanking Him for all good that you have received.*

# For Freedom, for Law and Order

At times, crime seems to have taken over our cities. In reaction, many citizens have called for "law and order." They want the laws enforced so they can, in the apostle's words, "live peaceful and quiet lives" (1 Tim. 2:2). While it is possible that law-and-order demands can suppress justice, human rights, and rightful freedom, it goes without saying that community life can exist only if there is law and order.

How do things stand in the city of God, the church, in our spiritual lives, in our relationship to God and to fellow Christians? Should there be "law and order," or is everything wide open, everyone having the freedom under the Gospel to do as he or she pleases?

St. Paul says in his letter to the Romans that we are saved through faith in the redemptive merits of Jesus Christ. This is the Gospel. We are not saved by doing the works of the Law. Because Christ has redeemed us from the curse of the Law, the Law can no longer dictate what we must do or not do to be right with God.

What happens, then, to the Law? May we overthrow it, disregard it, even transgress it, and say, "We are free under the Gospel; God's law no longer plays a part in our lives"? St. Paul's answer is, "By no means!" The Law is still needed to condemn sin.

Does God stand for both freedom and for law and order? He does indeed, and through the Gospel and the Law He provides for both.

*Prayer Suggestion: Thank God for the Gospel of Christ and for His Law to guide you in Christian living.*

# The Guest Became Host

Martha of Bethany meant it well when she busily prepared a meal for Jesus. Providing sustenance for the Master was an act of faith; it is likewise faith working by love when we feed the least of His brethren. He declares, "I was hungry and you gave Me something to eat" (Matt. 25:35). Not only our eating and drinking but also—and perhaps more so—the preparation of food and drink are acts performed to the glory of God when done in faith. As St. Paul said, "Whether you eat or drink or whatever you do, do it all for the glory of God" (1 Cor. 10:31).

So what did Martha do wrong? Her problem dealt with priorities. Hearing the Word of Christ, as Mary had chosen to do, supersedes all other activities, laudable as they may be. The Word is food for the soul, the true bread of life. In that Bethany home Jesus was serving it. He who had been invited as guest became the spiritual host to Mary and Martha.

Nothing is more important than to be daily nourished by God's Word. St. Paul tells his young coworker that he has been "brought up in the truths of the faith and of the good teaching that you have followed" (1 Tim. 4:6). The Word of God is true "soul food." Without it, spiritual hunger, even starvation, sets in.

Jesus Christ is the Bread of Life. Through Him God conveys the message that He so loved all people that He gave up His Son to be their Savior. He is also among us as the Word, whose words are spirit and life. In our homes, too, the invited Guest becomes the blessing-dispensing Host.

*Prayer Suggestion: In your prayer enlarge on this table request: "Come, Lord Jesus, be our Guest, and let Your gifts to us be blest."*

# A Time of Vigilance

The end of another church year calls on us to exercise vigilance. The "old evil Foe" is always at hand to divert our heart and mind from the coming of God's Son in the flesh to redeem us. St. Peter reminds us, "Be self-controlled and alert. Your enemy the devil prowls around like a roaring lion looking for someone to devour" (1 Peter 5:8).

The enemy is also the world, which in these pre-Christmas weeks tries to adorn itself with the glitter and glamour of a thoroughly commercialized Christmas from which Jesus Christ is excluded. And we are our own enemies when we lose ourselves in spending orgies.

Advent's call to vigilance is sounded not only because our foes are always near but especially because of the coming of our dearest friend. He is Jesus Christ, who honors us by taking us into His confidence and love, saying, "I have called you friends, for all that I learned from My Father I have made known to you" (John 15:15).

This true friend bears all our sins and griefs, for He comes as the Lamb of God who takes away the sin of the world.

There is a particular need for vigilance because our Lord's return will be at a time that is both unannounced and unexpected. Our Advent King declares, "You also must be ready, because the Son of Man will come at an hour when you do not expect Him" (Luke 12:40). Our response? "Amen. Come, Lord Jesus!" (Rev. 22:20).

***Prayer Suggestion:*** *In your prayer bid Jesus welcome in your heart and home.*

# The Blessed One Came to Bless

Someone has called the four gospels "Passion stories with long introductions." It is true because all the events the evangelists reported in earlier chapters—our Lord's birth, baptism, calling of apostles, preaching journeys, healings, encounters with opponents, prophecies—lead up to the grand finale: "The Son of Man will be betrayed to the chief priests and teachers of the law. They will condemn Him to death and will hand Him over to the Gentiles, who will … flog Him and kill Him. Three days later He will rise" (Mark 10:33–34).

Jesus Himself announced the agenda for the week that began on Palm Sunday. He knew ahead of time that all this had to occur so God's gracious will might be done, the Scriptures might be fulfilled, and the price might be paid for the redemption of the human race.

The Savior's entry into Jerusalem to open the week of His Passion is thus an event of shadow and light, of sorrow and joy, of tears mingled with shouts of Hosanna. Jesus Himself had wept over Jerusalem because of the unbelief that was at the heart of all sin making His own death necessary.

There is ground also for rejoicing. Jesus Christ, God's Son, came into the world—the world of sinners, whether in Jerusalem or in any other city or community—to lay down His life and take it again for our salvation. He came to bless. Therefore we call Him the Blessed One, and we join the multitude in Jerusalem singing, "Hosanna to the Son of David! Blessed is He who comes in the name of the Lord! Hosanna in the highest!" (Matt. 21:9).

*Prayer Suggestion:* *Give thanks and praise to Christ for coming among us to bless us with His salvation.*

# Why Jesus Rode a Donkey

In 1973 a Canadian artist provoked the British monarchists when he depicted Queen Elizabeth II as dressed in a regimental uniform and riding a moose.

A far greater incongruity seemed to have occurred when Jesus Christ, the King of kings and Lord of lords, entered Jerusalem riding a donkey. You would think, if ride He must, that a steed such as a conquering general would ride in a victory parade would have been more appropriate, or, if He entered New York City or Washington, D.C., today, that He would ride in a long, shiny limousine. But a *donkey*—it seems so unbecoming.

The truth of the matter is that it was not unbecoming at all, for our Lord had come into this world—and on that occasion had come into Jerusalem—for the express purpose of being the Servant who humbled Himself and was obedient to death, even death on a cross, to save us from sin and the fear of death. In His state of humiliation, Jesus, the Son of God, had laid aside His divine majesty, power, and glory so, as a true man, He might take the place of all sinners from the time of Adam and atone for their sins. So He chose a donkey to ride on, an animal used in the humble, everyday tasks of life.

We know how Jesus' self-denial affects us. St. Paul writes, "You know the grace of our Lord Jesus Christ, that though He was rich, yet for your sakes He became poor, so that you through His poverty might become rich" (2 Cor. 8:9).

*Prayer Suggestion: Express your gratitude to Jesus for having come in the humility of a servant to earn forgiveness for you.*

# The Sycamore: A Repentance Tree

The sycamore tree rates honorable mention in Holy Scripture. The prophet Amos, along with being a herdsman, was a dresser of sycamore trees. An excellent shade tree, the sycamore was often planted by the roadside. Such a tree stood at a street in Jericho. When Jesus came that way, the publican Zacchaeus climbed into it to get a better look at Him.

The biblical sycamore tree bore fruit—a kind of fig. That tree in Jericho with Zacchaeus in its branches represents another kind of fruit that our Savior longed to see—the fruit of repentance. Zacchaeus, a tax collector for the Romans, had been a thief. By the grace of God he repented of his wrongdoing. So our Lord paused in His journey to rescue also this sinner. He said to the man who was literally and figuratively up a tree, "Zacchaeus, come down immediately. I must stay at your house today" (Luke 19:5).

Zacchaeus wanted to show the fruit of repentance. Half of his goods he would give to the poor, and to all whom he had defrauded he would make a fourfold restoration.

The Lord still calls sinners to repentance, for He came to seek and save the lost. That journey to Jerusalem to suffer and to die was made in behalf of all people also today. Those who accept Him as Savior receive the Holy Spirit, who brings forth in them "love, joy, peace, patience, kindness, goodness, faithfulness, gentleness, self-control" (Gal. 5:22–23).

So if you're up a tree about Christian living, let Jesus into the home of your heart.

*Prayer Suggestion: Pray that God in Jesus' name would send the Holy Spirit into your heart.*

# Mary's Magnificat Is Also Ours

Mary was not the first Israelite woman to compose a hymn of praise. Deborah of old had resolved (Judges 5:3), "I will make music to the LORD, the God of Israel." Hannah, the mother of Samuel, opened her hymn with, "My heart rejoices in the LORD" (1 Sam. 2:1). Others before Mary had acknowledged God's favor with both joy and humility.

But there is something unique about Mary. She stands alone among all the women of the world—past, present, and future—because God chose her to be the virgin-mother of His Son, the long-awaited Messiah. She is right in saying, "From now on all generations will call me blessed" (Luke 1:48).

Note, however, that in her Magnificat, Mary doesn't rejoice primarily over a personal honor but over the salvation God is providing for His people as He has promised: "He has helped His servant Israel, remembering to be merciful to Abraham and his descendants forever" (Luke 1:54–55). When she rejoices in "God *my* Savior," she includes herself in the salvation all sinners need—the blood-bought salvation wrought by Jesus, her own Son. Not only is it true that at the fullness of time God's Son was born of a woman, namely Mary, but also *for* her as well as for all, without distinction—Jew and Greek, slave and free, male and female—for by faith they are all one in Christ Jesus.

We too are included. Therefore we can make Mary's Magnificat our own and sing of how God "has been mindful of the humble state of His servant" (Luke 1:48).

*Prayer Suggestion: In your own words repeat the expressions of thanks and praise to God such as Mary voiced in her Magnificat.*

# Our Response to Christ's Coming

When it was time for the world's Messiah to be born, the angel Gabriel was sent on two important missions. The first was to Jerusalem to reveal to Zechariah that the forerunner, John the Baptist, was to be born of him and his wife, Elizabeth. The second was to Nazareth to announce an even greater event to Mary.

Gabriel, who described himself as standing "in the presence of the Lord" (Luke 1:19), was an angel of high rank to whom important messages were assigned. In Old Testament times, God sent him to Daniel to interpret a vision and, at a later time, to reveal to him the prophecy of the 70 weeks.

To Mary Gabriel made known that she should bear a son who was to be named Jesus, "the Son of the Most High" (Luke 1:32). Conceived by the Holy Spirit, "the holy one to be born will be called the Son of God" (Luke 1:35), the angel went on to say. There was no mistake about it: Mary had been chosen to be the virgin mother of whom the long-expected Messiah was to be born.

Mary's response? She confessed a faith marked by obedience and humility: "I am the Lord's servant. … May it be to me as you have said" (Luke 1:38).

The Advent message of the coming Savior ought to find a similar attitude in us—an attitude of faith that says with God nothing is impossible, an attitude that reveals both the need for the Savior and a willingness to receive Him.

***Prayer Suggestion:*** *Give thanks to God for His Advent promise of the Savior, the Lord Jesus Christ.*

# The Two Serpents

The first serpent came to Adam and Eve in Eden and misled them into eating of the forbidden fruit of the tree of knowledge of good and evil. It was the devil who spoke through the serpent. The Tempter is identified in Revelation 20:2 as "the dragon, that ancient serpent, who is the devil or Satan."

The second serpent was the one that Moses in the wilderness affixed on a pole so when an Israelite, bitten by a fiery serpent, "looked at the bronze snake, he lived" (Num. 21:9). This serpent is a type of Christ, as our Lord Himself teaches: "So the Son of Man must be lifted up, that everyone who believes in Him may have eternal life" (John 3:14–15).

The two serpents thus stand for the two contestants in the showdown battle: Satan and the Savior. Genesis 3:15 foretold the outcome of that mortal combat: The promised Messiah would crush Satan's power. The wounds Jesus endured brought Him into the grave, but they could not keep Him from rising triumphantly from the dead.

Satan still bothers us. Therefore St. Peter tells us, "Be self-controlled and alert. Your enemy the devil prowls around like a roaring lion looking for someone to devour. Resist him, standing firm in the faith" (1 Peter 5:8–9). We can overcome Satan's temptations, for Christ has already won the victory over him.

***Prayer Suggestion:*** *Thank Christ for overcoming Satan. Ask Him for strength to resist his temptations.*

# God's Obedient Son

Jesus, the Holy One of Israel, atoned for all the sins of the unholy ones of Israel and of all human beings.

During their 40-year stay in the wilderness, the Israelites were tempted by the devil to every form of disbelief and disobedience: idolatry, immorality, grumbling, murmuring, putting the Lord to the test instead of trusting in His promises, wanting to live by earthly bread alone to the neglect of the Bread of Life. These sins are sufficient to bring humankind into eternal perdition.

St. Paul states the lesson, "We should not commit sexual immorality, as some of them did—and in one day twenty-three thousand of them died. We should not test the Lord, as some of them did—and were killed by snakes. And do not grumble, as some of them did—and were killed by the destroying angel" (1 Cor. 10:8–10).

But here comes Jesus Christ, whose 40 days in the wilderness balances out with the Israelites' 40 years. He, too, was tempted by the devil. But unlike the children of Israel, He remained obedient to the Word of God. His preliminary victory in the wilderness foreshadowed His complete rout of Satan when He went to the cross.

The devil tempts also us, not only in lonely places but also in busy marketplaces and in the midst of crowds. He is apt to borrow a line from a television program and say, "Let's make a deal." He wants us to live his kind of life. But we are not compelled to do so. Because Jesus withstood his temptations, we who are with Him by faith can likewise prevail.

***Prayer Suggestion:*** *Ask the heavenly Father to help you be an obedient son or daughter through faith in Jesus Christ.*

# Doing the Church's Business

Jesus objected when, in the temple courtyard, merchants sold animals intended for sacrifice and when other concessionaires operated currency exchanges for profit. He objects today when people turn God's house into a marketplace and transact their business in it.

Yet the church is a place of business—the Lord's business. The young Jesus did His Father's business when He occupied Himself with God's Word in the temple (Luke 2:41–52). When He said at the temple cleansing that the house of God is "a house of prayer" (Matt. 21:13), He stressed that it is for worship. We do our Father's business when we pray, proclaim the Word, partake in the sacraments, bring our offerings, and have fellowship with one another.

To us "church" is far more than a building. It is God's people who are redeemed by Jesus Christ, who serve Him on Sundays and weekdays, and profess Him before the world. Jesus made it the business of the church to "make disciples of all nations, baptizing them in the name of the Father and of the Son and of the Holy Spirit, and teaching them to obey everything I have commanded you" (Matt. 28:19–20).

The church's business is Gospel preaching and teaching, baptizing and celebrating Holy Communion, prayer and fellowship, ministry and mission. Are we doing this business also at a time when Christmas shopping so dominates the business world?

*Prayer Suggestion:* Ask your Lord to grant you zeal for His house and love for His Gospel.

# Closer Than Cousins

Jesus and John the Baptist were relatives. Their respective mothers, Mary and Elizabeth, were kinswomen, or "cousins" (Luke 1:36 KJV). That would make Jesus and John second cousins.

But their closeness to one another exceeds a blood relationship. John is herald and forerunner, the announcer of Christ's advent. To this day he prepares our hearts to receive the Savior by preaching repentance and faith. He preaches not only the Law but also the Gospel: "All mankind will see God's salvation" (Luke 3:6). Again, pointing to Jesus: "Look, the Lamb of God, who takes away the sin of the world" (John 1:29). How close was this witness bearer to Jesus!

And Jesus was close to John, at whose hands He was baptized. In John 5:35, He calls John a "lamp that burned and gave light." Further: "Among those born of women there has not risen anyone greater than John the Baptist" (Matt. 11:11).

At that point in time, Jesus was still lingering in the background. Only with His baptism in the Jordan would He come to the fore to begin His public ministry. And then Jesus would increase, but John would decrease.

"There is a friend who sticks closer than a brother," Proverbs 18:24 says. We know He is close to us like that kind of a friend. But how close are we to Him? Are we His friends in good times and trying times? Do we befriend the least of His brothers and sisters and thus show our friendship for Him?

*Prayer Suggestion:* Base your prayer on the hymn "What a Friend We Have in Jesus!"

# Test and Testimony in the Desert

In the desert of the Sinai peninsula, the children of Israel, bound for the Promised Land, frequently rebelled against God.

St. Paul recalls in 1 Corinthians 10 that God had provided His people with manna from heaven and drinking water out of a rock, saying that these bodily gifts represented also the spiritual blessings flowing from the Rock that was Christ. Yet Israel sinned, committing gross idolatry by worshiping the golden calf. In the desert, God had spoken to His people, but they ignored His voice.

It was in another desert that God again spoke to Israel. In the wilderness of Judea, reaching to the Dead Sea and northward along the Jordan River, John the Baptist witnessed against sin and bore testimony for Jesus Christ. There was also a pilgrimage of repentance where "the whole Judean countryside and all the people of Jerusalem went out to him. Confessing their sins, they were baptized by him in the Jordan River" (Mark 1:5).

So incisive was John's message that some people wondered whether he was the Messiah. "But [John] confessed freely, 'I am not the Christ.' They asked him, 'Then who are you?' … John replied … 'I am the voice of one calling in the desert, "Make straight the way for the Lord"'" (John 1:20–23).

John's testimony was clear: Jesus of Nazareth is the Lord, the Lamb of God who takes away the sin of the world.

John's testimony is still the message for Advent.

*Prayer Suggestion: Thank Jesus, the Lamb of God, for taking away your sin.*

# In the Savior's Footsteps

Time was—in European history from approximately A.D. 1100 to 1300—when "taking the cross" meant to go on a crusade to wrest the Holy Land from the infidel. The crusaders wore the cross as a badge.

Today, taking up the cross does not mean joining an overseas military expedition in behalf of Christ's kingdom. Our crusades are apt to be much closer to home. The battlefield is right in our hearts, and the cross we are asked to carry is every affliction we must endure as the disciples of Christ.

Our Lord carried the great cross to Calvary and died on it for our salvation. As His followers we are now both willing and able to deny ourselves, take up our crosses, and follow Him. The crosses we bear are small in comparison with Christ's great cross; they are in fact crucifixes.

Nevertheless, some believe that Jesus is asking too much when He tells us to follow in His footsteps. They do not want to say no to selfish ambitions and pleasures; ridicule for the faith is too hard to bear; serving Christ seems unrewarding.

But that is a great delusion. There is joy in following Jesus—joy in being in His presence, joy in hearing His life-giving words, joy in celebrating His birth at Christmas time and His resurrection on Easter morning. There is much on the plus side of Christianity.

What about you and me? The cross of Christ was placed on us in Baptism, making us followers of Christ.

*Prayer Suggestion: Ask Jesus to let you experience the happiness to be found in following in His footsteps.*

## Building a Solid Life

God grounds every work of His on rock bottom. The psalmist declares, "In the beginning You laid the foundations of the earth" (Ps. 102:25)—layer upon layer of rock.

The church of Jesus Christ likewise rests on a solid foundation. The apostle declares, "No one can lay any foundation other than the one already laid, which is Jesus Christ" (1 Cor. 3:11). The Word of God that Jesus taught and the work of redemption that He wrought, that is the rock on which God's kingdom is built. This kingdom is "the city with foundations, whose architect and builder is God" (Heb. 11:10). In it we are safe, as Isaiah said long ago, "The Lord has established Zion, and in her His afflicted people will find refuge" (Is. 14:32).

Since God lays solid foundations for what He constructs, we ought to do the same for the life we are building from day to day. Our Christian faith is sure, for it rests on Christ's Word and work. Just as sure will be our Christian life when we hear Jesus' words and do them. When we do this, we will be "like a wise man who built his house on the rock. The rain came down, the streams rose, and the winds blew and beat against that house; yet it did not fall, because it had its foundation on the rock" (Matt. 7:24–25).

What the world offers—tainted riches, the tinsel, tarnish, glitter, and glamour of the commercial world at Christmas time, the "rock and roll" of passing pleasures, the latest technological gadgets—is shifting sand and therefore an unreliable basis for life. Therefore, on Christ, the solid Rock, we build. This is true wisdom.

*Prayer Suggestion: Pray the Lord that He may help you build your life on the solid foundation of His Word.*

# The Breakthrough of the Light

Although he was baptized in Judea and emerged triumphant from His temptation in a Judean wilderness, Jesus did not launch His ministry of preaching and healing in this south country. Because of unrest at the arrest of John the Baptist, our Lord traveled to Galilee, the northern part of Palestine. There He established His headquarters in Capernaum.

Jerusalem, deemed itself the seat of correct religious teaching and worship. Its inhabitants looked down on "Galilee of the Gentiles" as the "sticks" or "back woods." There heathen colonies had been planted when large numbers of Israelites had been carried into captivity in Assyria. At Jesus' time, a strong Grecian influence was felt in Galilee, making this area suspect of espousing a watered-down Judaism. It was thought to be a land of darkness. And, usually, where paganism holds sway, the darkness of sin and death prevails.

Yet Galilee, not Judea, was chosen for the opening of our Lord's preaching mission: "Repent, for the kingdom of heaven is near" (Matt. 4:17). There, where long ago the tribes of Zebulun and Naphtali were assigned their heritage, Jesus began to gather together the lost sheep from the house of Israel. There He first shone forth as the Light of the World.

Matthew sees this as the fulfillment of Isaiah's words: "The people living in darkness have seen a great light, on those living in the land of the shadow of death a light has dawned" (Is. 9:1–2). Today we thank God that the light of the Gospel illuminates the road to heaven through faith in Jesus Christ.

**Prayer Suggestion:** *Thank the heavenly Father for sending His Son to be the Light of the world.*

# Jesus, the Father's Special Emissary

Hebrews 3:1 calls Jesus "the apostle and high priest whom we confess." The Advent theme is that Jesus was the Father's "Apostle," sent to deliver a message. The message was, in a nutshell, "This is life eternal: that they may know You, the only true God, and Jesus Christ whom You have sent" (John 17:3).

The transmission of the message was at times difficult because of various obstacles and interferences. Inborn sin caused static. The disciples were slow learners, having comprehension problems especially when Jesus spoke in parables. Along with their countrymen, they were caught up in a spirit of nationalism that interpreted Christ's rule as an earthly one. Right up to the Ascension, they were still asking a question with political overtones, "Lord, are You at this time going to restore the kingdom to Israel?" (Acts 1:6).

Yet for the most part the message had come through, awaiting further clarification with the coming of the Holy Spirit. Peter's confession showed the true faith: "You are the Christ, the Son of the living God" (Matt. 16:16). On another occasion, the Twelve joined Peter, their spokesman, in saying, "You have the words of eternal life" (John 6:68).

Therefore Jesus, shortly before His departure from the disciples, could say to the Father, "I gave them the words You gave Me and they accepted them. They knew with certainty that I came from You" (John 17:8). His work done, He was ready to return to the Father. For Jesus it was "mission accomplished," but for us the assignment still reads, "Therefore go and make disciples of all nations" (Matt. 28:19).

***Prayer Suggestion:*** *Ask the help of the Holy Spirit to bear witness to Jesus.*

# What Do You Want for Christmas?

In one holiday song, a youngster does not ask for expensive Christmas gifts but only for his "two front teeth." Perhaps he wanted them because they related closely to him as a maturing person. After all, children get tired of being teased about the missing-teeth aspect of growing up. They want a feeling of well-being. Whatever does that is a precious thing, although no price tag may be attached to it. It is not to be described as "mere" or "only" or "just."

So it is with the great love God revealed to us when He sent His Son into the world as our Savior. The Son came as an infant small, born in poverty, wrapped in swaddling clothes, laid in a manger. By all outward appearances there was little to impress the people for whom He came. Even then "He had no beauty or majesty to attract us to Him, nothing in His appearance that we should desire Him" (Is. 53:2). Yet in this Child the fullness of God dwelled. In Him, and in none other, is our salvation.

So we can say: Never mind the expensive gifts, the glitter and glamour, the royal trappings of a "Christ" who never was but exists only in peoples' imagination—a "Christ" with a halo and other heavenly features as artists like to picture Him. All we want for Christmas is the Christ Child, the Baby born in deep poverty and humility, for He communicates God's saving love for us. He brings life and salvation. In Him we find true happiness.

***Prayer Suggestion:*** *Express your gratitude for Christ's coming in great humility to be your Savior.*

## What Is Life?

Many thinkers have tried to answer the question, "What is life?" Marcus Aurelius called it "a battle"; Robert Browning, "an empty dream"; V. E. Cooke, "a hollow bubble"; James M. Barrie, "a cup of tea"; Roy Campbell, "a dusty corridor, shut at both ends."

These concepts show a failure to grasp life in all its dimensions. Some are cynical, some pessimistic, some frivolous.

So we turn to our Lord and ask Him, "What is life?" He tells us that the full life includes more than the physical—breathing, eating, drinking, working, resting. The full life embraces also and especially the heart, mind, and spirit or soul. The spiritual side of life has its source in Jesus Christ, who is the Word and who speaks words of life. He tells us, "I am the Way and the Truth and the Life" (John 14:6). And the words He speaks, He says, "are spirit and they are life" (John 6:63).

The life in Christ has its inception with conversion, with the Holy Spirit through Gospel, leading us to faith in Jesus as the Redeemer from sin and the Giver of life from here to eternity. Our Lord said to the heavenly Father in His High Priestly Prayer, "This is eternal life: that they may know You, the only true God, and Jesus Christ whom You have sent" (John 17:3).

What is life? It is the outcome of a heart given to Jesus Christ in faith—a faith accompanied by love to God and love to the neighbor, with all good thoughts, desires, words, and deeds springing from it. This life is available to you.

*Prayer Suggestion: Ask God the Holy Spirit to lead you closer to Christ and thereby to strengthen your life in Him.*

# God Himself Is Present

What a view God must have! "From heaven the LORD looks down and sees all mankind; from His dwelling place He watches all who live on earth—He who forms the hearts of them all, who considers everything they do" (Ps. 33:13–15).

But God does more than look down, as though He were a distant, absentee landlord. He is present everywhere in His universe as Creator and Preserver. " 'Do not I fill heaven and earth?' declares the LORD" (Jer. 23:24). What is more, God was present in our world in His Son, who as the Word made flesh dwelt among us. In Jesus Christ, the true Immanuel, God is with us. When we worship the God-in-Christ and receive His Word, it is exactly as we sing in the hymn, "God Himself is present."

Our Lord, before ascending into heaven, promised to establish His comforting presence among us through the Holy Spirit, proceeding from Him and the Father. That promise was redeemed when, at Pentecost, the Spirit with all His graces was outpoured. Christ did what He said: "I will not leave you as orphans; I will come to you" (John 14:18).

The Christ once born in Bethlehem is here with us today in His invisible presence as our Creator and Preserver, with the Father and the Holy Spirit. In a special way He is also with us in the Word. His promise stands: "I am with you always, to the very end of the age" (Matt. 28:20).

*Prayer Suggestion: Thank Christ for His continual presence with you and your dear ones, whether at home or away.*

# The Anointed One

In Old Testament times, prophets, priests, and kings were anointed with oil to consecrate them for their office. Examples of this are Elisha (1 Kings 19:16), Aaron (Ex. 29:7), and David (1 Sam. 16:13). To anoint was to inaugurate.

Jesus of Nazareth is in the true sense the Anointed One, the Messiah, the Christ. He was anointed as Prophet, Priest, and King, not with olive oil but "with the Holy Spirit and power" (Acts 10:38). This anointing took place at Jesus' baptism, with the Father acknowledging Him as the beloved Son in whom He was well pleased and the Holy Spirit descending on Him like a dove.

In the power of the Spirit, Jesus came to the synagogue in Nazareth and announced, on the basis of Isaiah 61:1–2, "The Spirit of the Sovereign Lord is on Me, because the Lord has anointed Me to preach good news to the poor. He has sent Me to bind up the brokenhearted, to proclaim freedom for the captives and release from darkness for the prisoners, to proclaim the year of the Lord's favor" (Luke 4:18–19).

As Prophet, Jesus preached the Good News of salvation. As our High Priest, He offered up Himself on the altar of the cross to redeem us. And as King, He rules in our hearts with grace and truth. As an old hymn puts it,

> Christ is born, the great Anointed;
> Heav'n and earth, His praises sing!
> Oh, receive whom God appointed
> For your Prophet, Priest, and King!

**Prayer Suggestion:** *Thank Jesus Christ for serving you through His threefold office.*

## "This Is the Son of God"

The Child that was born and the Son that was given us—does He not seem to be an ordinary human baby?

Yes, the baby Jesus was truly human. He was born of a mother. He needed milk to grow. When uncomfortable, He cried. The swaddling clothes had to be changed.

As the years passed, Jesus grew normally. He learned His ABCs in school. He went with Mary and Joseph to God's house to study the Scriptures and to worship the heavenly Father.

Having reached His thirtieth year, Jesus was baptized of John in the Jordan and began His public ministry. Many who saw and heard Him thought Him to be no more than a human being. People said of Him, "Isn't this the carpenter? Isn't this Mary's son and the brother of James, Joseph, Judas and Simon? Aren't His sisters here with us?" (Mark 6:3).

But here is the testimony of John the Baptist: "I have seen and I testify that this is the Son of God" (John 1:34). As far as His divine nature is concerned, He is "very God of very God, begotten, not made, being of one substance with the Father" (as we confess in the Nicene Creed).

John testifies further that Jesus is "the Lamb of God, who takes away the sin of the world!" (John 1:29). That is why His coming is of such great importance. That is why St. Paul exclaims, "Beyond all question, the mystery of godliness is great: [God] appeared in a body ... was preached among nations, was believed on in the world, was taken up in glory" (1 Tim. 3:16).

**Prayer Suggestion:** *Give thanks to God for His unspeakable gift: His own Son, to be your Savior.*

# Interpreting the Signs of the Times

Each sunrise and sunset has a message. It tells us that time is passing, that the Day of the Lord is approaching when the old cosmic order will be dissolved and "a new heaven and a new earth, the home of righteousness" will be ushered in (2 Peter 3:13).

Sun, moon, and stars were created "as signs to mark seasons and days and years" (Gen. 1:14). Jesus, in a conversation with the scribes and Pharisees, referred to the way people read the signs when He quoted them as saying in the evening, "It will be fair weather, for the sky is red." Jesus then made the application: "You know how to interpret the appearance of the sky, but you cannot interpret the signs of the times" (Matt. 16:2–3).

When Christians are aware of the signs of the times and know what they mean, they cannot but be alert and faithful in their calling, particularly because they don't know the precise time of the Lord's return, foreshadowed by these signs. Our Lord tarries, like a man on a journey who has not announced the time of his homecoming, "whether in the evening, or at midnight, or when the rooster crows, or at dawn" (Mark 13:35).

Christians are called to watchfulness and similar virtues, as the apostle declares, "Be on your guard; Stand firm in the faith; be men of courage; be strong" (1 Cor. 16:13). "Keep watch," said He who gave His all for us (Mark 14:34). Advent reminds us to interpret the signs of the times correctly and to be ready to receive the Lord when He comes.

***Prayer Suggestion:*** *Ask the Lord Jesus to keep you alert and watchful so you may be ready to receive Him when He comes.*

# An Exchange of Roles

Time was when Kansas City was a suburb of President Truman's hometown, Independence, Missouri. In later years the role was reversed; the smaller Independence eventually became a suburb of Kansas City.

In the course of human events, people too at times exchange roles. Parents take care of their children; in later years children look after their aging parents. In business, someone on "the fast track" may eventually give orders to a previous boss.

Such a reversal of roles is no more pronounced in anyone's life than in the life of Jesus Christ. Eternally the Son of God, whom angels worshiped, Jesus became a true human being when He was born of the Virgin Mary. He laid aside His divine majesty and put on the robes of a servant. The Creator exchanged roles with the creature, with the sinful human race. As St. Paul declares, "You know the grace of our Lord Jesus Christ, that though He was rich, yet for your sakes He became poor" (2 Cor. 8:9). In Philippians 2:7–8, Paul says that Christ, who was equal with God, who in fact was God, "made Himself nothing, taking the very nature of a servant." More than that, "He humbled Himself and became obedient to death—even death on a cross!"

St. Paul explains why Jesus exchanged places with us: "so that you through His poverty might become rich" (2 Cor. 8:9)—rich in the forgiveness of sins and in the sure promise of eternal life. To Him be all glory and honor!

*Prayer Suggestion: Pray for willingness and strength to follow in the footsteps of Jesus, our Servant-King.*

# Jesus Cheered and Comforted

At Florida, Missouri, which now is just a wide spot in the road, a sign says, "In this village Mark Twain was born, November 30, 1835. He cheered and comforted a tired world." The small, two-room shack of a house where he was born is preserved in a nearby park.

Some 2,000 years ago Jesus was born in Bethlehem, which the prophet Micah (5:2) described as "small among the clans of Judah." The place of His birth was not even a small house but a stable.

Jesus the Messiah was needed by a sin-tired, suffering world. The believers ardently longed for the fulfillment of the promise of a Savior. And God did keep His Word. As the carol states, "The hopes and fears of all the years Are met in thee [Bethlehem] tonight."

Jesus, nevertheless, cheered a tired world. Joy and cheer do result from the Gospel He preached and performed. In forgiving the sins of the paralytic man, Jesus said, "Take heart, son; your sins are forgiven" (Matt. 9:2).

Our Lord also comforted a tired world, fulfilling what God stated through Isaiah, "Comfort, comfort, My people" (Is. 40:1). The four gospel writers relate that Jesus comforted Mary and Martha at the tomb of Lazarus, that He comforted and welcomed penitent sinners, and that He spoke comfortingly and tenderly to little children.

Jesus still cheers and comforts a tired world, today's world of sorrow and suffering. Yes, Jesus cheers and comforts you and me.

***Prayer Suggestion:*** *Pray that Jesus' words of cheer and comfort may penetrate your heart and mind.*

# What Our Eyes Have Seen

At Christmas time, we can borrow the opening line of Julia Ward Howe's popular hymn and say, "Mine eyes have seen the glory of the coming of the Lord." Although Mrs. Howe was inspired to write her stanzas after seeing "the watchfires of a hundred circling camps" at Washington, D.C., during the Civil War, we are moved by God's glory that shone around the shepherds as they were watching their flocks by night.

The shepherds hurried to the manger that they might "see this thing that has happened, which the Lord has told us" (Luke 2:15). With both their physical and spiritual eyes, they saw the newborn Savior, Christ the Lord. What their eyes had seen they published with their mouths, as they praised God and proclaimed the Gospel of Christ's birth.

Shift the scene from Bethlehem's stable to the temple in Jerusalem, and you hear aged Simeon, one of God's senior citizens, exclaim, "My eyes have seen Your salvation which You have prepared in the sight of all people, a light for revelation to the Gentiles and for glory to Your people Israel" (Luke 2:30–32).

Our eyes, too, have seen the Christ Child, and we are thankful. We invite all, "Come, see in the manger our Savior and King!" Come, see the one of whom Isaiah said, "To us a child is born, to us a son is given" (Is. 9:6). Come, worship Him who is called "Wonderful Counselor, Mighty God, Everlasting Father, Prince of Peace!"

*Prayer Suggestion:* *Give praise to God, from whom all blessings flow, especially the gift of His Son, Jesus Christ.*

# A Night to Remember

O God, because You once caused this holy night to shine with the brightness of the true Light, grant that we who have known the mystery of that Light here on earth may come to the full measure of its joys in heaven; through Jesus Christ, our Lord, who lives and reigns with You and the Holy Spirit, one God, now and forevermore. Amen.

1987 CPH

The Collect for Christmas Night is one of the great gems of our devotional and liturgical literature. It sparkles in its open simplicity, even as it reserves some of its splendor under a symbol of mystery.

Picture a midnight service in a candlelit church. The Christmas tree lights shine, but they do not totally dispel the darkness. There is an air of mystery, sustained by music and message proclaiming Christ's birth.

The events of that most holy night are rightly narrated, but they cannot tell the whole story of God's love nor show us all the brilliance of the Light Christ came to be in our darkening world. So we simply but rehearse the great deeds of God.

"Today in the town of David a Savior has been born to you; He is Christ the Lord" (Luke 2:11).

"The true Light that gives light to every man was coming into the world"(John 1:9).

The night of sin and despair is no longer as dark as it was. There is still mystery in the incarnation of God's Son, but we have enough light to see the road to heaven.

***Prayer Suggestion:*** *Thank God for the gift of His Son for the salvation of all.*

# We Adore the Christ Child

Children sometimes blend fiction with fact as they retell the story of Christ's birth. One youngster confidently told his Sunday school teacher, "Mary and Joseph had to stay in a cheap motel at Bethlehem because a party was going on in the Holiday Inn, and there was no room for them there."

If fellow travelers that night were singing, laughing, and having a party in the Bethlehem inn, they certainly weren't celebrating Jesus' birth. The event of the ages—the coming of the Son of God in the flesh—at the time made about as much of an impact on the world as a snowflake falling softly on the roof.

But how different it was in the humble Bethlehem stable where shepherds were on their knees! They heard and believed the angel's message that Christ, their Savior and Lord, was born. And they adored Him. Later, the Wise Men also "bowed down and worshiped Him" (Matt. 2:11).

Charles Lamb, of English essay fame, wrote, "If Shakespeare would come into this room, we would all arise. If Christ came in, we would fall down at His feet." Christ has come into our presence; let us fall down and adore Him.

In the mystery of the Word made flesh, God has given us a new revelation of His glory. Above all, He has revealed His grace in the person and work of His Son, our Redeemer from sin. Therefore, with angels and archangels and with all the company of heaven, we laud and magnify His glorious name. We invite one another, "Oh, come, let us adore Him!"

***Prayer Suggestion:*** *In your prayer, express your joy and thankfulness for the birth of Jesus Christ, the Son of God.*

# God's Good News Reaches Us in Time

For one James M. Utz, Christmas Day was followed by execution. On December 26, 1864, he was hanged for spying for the Confederates. A pardon from President Lincoln was on the way, but it didn't arrive in time.

"Too late" implies tragedy. Several years ago, many vacationers in the valley of the Big Thompson River in Colorado drowned because the flood warning came too late. Many accident victims have lost their lives because they could not be taken quickly enough to trauma centers.

The "too late" factor affects also the mission of the church. The well-known missionary Stanley Jones once spoke to a Hindu woman about the God of Christianity, the heavenly Father, who in Christ Jesus loves and forgives. The woman replied, "I always knew there was a God like that; but for me, you are too late." Of course, she only thought it was too late.

For the living, God's Good News is never too late—never too late because the time of grace continues. The day of salvation is still in effect. There still is time for all who in repentance and faith respond to Christ's invitation. Those who do can confess, "The blood of Jesus, [God's] Son, purifies us from all sin" (1 John 1:7).

Further, for us the living, it is not too late to show love to persons around us, to forgive them, to share the love of Christ with them.

***Prayer Suggestion:*** *Praise the heavenly Father for sending His Son, Jesus Christ, for your salvation and for bringing you to faith in Him through the Gospel.*

# A Lesson in Service

An interesting floral display seen in a church showed red poinsettias arranged in the shape of a Christmas tree, with white poinsettias in the middle forming a cross.

From the time the Savior was born, the cross was in the background of His life. With prophetic foresight, aged Simeon spoke of the infant Jesus as "this child … destined to cause the falling and rising of many in Israel, and to be a sign that will be spoken against" (Luke 2:34).

The road from Bethlehem's manger to Calvary's cross was marked by many intermediate steps. All were stages in our Lord's deepening humiliation. The painful experience of being rejected by His own townspeople, the mounting resentment at His ministry, the fickleness of His disciples, the need to teach them the ABCs of humble service by washing their feet—all this was a foretaste of and a rehearsal for the time when the Son of God would be obedient unto death, even death on a cross. Having emptied Himself of divine glory and taken the form of a servant, He was the supreme sacrifice for our redemption.

Having learned that lesson well—the lesson of how we came to be at peace with God through Jesus Christ—we learn the further lesson of Christian service. There is no better paragon of self-giving service to one another than the example of the Son of Man, who "did not come to be served, but to serve, and to give His life as a ransom for many" (Matt. 20:28).

*Prayer Suggestion: Render your thanks to Christ for coming into the world to save you, and ask Him to teach you the meaning of service.*

# The Presence

The children of Israel, in obedience to God's direction, provided their place of worship, the tabernacle, with a "table with all its articles and the bread of the Presence; the pure gold lampstand with its row of lamps and all its accessories" (Ex. 39:36–37). The "bread of the Presence," translated in the King James Version as "showbread," consisted of 12 loaves that represented God's presence and His constant communion with His people.

Less pretentious was the setting in the Upper Room as Jesus distributed Holy Communion to His disciples. Yet the scene is reminiscent of the tabernacle. There was a table, from which came "the Lord's Table" as another term for Holy Communion. And there were bread and wine, which Jesus consecrated and of which He said, "This is My body ... this is My blood." Here too is "bread of the Presence," Christ's real presence.

In His final talks, Jesus comforted His disciples with the assurance of His presence. In His invisible presence He would be with them "always, to the very end of the age." Further, He assured them of the presence of the Holy Spirit, who "lives with you, and will be in you" (John 14:17). The Holy Spirit comes through the Word Jesus has spoken. In yet another very special way would Jesus be in our midst as He was with the disciples: present in His body and blood. He who is with us in the Spirit, the Word, and the Lord's Table is the living Christ. And because He lives, we will live also.

***Prayer Suggestion:*** *Ask the Christ once born in Bethlehem to keep coming to and to be with you.*

# Worship in Spirit and Truth

In the Old Testament, God said, "Make an altar of earth for Me and sacrifice on it your burnt offerings and fellowship offerings, your sheep and goats and your cattle. Wherever I cause My name to be honored, I will come to you and bless you" (Ex. 20:24). After Israel's settlement in the Promised Land, the temple in Jerusalem came to be the place where God had written His name, and there He required that the prescribed worship be performed.

Jesus Christ came into the world to usher in the time of the New Testament with a new approach to worship. Sacrificial rituals and visual types pointing to something to come were now obsolete, for the Lamb of God was offered once for all to atone for the sins of the world. In Christ, God has direct converse with His children. New Testament worship reflects this personal relationship between God and Christians. He speaks to them in His Word, and they speak to Him in prayer.

Is Mount Gerizim in Samaria or the temple in Jerusalem the right place for worship, the woman at Jacob's well asks. Jesus says that the question is irrelevant. The time has come, He says, when true worshipers will worship God, who is a Spirit, "in spirit and truth," that is, in keeping with the new relationship of faith and love in which they now stand before God.

The place of worship with its appointments is still important and dear to us, but only because it helps us worship God in spirit and truth.

*Prayer Suggestion: Express your thankfulness to God for the privilege of praying to Him directly.*

# Time Marches On

Some years ago, the hands of a clock on the cover of *The Bulletin of Atomic Scientists,* stood at four minutes to midnight. These scientists were saying that the midnight hour of nuclear destruction would soon strike unless measures were taken to reverse the trend. If uninformed people had said this, we might have called them alarmists. But what scientists said could not be lightly dismissed. We are thankful that the clock has been turned back since that cover was printed.

Someday, though, a world dissolution will come—one by the direct intervention of God. The prophets in the Old Testament, then Jesus and His apostles, spoke of it. This universe once had a beginning, and it will also have an end. No time schedule has been announced. Jesus said, "No one knows about that day or hour, not even the angels of heaven, nor the Son, but only the Father" (Matt. 24:36).

We bear in mind that time marches relentlessly on and carries us with it in its advance toward eternity. Time is like a stream that flows onward until it reaches its destination.

Since we know this, we ought to watch and pray and be ready, always looking forward to our eternal home in heaven. By His atoning work, Jesus prepared a place for us.

In the meantime, we go about our work and other activities. We take an interest in the world around us and work for its betterment—but always with a detachment, always with the desire that our day-by-day life with Jesus may become eternal life with Him at God's right hand.

*Prayer Suggestion: Pray that the signs of the time may deepen your love for Jesus, your Lord.*

# Our Abiding Home

In the physical world, well-constructed buildings usually outlast their builders. Many century-old houses of brick and stone are still inhabitable. Although the architects who designed them, the contractors and crews who erected them, and the families who first owned them have long ago vanished from the scene, the houses remain. Sometimes temples and tombs, fortresses and fountains, highways and aqueducts survive the original builders by several millennia.

Everything long-lasting that humans can build is, in turn, overshadowed by the world God has made. God's mountains, lands, and seas outlast the works of man.

God, however, outlasts even this durable universe. He is immortal, from everlasting to everlasting. When at long last the granite mountains lie in dust, the last of the giant redwood trees have decayed, and the heavenly bodies have fallen from their orbits, God still will be.

Because God is eternal, also heaven, His dwelling place, will last forever. Heaven is "the city with foundations, whose architect and builder is God" (Heb. 11:10). Here on earth, we are reminded that "here we do not have an enduring city, but we are looking for the city that is to come" (Heb. 13:14). Therefore we do well not to become too fond of the world or its things. They are material and temporal. Only the things that are not seen are eternal.

Eternal life in an eternal home with an eternal Father is mine only through faith in Jesus Christ, who suffered, died, and rose again.

*Prayer Suggestion: Say your thank-You to God for all the blessings of the past year.*

# Devotions for Special Festivals and Occasions

# What the Ashes Mean

Ash Wednesday marks the beginning of Lent. On this day, you may see people on the street or at work with ash smudges on their foreheads. Then it dawns on you that this is Ash Wednesday and that these people are confessing their faith. We do well to let the general public know about our commitment to Jesus Christ. The ashes remind us of a truth encompassing us all: that we are dust and ashes and to dust we shall return.

Sackcloth and ashes in Old Testament times were outward signs of sorrow over sin. Similarly, Ash Wednesday worshipers who daub their foreheads with ashes—the ashes of last year's palms—indicate mourning over their sins. Sin made it necessary for Jesus Christ to suffer and die.

Not all Christians observe Ash Wednesday with outward signs of remorse. Nevertheless, in their hearts they grieve over their sins.

"It is my sins for which You, Lord, must languish." With this confession on their lips, Christians go to the house of God this day and, as is mostly the case, partake of Holy Communion. Thus the truth is brought home to them: Christ's body was broken and His blood shed for the remission of sins.

Ashes are gray and grim, but they remind us that through Christ (as Isaiah said), God gives us "beauty instead of ashes, the oil of gladness instead of mourning, and a garment of praise instead of spirit of despair" (Is. 61:3).

*Prayer Suggestion: Ask God to forgive you all your sins for Jesus' sake and to grant you joy at your forgiveness.*

# The Centrality of the Cross

Not everyone within the church agrees as to the nature and purpose of Lent. Some regard it primarily as a "closed" season, a time when the emphasis is more on what you don't do than on what you do. Fasting fits into this concept. Others see it as a time when we can focus on Jesus as our example, teaching us how to act under suffering. Many like to skip Lent altogether and observe only Easter. (One might wonder if the cross and Lent's reminder of our sin offend them.)

In *The Kingdom Beyond Caste*, Liston Pope of the Yale Divinity School wrote, "Christ in His suffering has revealed a new dimension of God. The idea that God Himself could suffer was new with Christianity. Other religions have gods who reign, or who help man avoid suffering, or who are indifferent to human suffering. But the central symbol of Christianity is a cross, and its Savior is a crucified Lord."

The cross stands at the center of the Christian faith. Salvation in other religious systems is made to depend on being good and doing good or doing one's own suffering to appease God. Holy Scripture, on the other hand, brings us the Gospel of God's Son suffering and dying on a cross for our salvation, full and free.

It may not have been a "green hill" where our dear Lord was crucified, but we are blessed nonetheless, for "He died that we might be forgiven."

*Prayer Suggestion: Ask the Lord for His presence in your heart as you ponder His passion.*

# Our Lord's Last Will and Testament

When Leonard Jerome, an American of considerable wealth and the father-in-law of Winston Churchill, was about to die, he said to his family, "I have given you all I have. Pass it on."

Shortly before His death, Jesus likewise revealed His last will and testament. He did not leave us earthly wealth, He had something much better. He gave us His life so we might have pardon and peace with God. On the cross of Good Friday, His body was broken and His blood shed for the remission of our sins. In the Holy Sacrament He imparts to us that body and blood. Here are His express words: "Take and eat; this is My body … Drink … this is My blood of the covenant" (Matt. 26:26–27).

All that our Lord speaks and does in this sacrament constitutes His last will and testament. Inasfar as it is His will, the words express what He wants us to do: "eat," "drink," "do this in remembrance of Me." As His testament it offers, conveys, and seals to us what Christ has gained for us by His life, death, and resurrection. Thereby He gives us the riches of spiritual life in Him and eternal life to come. This is His legacy.

The dying man said to his family, "Pass it on." We cannot, of course, do for others what only Christ can do: redeem sinners. But we can pass on the good news of the salvation He has procured. When we do that, Christ's bequeath becomes also that of others.

*Prayer Suggestion: Ask your Lord's help to prepare you for joyfully receiving His body and blood in the Sacrament as pledges of His grace.*

# One for All

In Charles Dickens' story of the French Revolution, *A Tale of Two Cities*, Sidney Carton changes places with a condemned man, Charles Darnay, and dies in his stead on the guillotine. His famous last words read, "It is a far, far better thing that I do than I have ever done … it is a far better rest than I have ever known."

Jesus did a similar thing, but in a perfect sense. He went to the cross so every sinner—every Charles Darnay—might be released from death, the punishment for sin, and go free and be declared innocent by God. This is the meaning of the Lenten story, particularly the account of our Lord's crucifixion on Good Friday. As proclaimed by Christ Himself and later by His apostles, the Gospel speaks of His obedience, suffering, and death as making atonement for our sins. Jesus, the sinners' Substitute, is the Lamb of God offered up for us. God made Him who knew no sin and deserved no penalty to be sin for us and to bear the divine judgment.

Jesus said, "Greater love has no one than this, that he lay down his life for his friends" (John 15:13). In another sense, that is what Sidney Carton did for his friend, Charles Darnay. But our Lord did more. He did not only lay down His life for friends but for enemies as well—in fact, for all sinners. The apostle writes, "God demonstrates His own love for us in this: While we were still sinners, Christ died for us" (Rom. 5:8).

The "One for all" theme of Good Friday has a reverse side: Out of thankfulness we all now pledge ourselves to the One, loving and serving Him in His kingdom.

***Prayer Suggestion:*** *Declare to your Lord and Savior that you are unspeakably thankful to Him for laying down His life for you.*

# Christ's Easter Victory

Most victories do not come easily; they are often preceded by frustration, even defeats. In 1858, Abraham Lincoln ran as a candidate for the United States Senate, engaging in debates with the then occupant of the seat, Stephen A. Douglas. Lincoln lost the election, but thanks to the debates, he became a national figure. Two years later, he was elected president.

Many people in Jesus' time considered Him a loser. He lost many followers, prompting Him to ask the Twelve, "You do not want to leave too, do you?" (John 6:67). The people of His hometown Nazareth were offended at Him, and for a while He lost the support of His family. His being sentenced to the cross and His subsequent death and burial seemed to spell out failure in large letters. In the words of Paul Gerhardt's hymn, when they "in the grave did sink Him, the foe held jubilee."

But by completing His work on the cross, down to dotting the last "i" and crossing the last "t," Jesus had won the victory over sin, death, and Satan. His resurrection on Easter morning attested to the fullness of this victory. We exclaim with St. Paul, "Thanks be to God! He gives us the victory through our Lord Jesus Christ" (1 Cor. 15:57).

Christ's victory assures us of the completeness of His work for our salvation and of the certainty of our own bodily resurrection. And, set free from the rule of sin and the fear of death, we can rise daily to the newness of life in Him.

*Prayer Suggestion: Express your joy and thankfulness to the Savior for His victorious resurrection from the dead and for granting you new life, today and forever.*

# The Era of Missions Begins

Pentecost Day ushers in the New Testament era of missions. In the book of Acts the story of missions can be summarized in these three words: "up, down, and out."

Jesus went up: The ascension of our Lord (Acts 1:9) is an important event in the history of missions. Now sitting at the right hand of God, He has full authority in heaven and on earth. He is especially concerned about the growth of the church, which is His body.

The Holy Spirit came down: Pentecost (Acts 2:1–13) marks the fulfillment of Jesus' promise to send His Spirit down upon His disciples. If the Spirit had not descended, Christ's mission would never have gotten off the ground. With the coming of the Lord and Giver of Life, the era of missions was born.

The disciples went out: "Those who had been scattered preached the word wherever they went" (Acts 8:4). This is but one of many passages reporting that not only the apostles but also the members of the early church went into all the world to preach the Gospel. The church assembled in Jerusalem scattered—by persecution, but especially in obedience to Christ's missionary command—to "preach the Good News to all creation" (Mark 16:15).

The ascent of Jesus and the descent of the Spirit on Pentecost are past events. But not yet completed is our mission of continually going out into the world to proclaim Christ's Gospel. Because Jesus went up and the Spirit came down, we are enabled to go out as Christ's ambassadors.

*Prayer Suggestion: Pray God the Holy Spirit to continue His sanctifying work in you and to bless the Gospel of Christ wherever it is proclaimed.*

# Why We Are in Church Today

People are not by nature thankful. For many, ingratitude is a step in the journey of moral and spiritual decline. St. Paul points out in Romans 1:21 how it went with pagan nations: "Although they knew God, they neither glorified Him as God nor gave thanks to Him." Then follow other sins to which God in His judgment abandons them.

The children of Israel, God's own people, were likewise notorious for their unthankfulness. God declares through Isaiah, "The ox knows his master, the donkey his owner's manger, but Israel does not know, My people do not understand. Ah, sinful nation … " (Is. 1:3–4). Israel did not stop to consider that "every good and perfect gift is from above, coming down from the Father of the heavenly lights" (James 1:17).

The nine leprous Israelites whom Christ had healed but who did not return to say thanks ran true to form. Our Lord felt hurt: "Were not all ten cleansed? Where are the other nine?" (Luke 17:17). Only one man, a non-Israelite, was grateful—and declared himself so by word and deed.

We have many reasons to be grateful. The one reason that stands like Mount Everest above all others is our healing from the leprosy of sin. Jesus went to another mount—Calvary—to shed His blood that cleanses us from all sin. In gratitude we do what the Samaritan did: turn back, praise God with a loud voice, and at Jesus' feet give thanks. That's why we are in church today. That's why we are thankful in our homes as we gather around well-laden tables and enjoy family fellowship. We cannot but give thanks to God for all His benefits to us.

***Prayer Suggestion:*** *In your prayer, enumerate the main blessings you have received from God and thank Him for them.*

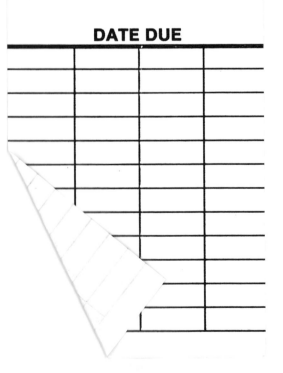

**DATE DUE**